Every Sales Leader knows they need a pipeline – but not just any pipeline.

For years, we've tolerated bloated forecasts, ghost deals, and pipeline reviews that are little more than wishful thinking in a spreadsheet.

Finally – someone had the guts to call it out.
Leslie Venetz didn't just write another sales book – she created the definitive blueprint for building a Profit Generating Pipeline.

Not a "feel-good" funnel.
Not a "trust the process" pipedream.
But a real, revenue-producing system that separates the top 5% from the rest of the pack.

If you lead a sales team, this isn't optional reading – it's required.
Because hope is not a strategy. But profit is.

Anthony Iannarino | 6x best-selling author and USA Today Best-Seller, The Only Sales Guide You'll Ever Need

Profit Generating Pipeline is a book written for the sales leaders who are tired of being told to do more without being told how to do better.

Leslie Venetz brings the kind of clarity and experience that earns trust quickly. Her frameworks are practical, her voice is direct, and her perspective is rooted in what actually drives results. This isn't a book about tactics. It's about leadership, strategy, and building systems that scale.

What I appreciate most is how much of Leslie's community-first mindset comes through in her writing. She doesn't just want you to hit quota. She wants you to build a sales culture your team is proud to be part of.

Sam Jacobs | Wall Street Journal Best Selling Author, Kind Folks Finish First

I've had the privilege of co-leading a sales workshop with Leslie Venetz and watching her in action. She's one of the clearest, most engaging voices in sales today. Her ability to teach, connect, and deliver insights with precision is rare—and Profit Generating Pipeline captures all of it.

As someone who lives and breathes sales messaging, I was blown away by how effectively Leslie breaks down complex concepts without watering them down. She doesn't just give you frameworks. She gives you the why, the when, and the nuance that turns a good strategy into a great one.

This book isn't just full of smart ideas. It's full of truth. Leslie knows what she's talking about, and it's a gift to have it all captured in one place. Any sales leader who wants to coach better, write better, or lead with more confidence needs this book in their hands.

Jen Allen-Kenth | International Keynote Speaker & Founder, DemandJen

Leslie and I don't agree on everything when it comes to sales—and that's part of why I respect her so much. She's sharp, thoughtful, and unapologetically clear in her thinking. There's no filler here, no buzzwords, no empty frameworks pretending to be strategy.

Profit Generating Pipeline is a straight-up useful book. It's the kind of book you actually highlight, then go back to when you're writing copy, coaching a team, or reworking a sales process that's gone off the rails.

Even when Leslie's pushing ideas I hadn't considered, I trust where she's coming from because she's done the work. She's not guessing. This book is proof of that.

Scott Leese | 6x Sales Leader, 5x Founder & Best-Selling Author

This book shows you how to build a pipeline that drives profit and a team that sticks around to keep it going. Leslie Venetz shows you how to earn trust, coach with clarity, and turn process into predictable revenue. If your sales model depends on people, not just output, this is the system you've been missing.

Bryan Howard | CEO of Peoplyst, Author of The Vanguard Edge

I rarely see sales advice that aligns so well with buyer psychology. Leslie nails it with her micro-campaign and personalization tactics.

Kumar R. Parakala | Chairman, Thriveco, USA National Bestselling Author, _Lead to Disrupt_

Finally, a book that tosses out outdated sales fluff and replaces it with actionable, ethical strategies. Leslie's approach to building trust is a breath of fresh air.

Tamara Nall | CEO & Founder, The Leading Niche

I've led high-performing teams across industries and continents, and I can confidently say this is one of the most practical and empowering sales leadership books I've ever read. Leslie doesn't just share a framework. The author rewrites what it means to build trust, lead with purpose, and generate real, lasting pipeline. If you're ready to stop chasing quick wins and start building something sustainable, this book is your blueprint.

Carl Grant III | Author, *How to Live the Abundant Life*

I found Leslie's clarity on segment-specific value propositions priceless. Profit Generating Pipeline is a modern classic for sales leadership.

Aaron Poynton | CEO, Omnipoynt Solutions and USA Today & WSJ Best Selling Author

Profit Generating Pipeline

A Proven Formula to Earn Trust and Drive Revenue

BY LESLIE VENETZ

ISBN **979-8-9985270-2-9** (pbk)
ISBN **979-8-9985270-3-6** (hcv)
ISBN **979-8-9985270-1-2** (ebook)

Library of Congress Control Number: **2025906303**

Table of Contents

Foreword

For you, a sales professional, reading a book like *Profit Generating Pipeline* represents an act of optimism.

You're seeking out new knowledge and new information about the art, craft, and science of selling because you believe that possession of it will enable you to become a better version of yourself.

This hopefulness that anyone can learn to do better and perform at a higher level is an integral element of the mindset of every top-producing sales professional I've worked with over a 50-year career at the highest levels in sales.

However, more than anything else, this optimism and hopefulness are engines of change.

In that regard, you should consider that in reading *Profit Generating Pipeline*, you are acting very much like one of your buyers.

Think about it for a second. The act of buying is all about change. A customer's purchase decision represents nothing more than their decision to make a change.

Well, in truth, a buyer's decision to change is actually four decisions:

1. What do we want to change? (i.e., What's the problem?)
2. Why do we want to change? (i.e., What's the business case?)
3. How do we want to change? (i.e., What's the product or solution?)
4. Who do we want to change with? (i.e., Which vendor do we trust to help us achieve our business case?)

The single biggest reason why most sellers underperform is that they work with a buyer all the way through their "selling process," without the buyer ever making all four change decisions.

Similarly, it's why so many deals end up in "No Decision." It's not because the buyer wants to stick with their current solution. It's because the seller didn't help the buyer make those four critical change decisions.

And that is really the core lesson of Leslie's book.

If you're reading this book just to cherry-pick a couple of new tactics you can use to boost your pipeline efforts, then you're unlikely to achieve the results you want. The quick fix is rarely the long-term change that is needed.

On the other hand, if you use the lessons Leslie presents (to answer the four change questions) to make the four change decisions about your pipeline generation processes, as well as your selling processes, then you'll find yourself committing to making substantive, informed changes that result in elevated levels of performance for you and for your team.

That is change that works. And that sticks.

More importantly, that improved performance you experience is how you'll convert your optimism into confidence. Meaning confidence that comes from understanding not just how you are selling, but why you are selling the way you do. And how that produces the results you want (month after month, year after year).

It goes full circle because it's that confidence you have in your ability to achieve the results you want that translates back into optimism about what's possible for you to achieve in your career.

I've had the pleasure of a front row seat to the development of this book over the past several years. I couldn't be more proud of Leslie and the valuable resource she's created for sellers and sales leaders alike.

I'm confident you'll feel the same way.

Good selling, everyone!

Andy Paul

Acknowledgements

Writing this book has been a powerful and rewarding journey, shaped by nearly two decades in sales and a deep commitment to evolving the way we sell. But it wasn't a journey I made alone. I was surrounded and supported by an extraordinary community of mentors, peers, colleagues, family, and friends, who made it possible.

My family has provided unwavering encouragement at every step of my life and career. You have encouraged me to bet on myself, both allowing me to find my own way and also making sure I knew I had a safe place to land. To my mom, dad, brother, and my husband, Chris - thank you for constantly reminding me that I can do hard things and for celebrating every milestone alongside me. Your love, patience, and enthusiasm fueled this journey.

To my extended family and chosen family, knowing that you're in my corner makes the hard work easier and more rewarding. To have the loudest cheering section at every event is truly a gift. You make me feel so loved and valued.

To Andy Paul, thank you for believing in me when I wasn't yet sure my expertise and perspective mattered, and for graciously contributing the foreword.

I've been incredibly fortunate to receive overwhelming support from the LinkedIn and broader sales community, as well as numerous mentors and the many incredible peer groups that I am proud to be part of. Thank you for continuously cheering me on, saying my name in rooms that I am not in, and reminding me of the positive impact my work has had on your lives. Special thanks to Brand Builders Group for their invaluable coaching and strategic guidance throughout the publishing process.

To all the sales professionals who came before me, thank you for laying the groundwork and inspiring conversations about integrity, trust, and buyer-centricity. I am especially grateful to the remarkable women in sales who have led the charge with courage and heart. With this book, I hope to further my dream of transforming sales into a respected, inclusive profession.

Finally, I must express deep gratitude to every single one of you. To every person who has supported my personal and professional journey in any way, thank you. I was able to write this book because friends, family, colleagues, and peers repeatedly showed up for me, believed in my work, and amplified my voice.

Thank you all, from the bottom of my heart.

Part 1

Sales Leadership Foundations

CHAPTER 1

Earn the Right

> *"Growth begins when we step outside our comfort zone. It can be intimidating to put ourselves in situations where we might fail, but it's in these moments of discomfort that we truly learn and develop."* —Adam Grant

Kevin stepped onto the bustling sales floor, his heart pounding with a mix of nerves and skepticism. He scanned the room, taking in the rows of reps hunched over their desks, deep in conversation, their voices rising and falling in a rhythmic cadence. It was his first real day on the job, but it already felt like he had somehow arrived late, like everyone else had been given a secret playbook he hadn't received.

After just three days of training, he was expected to start making calls. The reality of what that meant hadn't sunk in until this moment. His manager, Emily, walked him over to a desk tucked between two other reps. The space smelled faintly like a locked room and felt cramped, with just enough room for him to slide into his chair without knocking into his neighbor. On his desk sat a few chewed-up pens and a black phone with a cord that was so impossibly tangled it looked like it had barely survived previous sales reps.

There was no computer. No training manual. No lead list. Just a phone and high expectations.

Emily nodded encouragingly. "Time to start making some calls."

Kevin stared at her, waiting for more instructions, but none came. She was already sliding into her own chair, picking up her headset, and joining the chorus of sales reps around them. Emily wanted Kevin to succeed, but she made it clear that she had to catch up on coaching with the rest of her direct reports and make sales calls to ensure she hit her own quota.

Kevin gripped the edge of his desk. He wasn't sure what he had imagined, but it wasn't this. He had no idea who to call, what to say, or even where to start. For the first time since taking the job, he felt real doubt creep in.

This job wasn't something he had wanted. It wasn't even something he had pursued. He'd only taken it because his uncle owned the company, and after months of unsuccessfully trying to land a job elsewhere, he had given in to family pressure. Everyone had told him he would be great at sales. They said he had the personality for it. He was easy to talk to, good with people, and quick on his feet. But standing here, looking at an empty desk and a phone that might as well have been a brick, he didn't feel like someone who was about to be great at anything.

Kevin had convinced himself that this job would be temporary. Something to do until he figured out what he actually wanted. But now that he was here, staring at the mess of dated office supplies, he realized just how unprepared he was.

Kevin needed help, but he didn't want to interrupt Emily. She was nice during training, but he sensed that she was frustrated at not having a say in the decision to hire him. Instead, he glanced around, hoping for some kind of direction. To his left, a woman in her mid-thirties was nodding along to whatever was being said in her headset. Across the room, a rep was leaning so far back in his chair that Kevin was certain he was moments away from tipping over.

To his right sat a red-faced twenty-something with a five o'clock shadow and half-empty coffee cups scattered over his desk. The guy's tie was loose, his sleeves were rolled up, and his headset was shoved halfway off his ear. He looked exhausted.

Kevin leaned over. "Hey, man, uh... where do I get a list of people to call?"

The guy motioned vaguely at his own messy desk, covered in crumpled papers and printouts with highlighted names. "Figure out who we sell to. Find their numbers. Call them."

Kevin let that sink in. He ran a hand through his hair, feeling overwhelmed by the enormity of the task ahead of him.

Kevin wasn't a person who gave up easily. He had always been able to talk his way through things, to find his footing even in unfamiliar situations, but this was different. This was a job that required more than quick thinking and a good personality. It required a strategy and process.

He had neither.

Many of us have found ourselves in a situation like this. Hopefully, your first day of selling wasn't quite as chaotic as Kevin's, but if you're reading this book, you've likely asked yourself the same question Kevin was asking.

"How the heck do I build a qualified sales pipeline?"

What *Profit Generating Pipeline* Will Teach You

If any part of your job involves getting your buyer's attention, *Profit Generating Pipeline* is a must-read. This book shares the lessons that helped Kevin evolve from overwhelmed to overachiever.

We will cover the process that Kevin adopted, with Emily's support, and share their experiences to inspire your team to earn the right to their buyers' trust and business. You will learn how to develop top-performing salespeople while becoming a strategic sales leader. You will be empowered to achieve your personal best and even more proud that you've chosen sales as your profession.

This buyer-centric guide to the top-of-the-funnel is designed to help you and your team drive revenue through smart segmentation, exceptional sales copywriting, intentional prospecting, and repeatable processes.

We begin with the foundations of leadership, starting with the idea that before you lead others, you must first *earn the right*. That means modeling the growth mindset, even when growth feels scary. You'll be challenged to become the sales leader you've always wanted to follow, one who creates psychological safety, drives accountability, and inspires excellence.

Earn The Right Litmus Test
At each step in your selling process, pause and ask yourself:
"Have I earned the right to make this ask?"

Whether you're asking for attention in the inbox,
time in a discovery meeting, or ultimately a prospect's business,
always hold yourself accountable to this standard.

You'll learn how to build a high-performing sales culture, abandon outdated methods that undermine your team's success, and embrace the discipline that drives long-term results. With that mindset, you'll be prepared to take a strategic approach to top-of-funnel excellence, laying the groundwork for scalable pipeline success.

In Part 2, we shift from mindset to methodology. You'll master a proven pipeline formula, starting with clearly defining your ideal customer profile and creating value propositions tailored to each segment. From there, you'll learn how to develop micro-campaigns, write sales copy that converts, and optimize your outreach channels for maximum impact.

I'll show you how to build effective sales sequences, respond to objections with curiosity, not defensiveness, and run discovery meetings that deepen relationships. Along the way, you'll be invited to apply this formula so you can build repeatable processes that make durable growth achievable.

It is okay if, like Kevin, you feel like figuring out how to effectively generate quality sales leads is as difficult as fixing the impossibly tangled phone cord he encountered on his first day at work. We'll follow Kevin and his manager, Emily, throughout this book. Their story, as well as countless others, will help you develop your own formula to earn trust and drive revenue.

Because here's the thing: most of us don't receive a step-by-step manual on how to become a great sales leader. You take the job, and suddenly, you're expected to know how to motivate a team, hit revenue goals, and navigate constant changes in the market, all while keeping your boss(es) happy.

Profit Generating Pipeline will empower you to lead with less stress so that your team can sell more.

My Accidental Sales Career

Like Kevin, I didn't aspire to a career in B2B sales. I aspired to greatness, and admitting I was in sales didn't feel great.

I was a recent college graduate still laboring under the delusion that I would directly apply my college degrees to my life and livelihood. I spent years learning about social behavior, business marketing, and international relations. I'd spent the previous 10 years traveling for Model United Nations (MUN) and policy debate tournaments. I'd dedicated my time to fundraising for non-profits and volunteer leadership roles, like acting as the Student Body Vice President (VP). Now that I was getting a "real" job, I aspired to do work that I believed mattered.

I always knew following my ambition would mean leaving my home state of Montana for the big city. I arrived in Chicago in the summer of 2007 with no job, but I was sure that I would do something significant with my life. I was confident in my abilities and certain, in the way that only 20-somethings can be, that I was meant to do great things with my career.

I chose to move to Chicago because it gained the most points in a competition that was entirely made up, but I will share it with you because it gives you a true insight into how my brain works.

In my last year of college, I created an Excel spreadsheet for more than 30 cities with populations of over 250,000. They were mostly domestic, with a few recognizable global destinations like London, Paris, and Madrid. On the other axis, I listed everything that was most important to me at the time – access to music, food, and travel. After assigning point values based on the level of importance, I filled in the blanks. At the end of the exercise, Chicago had the most points, which is how I found myself, five days after wrapping my final college course, moving from a town of 60,000 to a city of six million, positive I'd be able to make it work.

I began applying for jobs where I could use what I'd learned in college or where I was sure I could make an impact. It was a jarring experience. Despite having recently managed a three-quarters-of-a-million-dollar budget as Student Body VP, the only roles where I could score interviews were entry-level positions paying $30,000 a year. The idea that, even if I did a truly spectacular job, even if I poured my heart and soul into a role and made waves for a company, I would be eligible for (at most) a 3% pay increase in one calendar year made me sick. I rejected the idea that my hard work would never be truly rewarded.

Sales Chose Me

As I was coming to this realization, I had an interview with a global business intelligence firm. It was for an entry-level inside sales job. I'd only agreed to the interview because I figured I could prove myself, then move into a different department when a "good" job came up. I convinced myself that taking a sales job for a few months until I could find something better wouldn't be the worst thing.

After weighing my options, I turned down the $30,000 jobs and accepted an $18,000 annual base salary with the promise of uncapped commission.

I had finally made it to the big city, working a corporate job in a fancy office tower in downtown Chicago. I had the title. I had the badge that got me through security every morning. I had everything I thought would make me feel like a real professional.

And yet, for months, I was skipping meals to pay my rent. I could hardly afford to exist on $18,000 a year. Every single expense was a strain, but I had a job where I felt in control of my financial future, and I was finding out that I also had a knack for selling.

Within weeks, I had a sneaking suspicion that sales was my calling. At the time, I wasn't willing to admit it out loud, but I was shocked to realize that what made sales conversations feel so natural to me were the years I'd spent practicing rhetoric in MUN, the endless weekends spent practicing my listening skills in policy debate, and the tens of thousands I raised for non-profits by telling them what's in it for them. I'd been practicing for a career in sales my entire life, and this is where the magic of *Earn the Right* begins.

Why I Stayed (Even When It Was Tough)

Nobody told me that the skills that make a person great at sales include curiosity, empathy, and active listening. It floored me. As a child of the '80s and '90s, my conception of sales was almost entirely based on Hollywood tropes like *Glengarry Glen Ross*, *Wall Street*, and *Boiler Room*. Movies steeped in toxic masculinity, the glory of capitalism, and sales as a profession of men who will do anything to close a deal. I saw that culture and many of those behaviors on the sales floor in that first job. They felt wrong, so I found myself resisting them, even when the top sellers assured me that this type of selling was the only path to success.

After only two months, I was promoted. Not just promoted—I beat the record for the fastest speed to merit-based promotion by an entire month. In two months of trusting my instincts and rejecting old ways of selling, I beat a record that had stood for as long as any employee could remember.

In a few weeks, I went from "Ew, sales is gross," to "Oh my gosh, I think I'm going to do this forever."

I accepted the $18,000 base confident that I could not only exceed the $30,000 other jobs were offering me, but that I could also double, maybe even triple that number. I did. Later in my career, I'd even 10x that number. I have 113% career quota overachievement and made every performance-based President's Club I had access to during my career. I've led hundreds of sellers and trained thousands more to achieve their goals and quotas.

Despite my initial resistance to a career in sales, I've thrived as a seller and sales leader, and I'm going to give you all my secrets in this book. You'll learn how rejecting old ways of selling and embracing a buyer-centric mindset will explode your earnings and love for sales.

You Deserve to Love the Work You Do

Reflecting on my journey in sales, I realize that sticking to my values was crucial. Had I chosen to conform to traditional sales methods that felt wrong to me, I might have seen success, but at a great cost to my emotional and mental health. Thousands of high-potential sales reps face similar struggles.

Too many sellers enter toxic sales environments and leave the profession before they get a chance to work for a great sales leader, maybe even to become one themselves. What I've absorbed about being a leader came as much from witnessing bad leadership as it did from learning how to embody good leadership practices.

> **"The old ways of selling weren't designed with today's buyers in mind. They also weren't designed with the health, happiness, and longevity of today's sellers in mind."**

Sales teams today are filled with talented professionals who are capable of doing incredible things when given the right guidance. But, too often, they're handed outdated sales playbooks and left to sink or swim. The old ways of selling weren't designed with today's buyers in mind. They also weren't designed with the health, happiness, and longevity of today's sellers in mind.

Early in my career, I stayed in sales out of sheer stubbornness. I faced internal doubts and external pressure to conform to toxic cultures, but I refused to let them drive me away. My early success gave me the confidence to challenge these norms and prove there are better ways to sell. In those early years, I stayed not because I loved the environment but to prove a point and pave the way for others who felt the same.

I never aspired to a career in sales. But my career proves that when done the right way—with integrity, curiosity, and a focus on the buyer—sales is one of the best professions out there.

Now, I want to show you how to do the same.

CHAPTER 2

Growth Can Be Scary

"Vulnerability is the birthplace of innovation, creativity, and change." –Brené Brown

Growth can be scary. We don't need to look further than famous brands like BlackBerry, Myspace, Toys R Us, or Blockbuster for reminders of companies that seemed unstoppable...until they weren't. They didn't fail because they lacked resources or brand recognition. They failed because they stopped growing. They ignored shifting customer preferences and resisted change. By the time they reacted, it was too late.

The Netflix Playbook: Listen, Adapt, Evolve

Blockbuster was the undisputed leader in video rentals. At its peak, it had over 9,000 stores worldwide and dominated the market. But as customer preferences evolved, the world of movie rentals started to shift. People wanted convenience: options beyond driving to physical stores, fewer late fees, and more flexibility.

Netflix saw this shift early. What started as a DVD rental service by mail quickly evolved into something much bigger. Reed Hastings and his team recognized the potential of streaming technology and leaned in, testing, iterating, and reimagining how people consumed entertainment. They didn't just guess what customers wanted - they listened. They experimented with pricing, subscription models, and platform features until they found a model that resonated.

At one point, Blockbuster had the opportunity to purchase Netflix for just $50 million. They laughed at the idea. After all, why would they need to change? They were the leader, a giant. But leadership doesn't come from being the biggest. It comes from being the most strategic and willing to adapt.

Netflix did what every winning sales organization must do. They paid attention to their customers. They experimented with new models. They made bold moves, even when they were risky. They continued to evolve as the market evolved.

Meanwhile, Blockbuster clung to its outdated model, refusing to evolve and confront changing demands. Later, they tried to adapt, but by the time they made real changes, Netflix already dominated the space. In 2010, Blockbuster filed for bankruptcy.

If you're leading a sales team, this isn't just a story about movies and streaming. This is your story too, and the moral is – adapt or die.

Change Isn't Optional – It's Table Stakes

Buyers are changing the way they research and purchase. Decision-makers have more information at their fingertips than ever before. They expect sellers to provide insights they can't find online. They're engaging on their terms and in their preferred channels. They expect personalization, relevance, and value before they ever take a meeting.

The way sales organizations respond to this shift will determine who thrives and who fades into irrelevance.

Right now, you are at the same crossroads that Blockbuster and Netflix once faced. You can continue doing what's comfortable, relying on outdated sales methods, and resisting shifts in buyer expectations. You can hope that what worked five years ago will still work today, or you can be like Reed Hastings.

Reed Hastings didn't start as a tech visionary. He was a business leader who recognized that the world was changing and decided to embrace it rather than fight it. He didn't have all the answers, but he tested, refined, and built a business that grew with its customers instead of falling behind them.

Committing to growth isn't just scary because it's new; it's deeply emotional. When sales leaders look toward change, it brings forward uncomfortable truths, anxieties, and fears.

What's *Really* Holding Sales Leaders Back?

Many sales leaders feel stuck. They sense buyer behaviors shifting but don't fully understand why or how to respond. They fear not knowing what comes next, terrified they'll make the wrong decision and end up looking foolish in front of their teams. Deep down, they want sales to be easy again, like it used to be – predictable and straightforward. They dread the possibility of underperforming, losing money, or even losing their jobs because they didn't hit quota. These fears aren't irrational – they're real, persistent, and deeply felt.

Behind these fears are powerful emotional and psychological blockers: fear itself, ego, pressure for immediate results, attachment to past success, and lack of psychological safety. Sales leaders and sellers alike fear making mistakes or being judged as inept. This emotional landscape creates paralysis, making even the most obvious changes feel unattainable.

Layered onto these fears are broader organizational issues. Many leaders face toxic internal cultures filled with greed, complacency, and selfishness. There's a persistent disconnect – CEOs not trusting their sales leaders, leaders not trusting the Board or Executive Leadership Team (ELT), sellers not trusting their managers, and managers not trusting their sellers. Trust becomes fractured at every level.

Toxic internal culture leaves teams trapped in the status quo. They become risk-averse, held back by ego, uncertainty, and an "it's the way we've always done it" mindset. Misalignment and unrealistic expectations lead to insecurity and overwhelm. Distraction and cognitive overload sap energy and clarity, further exacerbating feelings of helplessness.

> *"Toxic internal culture leaves teams trapped in the status quo. They become risk-averse, held back by ego, uncertainty, and an 'it's the way we've always done it' mindset."*

These emotional barriers manifest in practical challenges across sales teams. Seller-centric mindsets rooted in outdated methods, selfishness, and toxic sales-bro culture prevent meaningful buyer connections. They continue to view us on a spectrum from unnecessary to fraudulent, and those negative buyer attitudes deepen the environment of mistrust.

Leaders and teams alike become stuck in insular thinking and ignorance, refusing to seek external insights that could challenge their comfort zones.

At its most destructive, this cycle of mistrust leaves sales leaders feeling disempowered. The salespeople who work for them also feel the burden of working for leaders with no power to enact positive change and in a profession that often lacks respect. This pervasive sense of disrespect and mistrust becomes the silent undercurrent preventing real growth.

Break the Cycle: Build Psychological Safety

If you recognize yourself or your team in any of these fears or emotions, you are not alone. Growth is inherently uncomfortable, but naming these fears is the first critical step toward overcoming them. As a sales leader, your role doesn't stop at managing pipeline or hitting quotas. You must also guide your team through uncertainty by openly acknowledging these anxieties and fears and providing practical pathways forward.

Creating psychological safety within your team can significantly reduce emotional barriers. Normalize experimentation and frame mistakes as learning opportunities. Encourage transparent conversations about fears and doubts. Invite your sellers into the change process, showing vulnerability by sharing your own growth challenges. Psychological safety empowers sales teams to openly discuss concerns, experiment with new strategies, and confidently share feedback, creating a powerful culture of continuous improvement and innovation.

Leaders who model emotional openness, courage, and a willingness to adapt create powerful examples for their teams. Sales leaders earn trust through specific behaviors such as sharing company goals, transparently communicating both successes and failures, and keeping their promises. By consistently following through on commitments, you show your team that your words have meaning, which reinforces their trust in your leadership. You not only reduce resistance but also inspire genuine buy-in.

The results of a high-performance, psychologically safe culture extend beyond team dynamics. Organizations with this culture consistently experience accelerated revenue growth, higher customer satisfaction due to more meaningful interactions, and improved employee retention as team members feel valued and supported.

That's your job as a sales leader. Your mandate isn't just to deliver revenue this quarter. It's to build a sales team that thrives next year, five years from now, and beyond. Winning sales organizations aren't stagnant, relying on the same playbook year after year. They test, refine, and evolve. They study buyer behavior and adjust their messaging, sequencing, and outreach accordingly.

Applying these lessons will require trust, experimentation, and the willingness to put yourself out there. Trust isn't something you build once. It requires consistent and deliberate action.

From Manager to Coach: Your Real Job Starts Now

If you're reading this book, you might be standing at your own Netflix moment. You may be feeling the pressure of change. Maybe your response rates are declining. Maybe the sales playbook that once worked for your team isn't generating the same results, or your prospects aren't engaging the way they used to. Maybe your leadership is asking for more pipeline, but you know that what got you here isn't enough to get you to the next level.

Growth is always uncomfortable, but staying the same is far riskier. The sales leaders who win are the ones willing to evolve, experiment, and meet their buyers where they are. Reed Hastings faced that same fear. He could have played it safe. He could have doubled down on DVDs. Instead, he built Netflix.

Adapting to change isn't something you do alone. Your success doesn't just come from naming shifts in buyer behavior; it comes from getting your team to embrace those changes with you.

For organizations and sales leaders to stay on top of, if not in front of, changes in buyer preferences, you have to inspire your sellers to follow your lead. While you are teaching your sellers how to capture their buyers' attention so they can earn trust and drive revenue, you must earn the right to your team's trust. It's essential that we acknowledge that even sellers with a growth mindset are scared of change.

Your job as a sales leader goes beyond teaching your team the top-of-funnel techniques discussed in Part 2 of this book. Step one is acknowledging your role as a change management agent. This requires creating a culture that indexes high on psychological safety and has enough appetite for risk that sellers are open to trying new, creative approaches.

Only by taking creative risks to test what buyers respond to can a sales organization successfully iterate its pipeline strategy and ensure revenue growth.

The Tiger Woods Moment: What Got You Here, Won't Get You There

Tiger Woods was already at the top of his game. He had just won the 1997 Masters by a record-breaking 12 strokes, a level of dominance the sport had rarely seen. He could have kept doing what was working. He could have assumed that because he had already reached the pinnacle of success, the best move was to hold steady. But Woods understood something that elite performers in every industry eventually realize - what gets you to the top isn't always what keeps you there.

Despite his unprecedented victory, Woods made a radical decision. He completely rebuilt his golf swing. It wasn't a minor adjustment. It was an overhaul that forced him to unlearn years of muscle memory and start over with new mechanics. It was a move that looked reckless from the outside. He was winning. He had no reason to change. But Woods saw what others didn't. He knew that if he wanted to stay at the top, he needed to evolve before the game evolved past him.

For a period, he struggled. His performance dipped, he lost tournaments, and he faced criticism. Through that discomfort, he kept working and trusting the process. His coach Butch Harmon reinforced that the temporary setback was worth it in the long run. Harmon helped Woods stay committed to the bigger picture. When Woods came out on the other side, he wasn't just as good as he had been before - he was better.

By 2000, he was winning again. His refusal to accept complacency cemented his place as one of the greatest athletes of all time.

Lead the Change You Want to See

You shouldn't be surprised if even the sellers who have been hitting quota for 20 years are starting to fall behind. Buyer expectations are evolving so rapidly that no one is immune. What worked for them last year, or even last quarter, might not be working now.

It's not that they suddenly forgot how to sell. It's that the game has changed, and just like Tiger Woods, they have two choices. They can cling to what worked in the past, pretending the market hasn't shifted. Or they can embrace the discomfort of change, put in the work, and come out better on the other side.

This is where you come in. You are not just a manager of quotas. You are a coach. Like Harmon, your job is to help your team see that adaptation is the only choice and to guide them forward. Just like Butch Harmon ensured that Woods had the right coaching to navigate change, you need to be the leader that creates the space for your sellers to test new strategies, refine their approach, and push through the learning curve that comes with growth. You want to be a Butch Harmon growing a team of Tiger Woods-level sellers.

If you create a culture where it's safe to try new things and where experimentation is encouraged instead of punished, you will build a sales organization that thrives for years to come.

The mark of a true leader isn't in delivering short-term results but in the relentless pursuit of growth. To inspire confidence in your team and foster a continuous improvement mindset, you must showcase opportunities to amplify strengths and uncover growth areas. Start by identifying what your team does best. Recognize and celebrate these strengths and find ways to leverage them more effectively. When your team sees their skills being valued and utilized, their confidence grows. This sets a standard of excellence, encouraging everyone to perform at their highest level.

At the same time, acknowledge areas where improvement is needed, both in yourself and your team. Approach these areas with a mindset of growth and development rather than criticism. Provide support, resources, and encouragement to help your team turn weaknesses into strengths. Recognize that growth often comes with discomfort, but it is within this discomfort that true greatness lies.

Growth will be scary for your salespeople, too. Your reps need to believe that the effort they put into growth will pay off. Your job is to earn the right to ask for their trust by demonstrating your own commitment to continuous learning and development. By doing that, you'll be equipped to build a high-performing sales team where everyone thrives.

"The question isn't - is change coming? It's already here. The real question is - will you be the leader who helps your team embrace it?"

The question isn't - is change coming? It's already here. The real question is - will you be the leader who helps your team embrace it?

From Clueless to Closer: My Sales Journey

I know how scary this growth journey can be because I've lived it.

I was a recent college graduate who had just moved to Chicago with no job prospects. It was a leap into the unknown. I took a sales job with pay so low I skipped meals to pay bills—a job I never wanted. I was broke, living in a city where I barely knew anyone, and wondering if I'd made the right decision.

Yet, within weeks, I discovered something unexpected - I was damn good at sales. Not because I had mastered some high-pressure closing tactic, but because I had honed skills that mattered in ways I hadn't realized before: listening, curiosity, passion, and a deep desire to understand people.

Within two months, I broke the promotion track record. I closed deals faster than anyone before me, not because I had a perfect script, but because I refused to accept limits others imposed. I didn't believe that my financial worth should be determined by a slow-moving corporate process. I didn't believe that the only way to sell was through pressure and manipulation.

Instead, I found my own way. I challenged outdated norms. I leveraged my skills and values to prove that you don't have to choose between being good at sales and being a good person.

I didn't succeed because I followed the traditional sales playbook - I succeeded because I did what Netflix did. I tested, adapted, and refused to accept stagnation.

That's when I realized something bigger - I wasn't the only one struggling to fit into traditional sales environments. Thousands of high-potential sales leaders and their reps face the same battles every single day. Battles with toxic work cultures, outdated training, and expectations that you should just do what's always been done, even when it feels wrong.

Many of them leave, and many more never reach their full potential. I get it. Sales success can feel like an uphill battle. I am grateful I stayed in sales even when leaving felt easier and safer. Staying allowed me to prove a point - that there's a better way. You feel it too, and now you get to set the standard for what good looks like.

The Sales Leader's Mandate: Create a Culture of Evolution

Every single rep on your team, from day one to your most tenured top performer, needs a leader who will help them evolve. Woods didn't change his swing because he was failing - he changed it because he knew that if he didn't evolve, he would eventually fall behind.

Your sellers are in the same position. Even the best ones. The ones who have been closing deals for years. The ones who seem untouchable today. Their past success won't guarantee future success if the game changes around them. And right now, the game is changing fast.

Your job is to make sure they see that before it's too late. To create a culture where it's safe to test, learn, and grow. Where they aren't only measured by past performance but by their ability to adapt and thrive in a constantly evolving market.

Just as Reed Hastings didn't settle for running a DVD rental company, you cannot settle for being a sales leader who simply maintains the status quo.

Your job is to earn the right to ask for your team's trust by demonstrating your commitment to continuous improvement. The best way to prove that you are a leader worth following is to admit that you still have more to learn, to pursue that knowledge voraciously, and to apply it strategically.

By embracing change, pushing your team forward, and creating a culture of growth instead of fear, you don't just set your team up for success - you create a sales organization that wins in the long term.

CHAPTER 3

Becoming the Sales Leader You've Always Wanted to Be

"Our potential is one thing. What we do with it is quite another."
—Angela Duckworth

The Sales Leadership Crisis

Recently, I tuned into an episode of Sell Better's Daily Show. The guests were rehashing one of the biggest problems that sellers and company executives alike point to when sales teams fail – they promoted sales leaders who weren't ready for sales leadership.

The list of excuses why this keeps happening is long. You've heard them all.

Leadership moans that they had to promote the top performer because they were afraid that they'd quit if they weren't promoted, but the newly promoted sales leader has no emotional quotient (EQ). The executive team continues to be mystified when an individual contributor turned sales manager doesn't magically possess the skills necessary to have learner-centered conversations. The remaining individual contributors are frustrated when their manager has no training on how to coach or enable sellers…

I shook my head while listening to the guests circle around these issues, the same issues sellers griped about 15 years ago when I got my first corporate sales job. All of us know it's a problem, but none of us, including the guests on this show, have an easy solution.

Promoted Without a Playbook

Almost certainly, you are one of these sales leaders. You were promoted into management without any training on how to coach, manage, or lead. Maybe you eventually found a job that invested in leadership training, or, more likely, you figured it out as you went. You set your ego aside and learned what worked by getting it wrong as often as you got it right. You pieced together leadership mindsets and coaching frameworks from webinars, downloads, and books like this. You cared enough to keep learning and growing as a sales leader. Just in case nobody else has told you, that took hard work, and I am proud of you.

Now I am going to ask more of you. Adopting the principles in this book will require you, as a sales leader, to lead courageously and challenge the status quo. Embracing *Earn the Right* means committing to a mindset of continuous improvement and innovation, for yourself and your entire sales team.

If no one handed you a playbook when you got promoted, here it is: start by investing in yourself. The only way to become the sales leader you've always wanted to be is to build that leader from the inside out.

Investing in yourself doesn't stop at adopting a learn-it-all mindset. It requires action. It means setting aside time to grow and budget for leadership growth. That might be executive coaching, a paid leadership cohort, or attending a workshop outside of your company, but at the very least, prioritizing knowledge acquisition through reading. When you invest in your own growth with the same urgency that you bring to your pipeline, your leadership becomes sharper, faster, and more credible.

Your role is to create an environment where your team's success is inevitable. That is not an easy task. If you're trying to learn how to do it alone, you're significantly increasing your chance of failure.

Outside Looking In: Embracing External Perspectives

To truly excel as a leader and drive significant growth, it's crucial to look outside of yourself, your organization, and your normal way of doing things. Embracing external perspectives is the only way to leapfrog your growth and achieve breakthrough success. By investing in yourself, you set a positive example for your team and demonstrate the importance of growth and adaptability.

External perspectives provide fresh insights and innovative ideas that can challenge the status quo and spark new ways of thinking. When we remain within our familiar boundaries, we risk becoming stagnant and missing out on opportunities for improvement. By actively seeking out and incorporating external viewpoints, we can avoid these pitfalls and drive continuous innovation.

External voices can validate and strengthen your existing strategies. Having someone from outside of your organization provide feedback or support can lend credibility to your ideas and initiatives. It shows that you are open to diverse opinions and willing to consider different approaches. This can be particularly powerful when presenting new strategies to your team or the ELT and the Board. An outside expert can help reinforce your message and make a compelling case for change.

Leveraging proven external strategies can bolster your business case and show your commitment to effective leadership and growth. Many successful organizations have already navigated challenges similar to those you face. By studying their approaches and adapting their proven strategies to fit your unique context, you can accelerate your progress and avoid common mistakes. This not only demonstrates your dedication to continuous improvement but also highlights your ability to learn from others and apply best practices within your organization.

When you invest in your own development, you build the strategic muscle required to earn influence with your ELT and Board. You're not just executing. You're interpreting trends. You're pressure-testing ideas. You're bringing in frameworks and benchmarks from outside the org that elevate the conversation from anecdotal to evidence-backed. That's what makes a sales leader credible at the executive table.

Incorporating external perspectives requires humility and a willingness to admit that we don't have all the answers. It means being open to learning from others and recognizing that valuable insights can come from outside our immediate circle. This mindset is essential for personal and professional growth and sets a powerful example for your team.

Encourage your team to seek out external perspectives as well. Promote a culture of learning and curiosity where team members feel empowered to explore new ideas and bring them back to the organization. This collective openness to external insights will drive your team and company toward greater success.

The value of external perspectives lies in their ability to provide fresh insights, validate your ideas, and offer proven strategies for success. By expanding your perspective beyond your first-hand experiences and organization, you can accelerate growth and reach new heights in your career.

The Emily Effect: Leading with Humility and Curiosity

In Chapter 1, we briefly met Emily, Kevin's sales manager. Like most of us, Emily stumbled into leadership. She realized almost immediately that while she was an excellent seller, she struggled as a sales manager. Instead of taking what is commonly perceived as the easier route, relying on the status quo, and demanding more activity to get more results, she acknowledged her limitations. Emily thrived, not because she had all the answers, but because she was willing to admit that she didn't.

Most new sales managers assume they should already know how to lead. They tell themselves they were promoted for a reason, that they're supposed to have everything figured out. The thought of asking for help

Support Local Bookstores

Throughout this book, I reference some of my favorite authors and books that have helped evolve my sales style and philosophy. I'm an advocate of long-form reading as a path to genuine growth. That's why I host Business Book Club discussion every month, and part of why I was called to write this book. I'm also an advocate for supporting bookstores that create space for diverse voices, conversation, and community.

So, I have a big ask of you: where possible, please purchase your books through local or independent bookstores.

If you're not sure where to start, check out bookshop.org.

feels like admitting failure, but seeking external perspectives is essential to growth, because leadership is a skill that must be learned, not a position to be assumed.

A defining moment in Emily's career was deciding that instead of being a know-it-all, too afraid to seek help, she would lead with humility and curiosity. You can't coach others through change if you're not willing to change yourself.

Developing Mastery: Exposure, Skills Development, Fluency

Organizational psychologist and Wharton professor Adam Grant describes three key stages of developing mastery in any skill. First, there's exposure, where you start to familiarize yourself with the basics. Then comes skill development, where you focus on repetition, get feedback, and refine your abilities. Finally, there's fluency, where everything clicks into place and becomes second nature.

Most new sales managers get stuck at exposure. They assume leadership is simply an extension of selling, so they don't take the time to study it. They go through their first few weeks or months simply reacting to problems, managing as they were managed, and hoping that leadership will eventually "click." But leadership is not an instinct; it is a set of skills you have to learn actively.

Emily wasn't satisfied getting stuck at exposure. She didn't assume that being a great seller would make her a great leader. She treated leadership like a new skill, one that required study, practice, and deliberate effort. She sought out mentors, asked for feedback, joined external communities, and observed how the best leaders at her company operated. Instead of trying to prove she had it all figured out, she made skill development and fluency the priority.

Skill development is where many new managers hesitate. It requires putting yourself out there, admitting gaps in your knowledge, and actively seeking feedback. Most people avoid this stage because it can feel scary. Asking for guidance feels like exposing a weakness. Seeking mentorship can feel like an admission that you weren't ready for the job.

It's why many sales managers plateau early. Instead of developing new or expanded leadership skills, they double down on what they already know. They focus on pipeline metrics instead of coaching. They micromanage instead of enabling. They manage tasks instead of leading people.

Emily wasn't afraid to develop the skills she lacked. She tested different ways to coach. She paid attention to what got through to her team and adjusted when something didn't work. She stayed open to learning, even when it was frustrating. Every one of those steps was a choice to invest in her own growth. This is why she grew into a strong leader so quickly; she was willing to be uncomfortable to get better.

Empathy and Emotional Intelligence Are Superpower Skills

A significant part of Emily's early success came from focusing on developing empathy and emotional intelligence. Empathy allowed her to better understand her team's perspectives, motivations, and frustrations. By intentionally putting herself in their shoes, she became more effective at providing support and removing obstacles, rather than merely instructing them on what to do.

Emotional intelligence improved her self-awareness and her ability to manage emotions effectively, both her own and those of her team. Sales leaders can cultivate empathy and emotional intelligence by actively seeking feedback on how their behavior impacts others, reflecting regularly on their interactions, and practicing empathy-driven conversations. This effort helps create a culture where team members feel valued, understood, and supported, making them more open to coaching, experimentation, and adopting new strategies.

Unfortunately, most sales managers never reach the level of mastery that Adam Grant describes as fluency because they refuse to go through the learning process. Instead, they rely on the old way of selling, clinging to the outdated playbooks and leadership styles they experienced as sales reps. They repeat the same broken strategies because changing feels riskier than staying the same.

Great sales leadership requires growth. Sales leaders who never develop new skills reinforce the outdated sales methods that buyers hate. They focus on volume over quality. They push for more outreach instead of better outreach. They demand more pipelines instead of figuring out why their team is struggling to generate real opportunities. They react instead of strategizing.

Grow the Business by Growing Yourself

The shift from management to leadership doesn't start with a framework. It starts with you.

By doing the work, building trust, and committing to your own development, you create a ripple effect that transforms your team's performance and your company's outcomes.

True leaders are open to new perspectives and are willing to go above and beyond to succeed. If you are reading this book, I know you are committed to becoming a stronger leader, the strategic sales leader you are meant to be. You are committed to leadership over management. You are focused on inspiring and guiding your team rather than just monitoring tasks and metrics.

To be clear, being a manager isn't a bad thing; it's a crucial part of the leadership journey. The act of managing your teams, your quotas, and business expectations is essential. We all start our leadership journey as managers.

As former Vice Chairman of Wealth Management at Morgan Stanley, Carla Harris shares in her New York Times best seller, *Lead to Win*, "Leadership is a journey from execution to empowerment." Again and again, I've witnessed that before sales leaders learn to manage people, they default to managing metrics. The transition from (micro)managing metrics to enabling growth in others is the most important shift a sales leader can make.

Lead by Example: Earning Respect from Executives and Employees

The best sales leaders invest in their own growth first. When you model the behaviors you want to see in your team, like coaching, accountability, and curiosity, you make it easier for your reps to follow. When you learn to think strategically, not just tactically, you also earn more credibility with your executives. It starts with you.

The ELT and the Board appreciate leaders who are not only results-driven but also committed to the long-term success of the organization. Building trust with your ELT starts with speaking their language – connecting sales outcomes to broader business objectives, such as profitability, market share, and customer lifetime value. Show them that you can balance achieving short-term goals with strategic planning for the future. Advocate for your vision and strategy by effectively communicating how your team's efforts align with the broader organizational objectives.

"When you position yourself as a partner in business growth, not just a manager of sales activity, you earn the credibility and influence needed to drive meaningful change."

Executives are more likely to respect and trust leaders who demonstrate they're committed to their own professional growth. You earn a seat at the table by showing that you know how to work *on* the business, not just *in* it. When you position yourself as a partner in business growth, not just a manager of sales activity, you earn the credibility and influence needed to drive meaningful change.

Becoming the sales leader you've always wanted to be also requires accountability. Take responsibility for your decisions and actions – and encourage your team to do the same. By fostering a culture of accountability, you build trust and authority within your team, the ELT, and the Board.

The best sales leaders stay open to change. They evolve with their buyers. They test, iterate, and refine. They make coaching and enablement a priority instead of an afterthought.

Your team is always watching. When they see you invest in coaching, seek outside perspective, or challenge your own habits, they're more likely to do the same. It's not just what you say, it's what you model. The most consistent performers I've seen are led by managers who made coaching and self-development a priority.

The result of modeling the behavior you want to see in your team is that reps who feel valued and stay longer, reducing turnover and building stability. Sellers consistently hit quotas, not out of fear or pressure, but because they are deeply motivated by a shared commitment to team success. This creates a culture of genuine collaboration, trust, and unified purpose.

Bottom line: When you invest in yourself, you become the type of leader that sellers want to follow and that bosses respect.

CHAPTER 4

Fostering a High-Performance Sales Culture

"You don't have to be great to start, but you have to start to be great." –Zig Ziglar

From Sales Manager to Strategic Leader

When I met Stephanie, a new sales manager at a business intelligence organization with clients like J.P. Morgan, Boeing, and Apple, she had been managing a small team of individual contributors for nearly two years. The company had survived the pandemic and was preparing to grow. Stephanie was being tapped to take on a more strategic sales leadership role that included enablement responsibilities.

The Founder brought me in to support the growing management team and their reps. He asked me to focus on two key goals. The first was that he felt the team needed a fresh, external view of what good looks like in Business-to-Business (B2B) sales, from compensation and growth to sales techniques and strategies. The second was that his current managers were micro-managers, not strategic leaders.

During my first meeting with Stephanie, I understood why she was struggling with her new leadership and enablement responsibilities.

Stephanie was fiercely passionate about supporting and protecting her team. She was good at selling, but even better at ensuring her team felt like she was on their side.

That was the problem.

Her reps loved her. They went to her with every minor inconvenience and ask. At first, she saw it as a sign that she was doing something right. After all, isn't that what a great sales manager is supposed to do – listen to all of their team's frustrations?

Stephanie shared that her goal was to build a high-performing team, and she initially thought the best way to achieve it was by being well-liked. She believed that if her team liked her, they would be more motivated, more engaged, and ultimately perform better. But over time, she realized that likeability does not drive performance. Trust does.

Her initial approach was to advocate for everything her reps wanted, assuming that meeting their demands would naturally lead to better results. What she later realized is that her team did not need a manager who threw money at problems and fought for better breakroom snacks. They needed a leader who would challenge them, push them toward best practices, and align their success with a strategy that led to revenue.

Stephanie's breakthrough came when she stopped focusing on being liked and started focusing on earning trust. She reworked her approach, no longer just fighting for higher commission payouts but instead designing a comp structure that incentivized the right behaviors for outbound success. Even though her reps were resistant at first, they trusted that Stephanie was advocating for their success. She was no longer just giving them what they wanted. She was giving them what they needed to win in a changing market. To get executive sponsorship for her new strategy, Stephanie needed to earn the right to the Founder's attention, too.

Aligning with Organizational Goals

Stephanie was respected in the organization, yet her ideas on how to improve retention or increase sales performance were often dismissed by leadership. She needed them to see her as a strategic leader, not a sales manager with a narrow focus on her team.

Caring deeply about your team is table stakes to becoming an exceptional sales leader. However, if your leadership team doesn't believe you understand and align with organizational goals, you will never gain the sponsorship needed to drive substantial positive change.

Like Stephanie, to become the sales leader that you want to be, you may need to transform your approach. Fostering a high-performance sales culture requires you to acknowledge that trust, not likeability, drives revenue.

Understanding and aligning with the business's revenue strategy is crucial. Elevating your understanding of strategy to incorporate organizational goals and the leadership team's long-term vision of success is essential. Without this alignment, you cannot speak the language of the business, which is essential in effective sales leadership.

This skill gap came to a head when Stephanie asked me to review a proposal that she created after listening to feedback from her team. They wanted higher commission payouts, more incentives, and increased work-from-home flexibility. Stephanie agreed with them. She thought that if she could fight for these changes and win, it would prove to her team that she had their backs.

The proposal was not tied to organizational goals, nor was it backed by data. It read more like a wish list than the business plan Stephanie had aimed to create.

As we reviewed the proposal together, I illustrated to Stephanie that her job was not to ask for more money to throw at her sellers. Her job was to align incentives with the right behaviors that actually drove pipeline and revenue.

She thoughtfully constructed an updated compensation package. It was not about paying the team more. It was about aligning their compensation with the activities proven to move the needle. The existing compensation structure rewarded behaviors that kept the sales reps busy but were not driving a profit generating pipeline. Stephanie shifted the proposal to better incentivize the strategic outbound activities that earned trust with prospects and generated real revenue.

Once she pivoted her mindset and approach, something else happened - it became much easier for her to get time with and buy-in from the Founder.

Instead of asking for more money, she made a strategic argument for why realigning compensation to support different top-of-funnel metrics would lead to better long-term results. She started thinking like a business leader.

Your job is not to fight for your team's every whim. Your job is to help them win while aligning with company milestones. That means balancing what sellers want with what they need to succeed.

> *"Your job is to create an environment where winning is not just possible, but inevitable."*

You do not need to be universally liked by your team or executive leaders, but you do need to earn their trust and respect. They need to believe that the decisions you make, whether it's compensation changes, outbound strategy, or pipeline expectations, are rooted in best practices, not short-term appeasement. Your job is to create an environment where winning is not just possible, but inevitable.

Understanding What Drives Performance Beyond Money

Hopefully, it won't surprise you that money rarely breaks the top three when sellers list their motivations. According to Inc.com, top motivations also include doing work that matters, being part of an organization with great leadership and culture, and being recognized for their contributions.[1] This means that even in sales, a profession with profound intrinsic financial motivation, a paycheck is rarely enough to solicit game-changing work.

Becoming the strategic sales leader you want to be requires you to make big asks of your sales team. The paycheck might get them in the door, but inspiring them to strive for their personal best requires more than a paycheck. It involves understanding their deeper motivations and connecting with them on a personal level.

---

[1] Melanie Curtin, "What Best Motivates You at Work? When 200,000 Employees Were Asked, This Was Their Top Response," *Inc.*, August 20, 2018, https://www.inc.com/melanie-curtin/what-motivates-you-at-work-when-200000-workers-were-asked-this-was-their-top-reponse.html.

While this book does not aspire to be a guide to great leadership, I am hoping that I can share a bit of wisdom from the 15 years I spent as a sales leader. The majority of my career was dedicated to supporting full-cycle sales reps closing four- to six-figure deals. These reps had to care deeply about owning a relationship from the first phone call to the handover. As a result, they excelled at becoming subject matter experts, managing their time effectively, opening doors, and closing deals.

Every environment I managed in was a heavy commission split. Even the startup where I joined as employee number one was a 40/60 base-to-commission split. At the first sales leadership job I had, the split was closer to 25/75. This is to say that my reps *were* motivated by money, but money wasn't their only motivation. Had I relied solely on financial carrots to encourage performance, I wouldn't have spent 15 years leading quota-smashing teams.

What I discovered is that even when salespeople were heavily motivated by money, it was rarely because they aspired to get rich. These folks weren't spending their commission checks on fancy cars or popping bottles at the club (at least not every weekend). More often, they were motivated by the good that the money could do in the world.

Caring Personally versus Obnoxious Aggression: Finding Balance in Leadership

When I realized how to earn the right to ask my employees what their personal motivations were, it completely changed my ability to lead. It required me to acknowledge that I was asking them to trust me with their dreams. What I didn't know then was that I was tapping into a concept called "caring personally," which Kim Scott highlighted in her best-selling book *Radical Candor* as a core leadership value and the foundation for compassionate candor.

Before I'd read *Radical Candor*, actually before Kim had even written *Radical Candor*, I developed an exercise to help guide 1:1 conversations with my sales reps in pursuit of understanding their motivations and earning the right to tap into what made them want to show up as the best version of themselves at work.

You can download a copy here of that Source of Motivation Exercise, along with my PATH Goal Setting Framework at www.salesledgtm.com/leadership or use the QR code provided.

Use these exercises to better understand your sales reps' motivations and goals. This may not be the leadership advice you expected in a fairly tactical B2B sales book, but I've found that uncovering ways to connect with and care deeply about each of your reps is the surest path to earning the right to push them to greatness.

It is important that I lead by example and am radically candid with you. I was not a great sales leader when I was first thrust into a management role. I was 23 years old, and I'd only sold the product for six months. When my manager was fired quite suddenly, I became the Sales Manager of a team of six sales reps. All of them were older than me, most by more than a decade. All of them had considerably more sales experience than I did.

I found myself in the vicious cycle that I listened to the Sell Better Daily Show guests rehash nearly 15 years later. I was a brand-new sales manager, promoted because I was good at selling and, frankly, there was nobody else to give the job to. I was given no support or training and was expected to figure it out. In those first months of sales leadership, I described myself as an "iron fist, velvet glove" leader. How embarrassing! It makes me cringe to think back on how much pride I felt in that description. I thought I was nailing it. I was, in fact, not nailing it.

Instead, I deviated from what Kim Scott describes as "obnoxious aggression." I was proud to be "brutally honest." I thought I was being direct, transparent, and confident in my direction. I thought I was doing what a leader does. What I'd missed was making sure my team knew that I cared deeply. Of course, I knew that I cared deeply. I cared about their success so much that I felt sick with anxiety, so I pushed relentlessly to ensure they didn't fail.

My "iron fist, brutal honesty" approach was seen as direct but not kind. It got results, but hurt feelings just as often. Challenging my reps daily, on an open sales floor, eroded trust. Deals got done, bosses were happy, and reps were getting paid, but something was missing. Because sales reps are motivated by more than money, I was demotivating them more than money could motivate them. I was missing the importance of earning the right to challenge directly and the foundation of caring deeply.

Kim Scott even updated her book four years later to talk about "compassionate candor" versus "radical candor" because too many leaders were using her book as a reason to be jerks, justifying their behavior by saying, "Hey, I was only being candid."

Like many sales leaders, obnoxious aggression came to me naturally, so I can't use being misled by a book as an excuse. I got it wrong before I figured out a better way to lead.

Scott describes the balance as "caring personally while challenging directly." Once that clicked, it fundamentally changed my leadership style. My reps would still describe me as a hard ass. I have high expectations and a low tolerance for excuses, but I will also fight for my team. They deserve to love selling, get a fair paycheck, work for a sales leader they trust, and at an organization they're proud of.

I share this story of one of my earliest and most significant failings as a sales leader, in case any of you see yourself, to some extent, in this story and can learn from my mistakes.

The Trifecta of Trust Building

Now I teach the trifecta of trust-building behaviors.

First, actively listen to employee feedback and demonstrate your commitment by taking visible action based on their input or transparently sharing why the action is a challenge. When your team knows their voices matter, their engagement and sense of ownership increase.

Second, openly admit your mistakes and show vulnerability. This demonstrates authenticity and humility, reinforcing that trust is built through honesty rather than perceived perfection.

Finally, advocate for your team, ensuring they have the resources, support, and recognition they deserve. This confirms your genuine commitment to their success, deepening mutual trust.

Building and maintaining trust through transparency, consistency, active listening, vulnerability, and empathy is not a nice-to-have, it is fundamental to driving high performance. Teams with high levels of trust consistently outperform those without it. They collaborate more effectively, solve problems faster, and are more willing to take risks that lead to innovation and growth. Trust also fosters resilience, enabling teams to adapt confidently to change and uncertainty, ultimately enhancing long-term organizational success.

What I hope you will feel inspired to consider is:

How can I care deeply about my team?

How can I make sure they know that I care deeply about them?

Say it with words. Show it with actions. Truly give a shit. Only then have you earned the right to give direct, honest, and helpful feedback. If, like me, you have a tendency to jump to barking orders before you've earned the right for your team to trust your direction, let this book be a blueprint to becoming a better type of leader – the sales leader you've always wanted to be.

If you read that call to action and softly mumbled to yourself, "Well, that *is* what we pay them for," you're not exactly wrong, but I promise you this book will help you get better results from your team by earning the right to ask them to be overachievers in a world where checking the boxes and quota underachievement is the norm.

Gut Check Your Motivations

Before we move on, I have one final ask in your pursuit of becoming the strategic sales leader you're meant to be. I'm going to ask you to be honest about *your* motivations.

If personal glory motivated by ego is your North Star, you'll never be a great sales leader. If you only center yourself in your decision-making, you'll never have a consistently high-performing sales team or the respect of your executive team.

Your team's goals in the context of the organizational goals must come first. This means you need to make your team look good, you need to make the organization look strong, and then you, by default, shine. No, this doesn't mean you should sacrifice your mental health or be a door-mat. Quite the opposite, it means that your strength as a leader comes from understanding that your greatness is born from leading by example and helping others master the craft to achieve big goals.

To become the sales leader you've always wanted to be, learn from the examples provided. Understand the unique needs and strengths of your team and advocate for them while aligning with broader organizational goals. This dual focus will help you earn the trust and respect of both your team and leadership, guiding you toward effective and inspirational leadership.

Access Free Downloadable Worksheets

Download two of my favorite resources that you can use to tap into your team's greatness.

- PATH goal setting worksheet
- Sales Motivation Exercise

www.salesledgtm.com/leadership

CHAPTER 5

Rejecting Old Ways of Working (Because They Don't Work Anymore)

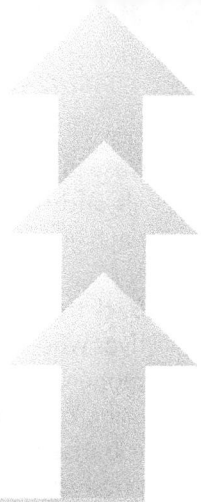

"You do not rise to the level of your goals. You fall to the level of your systems." –James Clear

Always Be Closing: The Sales Culture of the 1960s–2000s

In the late 1900s, the corporate world focused heavily on profitability, expansion, efficiency, and competition. This mindset shaped corporate cultures with rigid hierarchies, aggressive sales methods, and a singular focus on closing deals. Sales training prioritized controlling conversations and dominating interactions rather than genuinely understanding customer needs. The high-pressure, results-driven approach emphasized authority instead of empathy or meaningful connection.

Sales training manuals from major corporations like IBM, Xerox, and AT&T focused heavily on assertive selling techniques, strict sales processes, and robotic objection-handling scripts. Books that advanced this narrative, like Tom Hopkins' *How to Master the Art of Selling*, were widely popular in the 1980s and 90s. For nearly 50 years, salespeople were taught how to aggressively prospect, bulldoze over objections, and push for a close at all costs.

My Early Sales Career

When I started my sales career less than 20 years ago, the industry still relied heavily on many of these outdated tactics. My first sales job after moving to Chicago provided a stark contrast to today's environment.

Case in point: our sales team still relied on fax machines to send proposals and receive signed contracts. The entire sales floor would jump up each time the fax rang, hoping it was finally their deal coming through.

Back then, the sales leadership was composed almost entirely of executives who had come up through the ranks in the 1960s–2000s and championed those outdated approaches. Company policies reflected a strict adherence to traditional, rigid structures, with inflexible schedules and a transactional approach to customer relationships. The environment emphasized a culture of "work hard, play hard," which left little room for empathy, flexibility, or a deeper understanding of buyer needs.

I struggled with the aggressive sales tactics I was taught. The transactional, pushy style felt icky, and it certainly wasn't aligned with what my buyers wanted or needed. It felt wrong to approach prospects as adversaries instead of partners. Eventually, I realized I needed to reject those outdated norms. Instead, I developed my own approach, one built around genuine curiosity, deep listening, understanding needs, and consistently delivering real value.

Rejecting those outdated, aggressive sales practices allowed me to find new, better ways to sell. My personal approach, *Earn the Right,* allowed me to build trust and rapport with my customers, rather than relying on pressure or manipulation. My goal was to provide genuine value first and build long-term relationships. My success in sales grew significantly when I embraced this approach, and I discovered a more fulfilling and effective way to sell.

Same Script, New Era: Why Old Tactics Still Haunt Us

The reality is that much of the sales training, methodologies, frameworks, and strategies still taught today are rooted in those same old aggressive tactics. While some techniques remain useful, we can't pretend the sales profession hasn't evolved or that buyers haven't changed dramatically over the past 65 years. Continuing to apply outdated strategies simply doesn't serve today's buyers or sales professionals.

This book is about embracing new ways of selling and working. Ways of selling are built around buyer-centricity, trust, empathy, and psychological safety. We aren't throwing everything from the past away. Instead, we're choosing to learn from it, evolve our craft, and recognize that there is space and opportunity for better, more thoughtful approaches.

Rejecting old methods doesn't mean losing sales effectiveness. Creating psychological safety doesn't mean abandoning accountability. On the contrary, by embracing new strategies rooted in trust, value delivery, and a data-driven, disciplined approach, we can achieve better results. Our sellers and buyers alike deserve a modern sales approach that prioritizes solving genuine business problems and achieving shared success.

Radical Candor in Action

Obnoxiously aggressive leaders, as highlighted by Scott in *Radical Candor*, rely on blunt honesty, ignoring the negative emotional impact of their feedback. Unfortunately, this style has historically been common in sales environments, creating short-term results at the cost of long-term trust and team morale.

Obnoxious aggression was, and occasionally still is, my default management style. It is easy to fall into because, frankly, it works in the short term. Data shows that sales professionals generally prefer working for leaders who communicate transparently and directly, even if they are perceived as harsh, rather than leaders who fall into what Scott calls "ruinous empathy," where feedback is sugar-coated or withheld altogether. At least under an obnoxiously aggressive leader, team members always know where they stand.

However, sustainable growth and a high-performance culture demand more from sales leaders. The call for modern sales leaders is to intentionally balance clear, direct communication with genuine care for the individual. Leaders must push their teams to new heights while modeling graciousness, vulnerability, and openness to feedback. This balanced approach creates psychological safety, fosters accountability, and ultimately leads to stronger, more sustainable results for both teams and buyers.

> Qwerty Keyboard created in the 1870s, is named for the first six letters in the top letter row of the keyboard. Despite new keyboard designs being up to 74% more effective, the design continues to be heavily used.

The QWERTY Effect: Why Familiar Isn't Always Better

Even when we recognize the value of adopting new approaches and embracing change, letting go of outdated methods can feel daunting. It's easy to stay with what's familiar simply because it's comfortable. Clinging to old ways can hold us back. Just because something that worked in the past doesn't mean it remains the best approach today. A prime example of this is the QWERTY keyboard.

The QWERTY keyboard layout was designed in the 19th century for mechanical typewriters. Its primary purpose was to prevent jamming by spacing out commonly used letter pairs. While it did its job well in the era of typewriters, it was never meant for modern typing efficiency. Despite this, the QWERTY layout is still the standard today, not because it's the best, but because it's what we're used to.

As technology evolved, alternative keyboard layouts like the Dvorak Simplified Keyboard were developed to increase typing speed and accuracy. Studies show that the Dvorak layout can reduce finger movement and boost typing efficiency by up to 74%. Despite these benefits, QWERTY reigns supreme.

This resistance to change, despite clear data pointing us in a new direction, doesn't just apply to keyboards. It's also common in sales strategies, where holding onto familiar methods can prevent teams from adapting effectively to new market dynamics. Like using outdated sales practices from the late 1900s ignores the demands of the modern buyer, our continued use of the QWERTY keyboard is not based on effectiveness but familiarity.

In sales, clinging to outdated methods doesn't just slow you down; it actively hurts your ability to drive business growth. It leads to missed opportunities, lost deals, decreased market share, and ultimately diminished revenue. The sales profession evolves rapidly, driven by new technologies, shifting buyer behaviors, and heightened customer expectations. Companies that resist adapting their sales approach risk becoming irrelevant and losing ground to more agile competitors.

For sales leaders, this lesson is crucial. Sticking to outdated sales strategies can hinder your team's performance and your organization's growth. To stay competitive and drive success, you need to embrace new approaches and always look for ways to improve.

Curious Questions: Lessons from the Great Depression

Rejecting old ways of working means committing to continuous improvement and innovation. It involves questioning existing practices, exploring new ideas, and being willing to take risks.

The persistence of the QWERTY keyboard is a classic example of how we often stick to what we know, even when better options are available. What often holds us back from change is that we never question why something was created the way it was in the first place. We get so used to how things are that we forget to ask if there's a better way.

This reminds me of a story about our family's hamburger recipe. In my family, we always put breadcrumbs in our hamburgers. I never questioned why, assuming it was to improve the taste or texture. When I finally asked about the recipe, I learned the real reason: meat was expensive, so my grandparents used breadcrumbs to make the meat stretch further, and the practice stuck. If I had never asked, I would have continued adding breadcrumbs to my recipe, not because it created a better hamburger, but because it's how it has always been done. By practicing curiosity, I learned it was a holdover from times of financial insecurity and could make an informed decision next time I grilled up a burger.

Being curious about the status quo allows us to make better decisions about what habits to keep and which we can let go of because they no longer serve us. The QWERTY keyboard and my family's hamburger recipe show why it's important to ditch outdated methods and embrace more efficient approaches. Your willingness to challenge the status quo and drive continuous improvement will inspire your team and position your organization for long-term success.

Evolving with Empathy: What Today's Buyers *Really* Want

The cliché, "What got us here won't get us there," is truer than ever in B2B sales.

Psychology is universal, but values and expectations evolve with each generation. The foundational psychological principles of sales, like understanding human behavior and influencing decisions, remain constant. However, buyer demographics, expectations, and values have shifted dramatically.

Selling *and* buying have undergone a significant transformation. Modern B2B strategies focus on understanding the customer's needs and providing value through personalized, consultative, and data-driven approaches. The shift toward collaboration is evident in how sales professionals are increasingly trained to listen actively, build trust, and act as advisors rather than pushers or order takers.

Today's buyers expect a blend of traditional values like trust and familiarity with modern demands for data-driven insights, win-win mindsets, and digital competence. While traditional ways of interacting with buyers persist, they are now complemented by demands for clear pricing structures, transparency, and proactive information sharing. Buyers look to sellers as strategic partners, valuing industry knowledge, thought leadership, and innovative solutions to complex challenges.

"The shift from aggressive, hierarchical tactics to empathetic, collaborative, and data-driven strategies has transformed how sales professionals engage with customers."

The shift from aggressive, hierarchical tactics to empathetic, collaborative, and data-driven strategies has transformed how sales professionals engage with customers.

This evolution doesn't mean discarding every past lesson; it means thoughtfully examining past approaches, retaining timeless truths about human psychology, and updating our methods to match today's buyers and market realities. The underlying psychological drivers of buying behavior remain fundamentally true, even as our methods for engaging buyers continue to evolve.

The journey from the past to the present shows that what worked yesterday may not be the best choice for today or tomorrow. It's time to reject the old ways and become the catalyst for change. Embracing the modern sales approach discussed throughout this book empowers your team to build disciplined, profitable pipelines rooted in genuine buyer trust.

CHAPTER 6

The Discipline Behind the Results

> *"Often when you think you're at the end of something, you're at the beginning of something else." –Mr. Rogers*

Lessons from Mr. Miyagi

In the classic movie *Karate Kid*, Daniel is a teenager who desperately wants to learn karate to defend himself against bullies. He seeks help from Mr. Miyagi, an experienced martial arts master, but Mr. Miyagi doesn't teach Daniel fighting techniques. Instead, Mr. Miyagi assigns Daniel tasks that seem unrelated to karate: waxing cars, sanding the floor, and painting fences. Daniel becomes annoyed and confused because the chores feel pointless. He doesn't understand how they could possibly relate to karate.

Mr. Miyagi knows something Daniel doesn't. Each chore is carefully chosen, and every movement is intentional. Waxing cars in a precise circular motion, sanding floors with deliberate patterns, and painting fences with careful strokes build Daniel's muscles, reflexes, and instincts. These repetitive tasks equip Daniel with the foundation to be an exceptional fighter. Mr. Miyagi knows that if Daniel practices intentionally and builds the right habits through repetition, his success won't just be possible - it will be inevitable.

Trusting the Process: Kevin's Cold Call Comeback

Kevin, the new seller on Emily's team, feels embarrassed about cold calling. He hates interrupting prospects, and he doesn't fully believe in the product he's selling at his uncle's SaaS company. Kevin thinks Emily's recommended cold call opener sounds pushy. He'd rather talk about the weather or sports, anything but business.

Emily doesn't just tell Kevin what to do and leave it at that. She recognizes Kevin's discomfort not as defiance, but as a sign of underdeveloped confidence - a signal for personalized coaching. She knows Kevin has potential but lacks the confidence to use the call opener effectively. Like Mr. Miyagi, Emily knows Kevin needs practice, so they role-play repeatedly until Kevin's words flow naturally, and his tone conveys genuine confidence.

Emily doesn't stop at role-playing; she shows Kevin the data. Cold calls opened with a relevant reason for the call consistently outperform calls that start with small talk. Emily knows that being transparent with data and using it to help a seller trust her advice means they are much more likely to take the time to master the techniques she is teaching.

She even picks up the phone herself, modeling the behavior she's teaching Kevin. As multi-platinum recording artists, Migos would say, "she walks it like she talks it," demonstrating firsthand the effectiveness of the process she's asking Kevin to follow.

At first, Kevin resists, just like Daniel resisted Mr. Miyagi's chores. Kevin thinks he knows better and believes his conversational skills alone should carry him. He questions Emily's methods and feels frustrated by the repetitive drills. But slowly, as he sees the incremental improvements, Kevin starts to trust the process. He realizes the opener isn't pushy - it's clear, respectful, and relevant. He sees that practice builds skills and that skills build confidence. As a leader, it's not just your job to design repeatable sales processes, it's your job to help your reps believe in their value before they yield results.

This intentional process, designed and reinforced by Emily, ensures Kevin's transformation from hesitant and uncertain to confident and capable. The habits, skills, and mindsets that guarantee their success require practice.

Just like Mr. Miyagi did for Daniel, and Emily did for Kevin, your job is to design deliberate practices that feel as clear and straightforward as waxing a car or painting a fence. Processes that salespeople might question at first, but they'll thank you for later, when those processes turn them into winners.

DEVELOPING SKILLS MASTERY

- **Exposure:** Familiarize yourself with the basics.
- **Skills development:** Focus on repetition and refinement.
- **Fluency:** Skill becomes second nature.

Perfecting My Chaturanga: Exposure to Fluency

As Adam Grant discusses in his book *Hidden Potential: The Science of Achieving Greater Things*, "The way that you master knowledge and skills is by using them as you acquire them. If you don't even make enough attempts to make mistakes, then it's pretty hard to make progress." This concept is echoed in Angela Duckworth's best-selling book *Grit*, where she emphasizes the importance of "deliberate practice." Deliberate practice involves focused, goal-oriented training, where each attempt is an opportunity to learn and improve. It's not just about repetition but about making intentional efforts to enhance specific skills.

Incorporating these principles into sales training means understanding that exposure and repetition are essential for sellers to ramp quickly, but skill mastery can only happen with deliberate practice. Guiding your salespeople to mastery involves setting clear goals, providing immediate feedback, and encouraging them to push beyond their comfort zones. By embracing deliberate practice, sales leaders can help their teams develop the resilience and expertise needed to thrive, but it won't happen overnight.

Sales leaders often feel the urge to train their teams on all aspects of sales simultaneously, hoping to accelerate their development. However, this approach is rarely effective. Similarly, sales reps might expect to jump from zero to hero in a matter of days, but this isn't feasible. There is no silver bullet in sales. The only way to gain fluency and master sales as a craft is through intentional practice and experience.

Fluency requires you to stay dialed in on one skill at a time in your coaching conversations, your call reviews, and your feedback loops. By coaching and training on a singular skill before moving to the next, you enable your sellers to develop good habits, so they never feel like they need to rely on tricks or tactics to build a pipeline.

Over the past two years, I've been building a yoga practice. Yoga requires you to build strength and master simple moves and poses before you can execute the complicated ones. Speaking from personal experience, it's tempting to try to achieve those complicated poses right away, driven by ego and impatience.

When I first started practicing yoga, I was exposed to dozens of complex poses, and the instructor made each of them look effortless. I watched her demonstrate them, and, with her coaching, I tried to copy what I saw. That was exposure and skill development. But I didn't move into deliberate practice – the kind that leads to fluency – until I chose a single pose to work on - my chaturanga. I broke it down into how I was holding each part of my body and focused on deliberately improving one small part of the movement at a time. That was deliberate practice with a goal of fluency. Now, two years in, my chaturanga is strong – not because I'm a natural, but because I've practiced it with precision so many times.

The true path to progress lies in focusing on the foundational elements. Only by learning small, seemingly boring movements and positions can you eventually put them together to achieve the final pose. As a sales leader, your job is not to expose your reps to every 'pose' in the sales playbook simultaneously and hope they figure it out. Your job is to help them build a strong foundation through repetition and then coach one skill at a time until it becomes second nature.

On the spectrum of exposure, skills development, and fluency as outlined by Grant, building a yoga practice demanded that I move swiftly into skill development, while accepting that it will take years of practice before I develop fluency. Training sellers demands the same.

They need to practice the basics every day, but the journey to fluency won't happen by going through the daily motions. The basics become their foundation for specialized skill development.

Much like the yoga practice I've been diligently investing in, it's important to acknowledge that sales is a craft. You get better with each day of deliberate practice, but it will take you years to develop fluency (and that's okay).

In sales, as in *The Karate Kid* or yoga, the basics might seem tedious, but they are essential. Daniel didn't realize that "wax on, wax off" was training his muscles for real combat, just as reps may not immediately see the value in structured practice. However, consistent, intentional practice is what transforms raw potential into real skill.

The Sales Leader's Toolkit: Coach, Train, Manage

Your job is to create the structure for effective skills development on the path to fluency. You must ensure your reps aren't just going through the motions but are building the right skills, the right way. That requires mastering three distinct but equally important roles: coaching, training, and managing. Each plays a different role in a rep's development, and together, they create a team that consistently builds profit generating pipeline.

Coaching happens one-on-one. It's specialized to exactly what each rep needs at that exact moment in their development. Coaching isn't about general sales knowledge. Instead, it's about collaborating with each team member on their unique challenges. This could mean listening to their recorded calls together, helping them improve their cold call openers, or practicing how to handle specific objections. Coaching is about creating deliberate practice opportunities that build confidence, skill, and trust. It earns you the right to push your team toward higher performance.

Training is done with the whole team. It's broader, focused on improving everyone's overall sales skills and knowledge. Training sessions might cover new discovery techniques, best practices for running effective demos, or teaching sellers how to clearly communicate the value of your solution. Training raises the baseline skills of your entire team.

When done well, training also creates a shared language and set of best practices everyone can rely on.

Managing involves activities like pipeline meetings, forecasting, deal reviews, and setting performance expectations. It's about accountability and making sure your team stays on track. Managing is important because it gives you visibility into what's happening across your sales organization. It helps you spot problems early so that you can solve them quickly. But managing alone won't build a high-performing team. Managing needs to be supported by strong coaching and consistent training.

Great sales leaders know how and when to shift between coaching, training, and managing. They use coaching to build trust and personalize skill development. They use training to lift the overall capability of their team. They use managing to keep their team accountable and focused on achieving revenue goals.

Building a Team That Delivers

Getting results is not about doing more. It is about doing better. It is about creating a team culture grounded in intention, structure, and consistent execution.

In Part 1, we've focused on building leadership foundations. Now, you need a strategy.

Part 2 of this book will walk you through the exact nine-step formula I teach outbound sales teams to help them build a profit generating pipeline. You will learn the specific techniques, sample scripts, and tools that support each step. Then, you will learn how to bring those steps to life through your leadership, supported by strategy, repeatable processes, modern sales skill sets, and winning mindsets.

When you apply this formula with intention and consistency, your team won't just grow a pipeline - they will generate real opportunities that drive revenue.

Part 2

A Proven Pipeline Formula

CHAPTER 7

Taking a Strategic Approach to Top-of-Funnel Excellence

"Deciding what not to do is as important as deciding what to do."
–Steve Jobs

The following chapters are a blueprint for top-of-funnel excellence. This section of the book will help you refine your approach to territory management, sales messaging, sequence building, and leading sales conversations.

The goal of sharing an approach that blends high-level strategy and practical tips, under the umbrella of the *Earn the Right* mindset, is to empower an outbound motion that drives revenue for your team.

What you won't see is a reliance on tricks, tactics, or outdated beliefs. Instead, we'll focus on plays backed by data, buyer psychology, and 20 years of driving revenue for outbound sales teams.

Kevin's Climb: Building Foundations for Sales Success

Imagine yourself guiding Kevin, alongside his real-life manager, Emily. Emily is an accomplished sales leader who initially underestimated how difficult it would be to earn Kevin's trust and engagement. She discovered firsthand that structured outbound strategies and repeatable processes were critical not only for seller success but also for reinforcing her credibility as a leader.

Companies implementing structured outbound sales strategies experience higher per-rep revenue growth compared to those without such strategies. Emily learned this lesson when Kevin struggled initially with unstructured methods, causing his performance and her own leadership to be questioned. Emily had to intentionally rebuild trust and demonstrate strategic clarity before Kevin could see the value in structured processes. As she invested in becoming a better, more strategic sales leader, she also built repeatable processes to enable Kevin's success.

As you read in Part 1, after only three days of training, Emily showed Kevin to his desk and told him to start making calls. Kevin needed to figure out who they sell to and how to reach them first. The formula Kevin learned and followed in the coming months to go from Performance Improvement Plan (PIP) to top-performer is what we'll cover in the coming chapters.

Kevin started by identifying and understanding his ideal customer. Initially overwhelmed, he soon learned from Emily that targeting the right customers is crucial. With Emily's guidance, Kevin shifted his mindset from trying to contact everyone to focusing on those most likely to buy. Emily taught him how to build and segment lists effectively, ensuring he reached out to the most qualified and interested prospects. This targeted approach made Kevin more effective and successful, which meant he finally started enjoying his job.

Crafting segment-specific value propositions was Kevin's next challenge. Emily showed him how to develop messages tailored to specific buying groups. Using a structured framework, Kevin learned to map out features, advantages, and benefits so he could speak in the language that resonated with his audience. With Emily's mentorship, Kevin learned the importance of delivering a compelling value proposition, making his interactions with prospects more impactful. Kevin's next focus was to fully utilize sequences and a multichannel approach. With Emily's help, he explored various outreach channels, their importance, and strategies for optimizing each one. Kevin came to embrace making the best use of chosen channels to ensure his message was heard loud and clear.

At this point, Kevin started reaching out with an emphasis on using outcome-based messaging to earn the attention of the best-fit buyers on their Channel of Choice (CoC). Emily's encouragement and feedback helped him refine his techniques, leading to even better results.

As Kevin started speaking with prospects, he realized that active listening and responding to objections were vital skills that he needed to master. While hosting discovery meetings, he practiced listening to understand rather than to respond. Kevin learned to reframe success in handling objections as continuing the conversation, not just overcoming them. Emily introduced him to frameworks that prioritize curiosity, asking smart questions, and using the voice of the customer during sales conversations. Emily's coaching in this area helped Kevin become more resilient and effective in his interactions.

Creating Career Longevity

Throughout Part 2, Emily's role as Kevin's manager is crucial. She inspires and guides him. Emily understands her organization's goals and how her work ties in, allowing her to effectively communicate her strategy, build repeatable processes to support her strategy, and enable Kevin with the skills to execute those processes.

Sales leaders face high stakes. The average tenure for a Vice President of Sales ranges from nine to 17 months, depending on the industry. Chief Revenue Officers (CROs) have the shortest tenure of any C-suite Officer, with Harvard Business Review data sharing an average tenure of 25 months.[2] Without effective leadership and structured processes, sales leaders face high rep attrition, missed quotas, and teams that dread rather than enjoy their work. The ability to earn the right to your team's trust so that you can empower them to execute a blueprint to top-of-funnel excellence directly impacts both team morale and personal career longevity.

Profit Generating Pipeline will guide you through the systems, strategies, and skills to build strong top-of-funnel foundations. By the end of this book, you will know how to lead a team that builds qualified pipeline with consistency, earns the attention of your best buyers, and drives revenue with less guesswork.

---

[2] Toman, Nick, Bryan Kurey, and Dave Lingebach. "The High Costs of Chief Revenue Officer Turnover." Harvard Business Review, October 10, 2024. https://hbr.org/2024/10/the-high-costs-of-chief-revenue-officer-turnover?autocomplete=true.

CHAPTER 8

Identifying and Understanding Your Ideal Customer

> *"The best sales strategy is to win where you have the greatest likelihood of winning." – Anthony Iannarino*

IDEAL CUSTOMER PROFILE (ICP) DEFINITION

A clearly defined description of the types of organizations & individuals within your SOM that gain maximum benefit from your product or service.

A strong ICP focuses your sales team's resources on prospects who are most likely to see immediate value from your solution, spend more money, buy faster & ultimately become successful, loyal customers.

When trying to capture the attention of your prospects, it can be tempting to cast a wide net. This is often referred to as a "boil the ocean" approach, where companies attempt to appeal to the broadest possible market. The most successful companies I've worked with find traction not by going big, but by niching down. This principle comes to life in the story of Melody McCloskey, CEO of StyleSeat.

When she first pitched her "OpenTable for beauty" concept in Silicon Valley, it was met with skepticism. The beauty industry, despite its massive market size, wasn't taken seriously. Many dismissed it as frivolous, but McCloskey didn't waste time pitching to people who refused to acknowledge her vision. She doubled down on her belief that if she could solve a real problem for a very specific audience - independent beauty professionals - the rest would follow.

McCloskey famously said, "Know your customers so well that your product fits them perfectly and sells itself." She knew that understanding her buyers wasn't only about market research. It was about listening. Her earliest users weren't treated as data points; they were her advisors. She listened closely to what they needed: easier scheduling, faster payments, and better client communication. Then she built her platform around those needs.

Her laser focus on a single, high-potential segment allowed her to deliver a solution that felt personal and specific. That specificity made StyleSeat sticky. Her users didn't just like the product. They became raving fans, many of whom doubled their revenue within a year of using the platform.

What's powerful for sales leaders to consider is that McCloskey didn't try to boil the ocean. She didn't pitch her solution to every independent service provided in the gig economy. She didn't chase every possible buyer. She picked a segment where she could focus on delivering maximum value.

Her success didn't come overnight. She spent 18 months bootstrapping StyleSeat before generating enough revenue to attract outside investment, but her clarity of focus never wavered. She knew who her buyers were, what mattered most to them, and she committed to meeting those needs better than anyone else. For sales leaders, McCloskey's approach is a reminder: your greatest advantage comes from niching down.

This chapter will help you realize that your Total Addressable Market (TAM) is not the same as your Ideal Customer Profile (ICP). Even your ICP is not one static group. You can't write one message to speak to everyone. If you want your team to run effective outbound, you must teach them how to segment. Not only to build better lists but also to design micro-campaigns that reflect what different buyers in different parts of the market care about most.

Sales leaders and their teams spend more time talking to buyers than anyone else in the organization. That means you are uniquely positioned to collect insights about what matters most. The real win isn't having that information. It's using it.

Just like McCloskey, your job is not to reach everyone. Your job is to understand the right people so well that your message fits perfectly and sells itself.

Understanding TAM, SAM, and SOM: The Key to Strategic ICP Creation

When discussing market potential, it's essential to understand three critical measurement tools:

- Total Addressable Market (TAM)
- Serviceable Available Market (SAM)
- Sales Obtainable Market (SOM)

These metrics help gauge the size of a market and set realistic growth expectations.

TAM (TOTAL ADDRESSABLE MARKET)
Entire market demand for what you sell.

SAM (SERVICEABLE AVAILABLE MARKET)
Segment of TAM your business can realistically serve.

SOM (SALES OBTAINABLE MARKET)
Portion of SAM you can actually sell to now.

Understanding these measurement tools is crucial, not only for setting targets but also for avoiding common pitfalls. A frequent misstep sales teams make is interpreting SAM as a list of "qualified leads." Once that happens, things get messy. Territories get too big. Customer Relationship Management Systems (CRMs) get overloaded. Reps feel overwhelmed and under-supported. They're given huge lists of people who technically could buy, but with no direction about how to prioritize the most valuable accounts.

Kevin experienced this firsthand. Each day, he brought a new list of leads to call, but was mostly met with responses like "not a fit" or "wrong person." Kevin felt like he was spinning his wheels. Emily knew the "boil the ocean" approach led to burnout and missed opportunities. She had seen other new sellers get distracted by the temptation to reach everybody, so she committed to making sure Kevin didn't fall into the same trap.

One morning, she told Kevin, "I see you're working hard, but it's time to work smarter. Let's focus on your Ideal Customer Profile, your ICP."

Kevin was confused. He told Emily, "I've been calling everyone on the list because I figured more people meant better chances."

Emily smiled, understanding his logic but knowing its pitfalls. "It's natural to think that way, but that's not how you'll succeed here. We've talked about TAM, which is everyone who could possibly buy from us. But if you try to talk to everyone, you end up connecting with no one."

Kevin had heard this before, but only now was he beginning to truly grasp the importance of narrowing his focus.

Emily continued, "Think of TAM as the entire ocean. It's massive, and there are plenty of fish, but not all of them are the best fit for what you're offering. SAM is smaller and more manageable, but even then, we aren't looking for just any fish. SOM is the part of the ocean with the hungriest fish, those who are most likely to bite. That is where we will find our ideal customers."

Kevin was intrigued. He asked, "So how do I find out who these ideal customers are?"

"Your SOM is the slice of your SAM that we can realistically win, given our strengths, positioning, and competition," she explained. "Your ICP defines the customers who we are not able to serve but who need our product and are most likely to buy quickly and to remain loyal."

Instead of asking for more accounts, Kevin began focusing strategically on smaller, clearly defined groups of potential customers. As he applied this targeted approach, he noticed an immediate shift. His conversations became more relevant, prospects responded better, and his confidence soared.

One afternoon, after landing a meeting with a high-profile company that perfectly matched the segmented ICP list that they built together, Kevin told Emily, "I finally understand. It's so much easier to earn a prospect's attention when I understand what is most relevant to them. Targeting the right people has made all the difference."

Emily was proud, reminding him that his ICP can be continually expanded as he learns more about the market and what prospects respond to best.

Kevin's journey illustrates why focusing on ICP accounts transforms sales efforts from scattered and frustrating to targeted and rewarding. He discovered firsthand the power of segmenting territories, shifting from merely trying to "do more" to genuinely "doing better."

That's the mindset shift this chapter is here to spark.

The Dangers of the "Boil the Ocean" Approach

Imagine if Melody McCloskey had taken the standard route: launching StyleSeat by blasting her message to everybody in the beauty industry with a generic pitch. She might have seen a few short-term wins, but she never would have built the kind of company that helped users double their revenue by powering over 155 million appointments. Her impact came from focus. She knew her buyers so well that she created something only for them. If she had tried to boil the ocean, that relevance would have been lost, and her product would have been white noise.

Many sales leaders feel pressured to contact as many leads as possible as quickly as possible. The logic seems sound at first glance: more

TAM is the total market demand for a product or service. It represents the maximum revenue opportunity if a company captured 100 percent of the market. Think of it as the biggest possible pie your company could take a slice from. For example, if you're selling women's apparel, your TAM would encompass all potential sales globally within that market. TAM gives you a sense of scale, but it's more of a theoretical maximum than a practical target.

SAM narrows the focus. It defines the portion of TAM that your company can realistically target based on your current business model, geography, and capabilities. For instance, if your company only operates in the U.S. and targets women between the ages of 25 and 65, your SAM will reflect the potential sales within that specific demographic and geographic segment. SAM gives you a clearer picture of the market you can effectively serve.

SOM tells you who to sell to right now. SOM reduces

activity means more leads, which means more revenue, right? Wrong.

Attempting to reach everyone dilutes your resources and spreads your team's efforts too thin. Reps get overwhelmed chasing hundreds of leads with no clear strategy. Their messaging gets watered down. Conversion rates drop - their confidence takes a hit, and frustration rises. Instead of investing in deliberate skill development, they get distracted by doing more. They start putting up activity numbers instead of generating meaningful conversations. The work becomes a grind, and that's only the internal cost. The external cost to your brand reputation could be even worse.

SPAM the TAM: A Modern Sales Pitfall

A "spray and pray" approach is less effective today than it's ever been. However, the ease with which organizations can send generic messages using AI and automation has marked an increase in the approach. More is not a strategy. Blasting your entire TAM with irrelevant messages and hoping something sticks is a recipe for disaster. This leads to a flood of outbound that is neither personalized, relevant, nor welcome. Buyers don't see value. They feel harassed.

Lazy sales behaviors like "spray and pray" or "spam the TAM" are why sales still ranks as one of the most hated professions.

We've trained buyers not to trust us. Not because outbound doesn't work, but because we've diluted its value with poor execution. The constant onslaught of irrelevant outreach turns sales from a helpful, buyer-centric experience into unwelcome noise. It's no wonder your salespeople get ghosted. It's no wonder deals stall. It's no wonder buyers don't want to talk to us.

the size of your SAM to the accounts that are most likely to buy now. The terms SOM and ICP are sometimes used interchangeably because SOM focuses on the portion of the market you can capture with current resources. However, we want to use the concept of ICP segmentation to take a strategic, targeted approach to penetrating the SOM.

Yes, a generic, high-volume approach can get you some quick wins, but those wins come at a cost. You alienate so many of your prospects with generic, self-serving outreach that when you finally do have something relevant to say, they're no longer listening. You've trained them to ignore you. Rebuilding that trust is incredibly hard, especially when it's not just an individual seller's reputation on the line but your brand's.

Rebuilding What's Been Broken: The Cost of Lost Trust

Trust erosion isn't a philosophical problem. It's a business problem.

According to Deloitte, 41% of respondents who experienced a reputation risk event reported loss of revenue as the biggest impact.[3] AON lists damage to brand or reputation as the eighth biggest risk facing global organizations today.[4] Trust erosion leads directly to lost revenue,

---

[3] Deloitte Touche Tohmatsu Limited, *2014 Global Survey on Reputation Risk: Reputation@Risk* (Forbes Insights, 2014), https://www2.deloitte.com/content/dam/Deloitte/global/Documents/Governance-Risk-Compliance/gx_grc_Reputation@Risk%20survey%20report_FINAL.pdf.
[4] *Aon plc, Building Reputational Resilience in the Life Sciences Sector*, April 2021, https://www.aon.com/getmedia/b6f3d9d0-8d49-4b22-8099-6a620e268695/Reputation-risk_Life-Sciences.pdf.

longer sales cycles, and lower conversion rates. And it all starts with a choice to prioritize volume over value.

Instead of casting the widest net possible, a more strategic approach involves narrowing your focus to the most promising leads. These are the buyers who are not only qualified but also have a high likelihood of buying, buying soon, and buying at a premium price point. That's how you get results without wrecking trust. That's how you build a brand buyers want to hear from.

Case Study: Peloton's Wake-Up Call

To truly understand the importance of moving beyond TAM and homing in on your SOM, let's take a look at Peloton's journey. Peloton began as a high-end exercise equipment company, initially trying to appeal to a broad audience of fitness enthusiasts. Their TAM was vast, so it was essentially anyone interested in fitness.

However, as Peloton started to grow, they encountered significant challenges. Despite the potential market size, they found that many consumers were not willing to invest in their premium-priced equipment. Peloton's early attempts to market to everyone left them struggling to convert leads into sales, as the majority of potential customers either opted for cheaper alternatives or were not interested in the interactive, community-driven experience that Peloton offered.

The turning point came when Peloton realized that their broad approach was not sustainable. Despite having a theoretically large TAM, the company's growth was being hindered by a lack of focus on the right customers. Relying solely on TAM led Peloton to overestimate their market potential and underperform.

Peloton's leadership recognized that they needed to dig deeper to understand who their real customers were. Customers who were not only interested in fitness but were also willing to pay a premium for a high-quality, connected workout experience. As William Lynch, President of Peloton, put it: "We recognized early on that we weren't just selling a bike. We were selling an experience, a community, and a lifestyle. Understanding who our customers are and what they value has been key to our success."

"We recognized early on that we weren't just selling a bike. We were selling an experience, a community, and a lifestyle. Understanding who our customers are and what they value has been key to our success."

William Lynch, President of Peloton illustrating the importance of practicing Value Based Segmentation.

This insight was crucial. It allowed Peloton to refine their go-to-market (GTM) approach by focusing on this specific segment of fitness enthusiasts who were likely to invest in a premium product. It led them to the portion of the market they could realistically capture and serve effectively. By zeroing in on this segment of their audience, Peloton tailored its marketing, product features, and brand messaging to resonate deeply.

For instance, Peloton began emphasizing the community aspect of their product, highlighting the live classes and the ability to interact with instructors and other users. They also shifted their advertising to target higher-income households and positioned Peloton not as fitness equipment, but as an investment in a healthier lifestyle – a shift that proved critical.

Peloton transformed from a niche player into a leader in the connected fitness space. By focusing on their SOM, Peloton stopped trying to sell to everybody and started selling to the customers who were most likely to buy, buy now, and buy at a premium. This strategic shift allowed Peloton to maximize its market share, driving significant growth and building a loyal customer base.

Peloton's story underscores the importance of not getting lost in the allure of a large TAM or a "boil the ocean" approach. Like Peloton, by focusing on the customers most likely to buy now, you can create a more focused, effective, and ultimately successful sales strategy.

I'll note that as a diehard SoulCycle fangirl, I resisted including this story. However, it's relevant, and if you're somebody who loves riding a bike that goes nowhere, you are still my people.*

If your sales reps are telling you they need more accounts to hit their targets, they still believe that more volume means better odds. You know that it means more noise, frustration, and rejection. Chasing volume without strategic segmentation leads to diluted messaging and wasted effort. Eventually, it leads to burnout because your team feels like they're spinning their wheels without meaningful results.

Three Smart Strategies for Targeted Outreach

Effective segmentation is the foundation of successful targeted outreach. You can get as creative as you'd like with your segmentation, but here are my three favorite strategies to get sales teams to pivot from TAM to SOM.

Value Based Segmentation Filters

Firmographic Examples:	Psychographic Examples:	Demographic Examples:
Organizational attributes that define the business entity	Company mindset, priorities, and behavioral tendencies	Professional traits of the individual decision-maker
• Company revenue	• Technology stack	• Job title
• Number of employees	• Strategic initiatives	• Department
• Industry or sector	• Culture (risk tolerance)	• Seniority (influence level)
• Geographic location(s)	• Decision-making style	• Role-specific challenges
• Number of locations or offices	• Investment priorities	• Personality type (DISC, OCEAN)
• Ownership structure (private, public, VC-backed)	• Competitive posture	• Reporting structure
• Years in business	• Market position (leader, challenger, disruptor)	• Team or cultural dynamics

The first method involves using account and contact-level filters. These criteria include demographic data such as job title, department, seniority level, and reporting structure. They also include psychographic traits like technology stack, strategic initiatives, decision-making style, and

---

*Author's Note

investment priorities. Finally, firmographic filters include company revenue, number of employees, industry, geographic footprint, ownership
structure, and funding status. These filters help narrow your market and,
especially, your account lists to the most relevant segments.

The second method leverages existing internal data, such as revisiting
previously lost opportunities, creating Marketing Qualified Lead (MQL)
criteria, or identifying prospects who submitted demo requests but were
never successfully engaged. This method allows sales teams to revisit
leads who have already demonstrated interest, significantly improving
the likelihood of conversion.

The third approach involves signal-based targeting, using intent data or
trigger events that indicate buyer readiness. Common triggers include
a prospect's recent promotion, new rounds of funding, significant
company announcements, or recent awards. Examples of intent data
are prospects visiting the pricing page on your website, an incomplete
sign-up, or requesting product details. Gartner research highlights that
using deep intent data can boost conversion rates from six percent to ten
percent, underscoring the effectiveness of targeted outreach informed
by clear buying signals.[5] Forbes, in an *Agency Council* article, emphasizes that advanced segmentation tactics are crucial for high-value B2B
lead generation, significantly increasing the likelihood of converting
cold prospects into a profit generating pipeline.[6]

Great leadership means empowering your team to spend their valuable
time on accounts that are most likely to buy. When your team focuses
their energy on fewer, high-quality opportunities rather than chasing
endless prospects, their work becomes more meaningful and productive. This approach generates better immediate results but also strengthens long-term customer relationships, ensuring sustainable success and
growth.

---

[5] Gartner, *Sales Pipeline: A Complete Guide for Sales Leaders and Reps*, accessed
May 22, 2025, https://www.gartner.com/en/sales/topics/sales-pipeline.
[6] Jonathan Schwartz, "Advanced Segmentation Tactics for High-Value B2B Lead
Generation," *Forbes Agency Council*, November 21, 2024, https://www.forbes.com/
councils/forbesagencycouncil/2024/11/21/advanced-segmentation-tactics-for-
high-value-b2b-lead-generation/.

Why the Right Customers Matter

The benefits of targeting the right customers extend far beyond immediate sales. Targeting the right customers often leads to higher customer lifetime value (CLTV or LTV), as customers who are a strong fit for your product or service are more likely to stick around, make repeat purchases, and generate ongoing revenue. Additionally, satisfied customers who find value in your product are more likely to recommend it to others, leading to new, high-quality leads through referrals. Furthermore, by consistently delivering value to the right customers, your company builds a reputation for reliability and quality, which can attract more ideal customers and create a cycle of growth.

In contrast, focusing on a broad set of leads without considering long-term value can lead to churn, dissatisfied customers, and missed opportunities for sustained growth. By strategically targeting the right customers from the outset, sales leaders can ensure that their efforts contribute to the long-term success of the company.

A Blueprint for Smarter Sales Focus

To move from a broad, TAM-focused approach to a more strategic and focused approach, start by refining your territory. Instead of building massive account lists filled with every possible lead, focus on only adding accounts to your CRM that align with your SOM. This is the portion of the market you can reasonably sell to now.

Next, define your ICP segments. Develop a detailed profile of different groups of ideal customers within your SOM. These profiles should combine filters, signals, and internal data. This will help you prioritize efforts on the accounts most likely to close and deliver high returns.

This not only reduces the activity burden on your sales reps but also increases their chances of success by enabling them to concentrate on the opportunities most likely to lead to profit generating pipeline.

Shifting the focus from qualified leads to ideal customers by segmenting your SOM is the easiest way to build outreach lists that convert.

Territory Management Strategy: Qualified Accounts Versus Ideal Accounts

When you're managing thousands of accounts already sitting in your CRM, it can feel overwhelming to figure out where to start. However, the key to unlocking the potential within this vast database lies in identifying and refining your ICP segments. When referring to ICP, I am talking about many segments of buyers within your SOM, each of which is ideal for a unique reason. The ICP isn't a theoretical concept. It's a practical tool that can help you sift through the noise and decide who to contact now.

An ICP is a detailed description of the type of account that is most likely to benefit from your product or service. It includes but goes beyond simple filters like revenue, employee count, or location. Your ICP will be unique to your organization and will differ depending on your sales model, offerings, existing clients, strategic goals, and more.

Understanding and activating your ICP has the ability to shorten your sales cycle, increase your deal size, and ensure that you are selling to customers who have the potential to become raving fans.

You might already be thinking, "Ideal? We don't have time for that. We'll sell to anybody who will pay us." But taking the time to define and understand your ICP ensures you're investing your efforts where they'll matter most, avoiding the inefficiency of chasing every possible buyer.

A common mistake many sales teams make is equating "able to be sold to" with ideal. I've seen this gap manifest on many sales calls with Sales-Led GTM Agency prospects when I ask, "Who is your ICP?"

A sales leader confidently states, "Our ICP is midmarket organizations in Healthcare, Finance, Non-Profits & Tech." When pressed for details, such as how they define "mid-market" or what specific challenges these industries face that make them ideal, they rarely have a clear answer. Broad definitions like "midmarket is anywhere between $150 million and $1.5 billion in revenue" are common, but they don't provide the granularity needed to effectively target and convert leads. Naming multiple umbrella industries is just as common, but knowing who may potentially buy is different from understanding why different ICP segments are likely to buy.

Without a refined ICP, your salespeople are likely using the same copy to speak with vastly different audiences. The C-suite of a HealthTech organization will not respond to the same messaging as the Director of a nonprofit. Refining your ICP is about zeroing in on who will get the most value and may be ready to buy now, so you can craft messaging that reflects that knowledge.

Conducting a deeper dive into your existing CRM data can significantly streamline this ICP refinement process. By reviewing your current customers, identifying common attributes among your highest-value accounts, and segmenting based on clear characteristics like industry, company size, pain points, and buying behaviors, you create an accurate and actionable profile. This targeted approach helps you quickly recognize which prospects are not just potential buyers, but ideal customers who will likely buy faster, spend more, and remain satisfied longer.

It's important to remember that your ICP is not static. As your business grows, as markets shift, and as new data becomes available, your ICP segments must evolve. Revisiting and refining your ICP ensures your sales strategy stays aligned with market conditions, adapts to new insights, and consistently drives meaningful results. By doing so, you avoid the trap of relying on outdated assumptions and ensure that your sales strategy is always optimized for success.

Non-obvious Reasons a Prospect May Be Ideal

By now, you understand the importance of moving from simply identifying qualified leads to focusing on ideal accounts, but not all ideal clients are created equal. It's essential to recognize that some prospects may offer more strategic value than others. Understanding these non-obvious reasons a prospect may be ideal will help you further prioritize your efforts and maximize the impact of your sales strategy.

A few non-obvious reasons a prospect may be ideal include:

- A hierarchical structure, which means you connect with economic buyers earlier in the sales cycle, allowing you to close deals faster.

- Account types that may historically result in higher deal sizes, making them more valuable from a revenue perspective.
- A well-known, respected brand that can boost your credibility, attracting similar high-profile clients who see your product or service as a proven solution
- Clients who are willing to participate in testimonials or case studies, providing valuable social proof that can be leveraged in future sales efforts.
- Clients who may be more likely to refer you to other potential customers, creating a strong referral network that enhances your overall sales efficiency.
- Accounts that are likely to renew their contracts provide stable, recurring revenue, deepening the long-term value of the relationship.
- Land and expand accounts that present opportunities for up-selling or cross-selling additional products and services, allowing your business to grow over time.

By considering these factors, you can refine your ICP segments to focus on prospects who not only can buy from you, but who also bring long-term value and align closely with your strategic goals, allowing you to allocate resources more effectively.

Application: Refining Your SOM

Where they started:
Targeting all healthcare IT executives

Where they ended:
Demographic filter: CIO title only

Firmographic filters: U.S.-based: hospital sector; revenue exceeding $100 million; more than 100 employees in customer service

Signal: Did not appear on the *U.S. News & World Report* Best Of list

This example demonstrates how adding layers of segmentation plus signals to your ICP can transform your outreach, making it more targeted, relevant, and effective. Instead of trying to speak in terms that could apply to anybody in healthcare, this client found ways to identify who was likely to be in need of their solution and spoke directly to the outcomes they desired.

The Power of Value-Based Prospecting and Segmentation

VBS can be amplified by identifying external signals or trigger events that indicate a prospect might be ready to engage. Many sales teams have access to intent tools or signal data platforms, which can help identify these triggers. However, even if you don't have access to such tools, there are still ways to incorporate triggers into your prospecting. For example, Google Alerts can be a powerful, free tool to stay informed about relevant news and updates related to your target accounts.

Your buyers' time, attention, and consideration are valuable commodities. You need to show them that you understand their unique needs. This is where value-based segmentation comes into play, helping you refine your outreach strategy with precision.

Value-Based Segmentation focuses on dividing an already defined ICP into smaller groups based on the distinct problems and priorities those buyer groups have. It relies on an understanding of their different goals, pain points, outcomes, and needs to ensure sales messaging is highly relevant to each segment.

Take, for example, a global software development company that I worked with in New York City. They understood that a broad, unfocused approach would dilute their messaging, so they applied Value-Based Segmentation to home in on specific ICP segments. Instead of targeting all IT executives in the healthcare sector, they zeroed in on Chief Information Officers (CIOs) within US hospitals, specifically those with customer service departments of over 100 staff members. This approach went beyond industry targeting. It was about identifying which accounts within the industry were most likely struggling with capacity and quality issues in customer service, making them ideal candidates for the company's software solutions.

Going deeper, this company took a creative approach by using nontraditional triggers. They targeted hospitals that did *not* make the "Best Of" list in the US News & World Report but had revenue exceeding $100 million. This segmentation indicated that these hospitals had room for improvement and the resources to invest in solutions that could help them climb the rankings. They stacked five filters and one signal together based on the assumption that the accounts left on the list had a problem their software could solve. By crafting messaging that addressed these specific challenges, the company was able to engage prospects on a deeper, more relevant level.

TOP-PERFORMING SIGNAL EXAMPLES

Recent funding or investment round	Executive leadership change
Recent promotions or role changes	Significant hiring or department expansion
New product launch or market entry	Company award or industry recognition
Strategic initiative or publicly stated business priority	Mergers, acquisitions, or strategic partnerships

Connecting the Dots Between Signals and Relevance

While Value-Based Segmentation offers a powerful approach to targeting the right accounts, especially when paired with signals, there are several challenges to be aware of.

Marketing Qualified Leads (MQLs) often signal interest in topics related to your industry or product, but that doesn't necessarily indicate intent to purchase. While intent data like downloading a white paper or signing up for a webinar shows that a prospect is engaged, they shouldn't be mistaken for a sales-ready lead.

Prospects might be in a learning phase, so it's critical that you have MQL criteria that mirror your ICP criteria. This ensures your reason for outreach isn't, "I saw you downloaded a whitepaper," but instead focused on the value you can deliver for accounts in that segment of your ICP. The download indicates that the lead should be moved to the front of the line, but there still needs to be a buyer-centric reason for outreach. When we create processes that treat MQLs as "ready to buy," they often get sold to lazily and without relevance.

Some trigger events, like promotions or funding rounds, are easy to track, which means they become the most commonly used signals.

To stand out, you must build additional layers of criteria. For example, instead of congratulating a prospect on their promotion, consider adding context that connects their new role to a recent strategic move by their company, such as winning a prestigious award or the CEO's commitments.

Outreach should go beyond simply repeating back facts that your prospect already knows. Emails that start with "Congratulations on your promotion" or "I see you're the VP at XYZ company" are often ignored because they offer no additional value. Instead, focus on how the trigger event relates to the problems your product or service solves and why they matter to the prospect.

One of my favorite applications of this strategy, when I worked for a strategy development company, was setting a trigger to be notified of new Chief Procurement Officer (CPO) hires. When I saw the new hire trigger, I waited two weeks and then emailed over a "First 100 Days" guide that shared insights from their peers on how to make the most of that time. I knew that a significant undertaking, in the first quarter as a new CPO, is a customer roadshow, meaning the CPO spends time building relationships with all of their key stakeholders (their internal customers). Instead of asking for a meeting and rushing to sell based on the trigger, I showed my understanding of their role and shared a deposit. It was an effective use of a signal to build interest and earn attention.

If you do not connect the dots between what triggered your outreach and earning the right to your prospect's attention by leading with relevance and value, you will find that signals have limited return on investment.

Laying the Foundation for Success

In this chapter, we've covered why defining and refining your SOM and creating ICP segments is so important.

Melody McCloskey built StyleSeat by deeply understanding her customers. She knew StyleSeat wasn't just a booking platform; it was an experience. Peloton did the same, shifting from equipment seller to lifestyle brand. They won loyalty by focusing on what mattered most to their users.

This customer-centric approach is not only crucial for identifying your ideal customers but also forms the foundation for crafting a compelling value proposition. By deeply understanding who your customers are and what they need, you can create a value proposition that speaks directly to their pain points and desires. This mindset is what makes ICP segmentation work. It's about knowing what you offer, who it's for, and what outcomes matter most to them.

When your segments are in place, you're ready to move into the next phase: crafting and communicating your value proposition. In the next chapter, we'll explore how to take this knowledge and transform it into segment-specific messaging that not only captures attention but also drives action.

Head to www.salesledgtm.com/value or scan the QR code below to download a Guide to Micro-Campaigns worksheet that you can use to build an ICP segment and a matching segment-specific value proposition.

CHAPTER 9

Crafting Segment-Specific Value Propositions

"Your outbound strategy should be laser-focused on solving specific problems for specific people." –Lori Richardson

Jennifer Tejada, as the Chairperson and CEO of PagerDuty, has always championed a customer-centric approach. Under her leadership, PagerDuty has thrived by focusing relentlessly on solving customers' most pressing problems. This strategy is a great example of how crafting and communicating a value proposition drives revenue.

In the early days of PagerDuty, the company faced a significant challenge: the need to differentiate itself in a crowded market of digital operations management tools. Instead of focusing on the technical features of their product, Tejada emphasized understanding the core issues that their customers faced. PagerDuty's team conducted in-depth interviews with customers, mapping out their pain points and urgent needs. They found that many businesses were struggling with managing complex digital operations, leading to costly downtime and inefficient responses to incidents.

With these insights, Tejada and her team shifted their focus to crafting a value proposition that spoke directly to these pain points. They highlighted how PagerDuty's solution could help businesses respond to incidents faster, minimize downtime, and streamline their digital operations. The messaging was not about the features of the product but about the tangible benefits and value it provided: the impact of quicker response times, reduced downtime, and increased operational efficiency.

This approach resonated strongly with their target audience. PagerDuty's value proposition was clear, compelling, and relevant. The focus on solving pressing problems rather than merely showcasing product features helped them connect with potential customers on a deeper level. This alignment of the value proposition with customer needs led to significant growth and established PagerDuty as a leader in its field.

Tejada's strategy highlights a crucial truth: a strong value proposition isn't about flashy features - it's about solving real problems. When you deeply understand your customers and speak directly to their pain points, you don't just sell the product - you earn their trust.

VALUE-BASED SEGMENTATION

Value-Based Segmentation (VBS) focuses on dividing an already defined ICP into smaller groups based specifically on the distinct problems and priorities that matter most to your customers.

Value-based segmentation relies on understanding differences in goals, pain points, outcomes, & buyer needs, so sales messaging is relevant to each segment.

What Makes a Value Proposition *Truly* Compelling?

Crafting a compelling value proposition is essential for engaging potential customers. This chapter will guide you through the process of developing messages that resonate deeply with specific customer segments. To achieve this, we will explore frameworks for mapping out features, advantages, and benefits, ensuring that communications focus on the outcomes that matter most to the buyer.

A well-crafted value proposition is not about listing the features of your product or service. It's about translating these features, past generic advantages, into meaningful benefits that address the specific needs and pain points of your target audience. Jennifer Tejada's approach at PagerDuty is a great example: by focusing on the outcomes that mattered most to customers, she shifted the company's messaging from product-centric to problem-centric. That shift is what made their value proposition resonate, and it's what makes any message truly compelling.

To build a value proposition that stands out, you need to understand your customer segments thoroughly. This means applying techniques like Value-Based Segmentation to tailor your messaging. We will delve into how to use this segmentation to craft messages that are not only relevant but also compelling. By focusing on the unique characteristics of each segment, you can highlight the aspects of your offering that will have the greatest impact.

And here's the key shift to embrace: you don't have one ICP, so you don't have one message. Every time you perform Value-Based Segmentation, you unlock the opportunity to build a new value proposition tailored to that sub-segment. It allows your salespeople to narrow their focus and speak with precision.

Generic messaging is a symptom of lazy segmentation. When your team leads with the same value proposition across your entire territory, it signals to your buyers that you haven't done the work. Buyers have limited attention spans and even less patience. If your message doesn't feel relevant in the first line, they're moving on. When you build messaging that reflects the specific needs of each segment, you earn the right to their attention.

This chapter will equip you with practical exercises to refine your value propositions. The outcome is specific messaging that speaks directly to the needs of your audience. Like PagerDuty's growth was fueled by a clear, relevant value proposition, your success hinges on how well you speak to what matters most to your buyers. By the end of this chapter, you'll be ready to create segment-specific messaging that moves people, because if you're not changing your message, you're not changing your buyer.

AIDA: Earning Attention and Action

In this section, we'll call on a seasoned marketing framework to learn how to turn product features into messages that truly resonate with your customers. My journey with the AIDA model - Attention, Interest, Desire, Action - began while pursuing my business degree.

Developed by E. St. Elmo Lewis around 1900, AIDA is a framework that outlines the steps needed for effective advertising: attracting attention, generating interest, creating desire, and prompting action. It's one of the most widely used models in advertising and was still being taught in my bachelor's program over 100 years later. Because it's based on behavioral psychology, it continues to serve as a guide, helping marketers (and at least one sales professional) guide prospects through a structured decision-making process.

Contemporary marketing sometimes replaces "attention" with "awareness," reflecting a shift toward understanding how consumers first learn about a product or brand. This adjustment underscores the importance of making a strong initial impression and building recognition early in the customer journey.

Classic marketing models, including AIDA, are based on the stimulus-response principle. In this model, advertising serves as the stimulus that triggers a response from the consumer. In sales, cold outreach is the stimulus.

Many of these models share a common sequence: Cognition (awareness/learning), Affect (feeling/interest/desire), and Behavior (action). This sequence is often referred to as the CAB model, emphasizing the stages consumers go through before making a purchase decision.

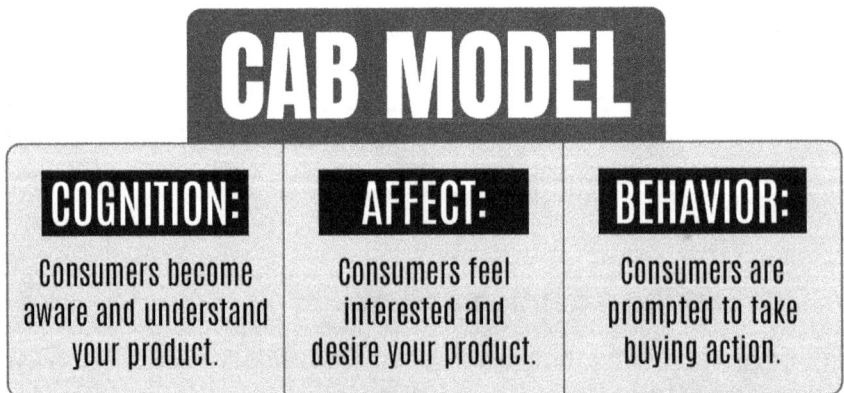

CAB MODEL

COGNITION:	AFFECT:	BEHAVIOR:
Consumers become aware and understand your product.	Consumers feel interested and desire your product.	Consumers are prompted to take buying action.

The CAB model gives you the psychological road map to shift from feature-focused messaging to benefit-led messaging. When you understand the cognitive, emotional, and behavioral journey your buyer is on, you can position your solution in a way that maps to what matters to them.

- *Cognition* is where your message must deliver clarity. This is your chance to teach your prospect something new or challenge how they think about their current approach. It's not about your product yet, it's about earning attention through relevance.
- *Affect* is the moment you connect your solution to something that matters. This is where benefits come in. Not the benefit to you or your company, but the benefit to them – their goals, their challenges, their KPIs. This is where desire gets built.
- *Behavior* is the final step. If you've done the first two well, this is where you earn the right to ask for action. You've created enough clarity and emotional relevance that your prospect is ready to engage.

When you use CAB alongside frameworks like AIDA and FABs, you're not guessing at what to say or how to say it. You're using proven models to build a message that earns attention, creates desire, and makes it clear why your solution is worth their time. Most importantly, you're leading with benefits – not features – because you've taken the time to understand what your buyer thinks, feels, and needs to act.

Since college, I've drawn on the lessons of AIDA and complementary frameworks like CAB and the Features, Advantages, and Benefits (FABs) framework. FABs provide a practical approach to implementing the AIDA model in sales copy. By identifying features, explaining their advantages, and linking them to benefits, you can craft messages that directly address the consumer's needs and desires.

Sales reps are facing challenges that go far beyond what traditional sales models were designed to address. Prospects are bombarded with constant streams of information, making it increasingly difficult for any single message to stand out. The traditional methods of reaching out to potential clients are becoming less effective as the dynamics of sales have fundamentally shifted. It's no longer sufficient to simply connect with prospects; sales reps must earn the right to their attention,

FABs Framework: A Quick Primer

Many sellers focus on features and advantages but stop short of detailing benefits. To create a compelling value proposition, you must understand your prospect's challenges and align your messaging to show how your solution meets their needs. The FABs framework – Features, Advantages, and Benefits – bridges that gap by translating what your product does into why it matters to your customer.

- **Features** describe what your product includes, like "real-time analytics."
- **Advantages** explain why those features matter, such as faster insights than the competition.
- **Benefits** connect directly to the prospect's needs, like helping them make faster, smarter business decisions.

By leading with benefits, you demonstrate to your prospects the real value your product offers—how it solves problems, makes work easier, or drives results.

especially in an environment that demands more relevance and value than ever before.

Applying the FABs Framework to Sales Copy

One of the most common mistakes in sales copywriting is focusing too much on the features of your product or service without connecting them to the prospect's needs. Features tell your prospect *what* your product does, but they don't tell them *why* it matters. That's why it's essential to frame your messaging around the benefits—how your product will make their life easier, solve a problem, or deliver value.

The FABs Framework helps sellers move beyond simply listing features and into the realm of explaining why those features matter to the prospect. Let's break it down and tie it to improving sales copy:

Features

Features are the inherent characteristics of your product or service. They describe what your offering does in a literal sense. For instance, if you're selling a software tool, a feature might be "real-time analytics" or "automated task tracking." Features help clarify what the product *is,* but don't go far enough in explaining *why* the prospect should care.

Advantages

Advantages explain *why* your features are valuable. In the case of real-time analytics, the advantage is clear: it provides up-to-date insights faster, which saves your customers' time. Advantages almost always come back to saving time, saving money, making money, or reducing risk. The issue is that all of your competitors are claiming the same set of advantages.

Benefits

Benefits are the most important piece of this puzzle because they connect the feature and the advantage directly to the prospect's needs. They answer the key question on every prospect's mind: *What's in it for me?*

For example, the benefit of real-time analytics isn't that it's fast or efficient; it's that it helps the prospect make data-driven decisions in real-time, leading to quicker, smarter business outcomes. In the case of automated task tracking, the benefit could be increasing team productivity, which means finishing projects sooner, so the company can take on more clients. Benefit-focused sales messaging talks about the outcomes the prospect can expect from investing in your product or service.

Why Benefits Are Your Sales Copy's Best Friend

While it's tempting to focus on features, especially when you're proud of your product's capabilities, prospects don't care about features alone. The most effective sales copy explains not just what your product is or does, but how it will improve the prospect's circumstances.

When you focus on benefits, you create a deeper connection with your prospect. You're showing that you understand their pain points and that your solution is designed to meet their needs. This shift from *what* the product does to *why* it matters makes your sales copy far more compelling and likely to generate attention, interest, and desire.

FABs Framework in Action

Let's review an example to show how you can apply the FABs framework if you're selling a project management tool.

FABS FRAMEWORK APPLIED

EXAMPLE BASED ON SALES MESSAGING FOR A PROJECT MANAGEMENT TOOL

Feature: **Advantage:**

Automated   Reduces errors and saves time compared
task tracking.   to manual tracking.

Benefit:

Increases team productivity, speeds up project completion, and allows your prospect to receive a bonus for finishing under budget. Additionally, this early completion enables the company to start working on a new Board priority a quarter sooner.

Notice how the feature alone—automated task tracking—might seem dry or irrelevant to a busy decision-maker. But by framing it as something that increases productivity, saves time, and even improves the prospect's own career outcomes, you make the message far more engaging. This transformation from feature to benefit is what will resonate most with your audience.

Most sellers stop at features, only sometimes touching on advantages, but the real magic happens when you push further to identify the benefits you unlock and higher levels of engagement. The challenge is helping your sales team understand the prospect's challenges deeply enough to communicate how your solution can make their life easier or help them reach their goals. Every piece of sales copy should ask and answer the question, "How does this help my prospect?"

Using the FABs framework, your team can write sales copy that is not only informative but also compelling - copy that speaks directly to the prospect's needs and motivates them to take action. This approach allows you to create messages that move beyond technical details and focus on what truly matters to the people you're reaching out to.

Most sellers stop at features, only sometimes touching on advantages, but the real magic happens when you push further to identify the benefits. That's how you unlock higher levels of engagement.

For instance, if your product enhances customer relationship management, the benefit might be improved customer satisfaction and retention. This approach is more impactful than simply stating your product has CRM capabilities that increase efficiencies.

To make that benefit feel relevant, you need to apply Value-Based Segmentation. That means moving beyond surface-level ICP definitions and narrowing your focus to the sub-segments that truly matter. For example, instead of targeting all IT executives in the financial sector, focus on only Chief Technology Officers (CTOs) at banks that specialize in commercial loans. Yes, IT titles in finance may be how you describe your ICP, but you must add further layers of segmentation to ensure that your messaging is both targeted and relevant.

FABs give you the structure to link product features to outcomes. Segmentation gives you the clarity to tie those outcomes to the right audience. When you combine the two, you create value propositions that are more compelling because they're precise. You're not just describing what your product does. You're showing it helps your buyer win.

Capturing Attention, the Canva Way

You know firsthand how challenging it is to break through the noise in a prospect's cluttered inbox. I audit hundreds, perhaps thousands, of cold emails every year, 80% of which focus solely on product and service features.

Just in case you are still writing feature-laden emails, let me assure you that a list of your product or service features will not capture and hold a prospect's attention.

Canva, a leader in graphic design tools, provides a clear example of how to effectively earn the right to a prospect's attention. Canva's email for their Pro offer starts with the subject line "Create presentations like a Pro, all the time." This subject line highlights a feature, but it also addresses a fundamental need: professionally designed presentations.

This approach captures the recipient's attention by immediately aligning with their core concerns and aspirations.

Once Canva has secured the prospect's attention, it maintains this engagement by showcasing the actual benefits of its Pro features. Instead of merely detailing what the features are, Canva's emails use practical examples to illustrate how these features enhance presentations and facilitate team collaboration. This method of storytelling highlights the real-world impact of the product, making the benefits clear and tangible.

By emphasizing benefits that address specific pain points and needs of its audience, Canva makes its value proposition not only relevant but also compelling. This approach ensures that the messaging resonates on a personal level, showing how Canva's solutions can make a meaningful difference in their work.

While this example is rooted in email marketing, this principle applies equally to sales. To earn and keep a prospect's attention, your message must go beyond what your product does and show how it meaningfully improves the prospect's life. Canva's approach exemplifies that benefit-driven messaging transforms outreach from noise into value.

The Southwest Lesson: Benefits Win Hearts, Not Just Wallets

Imagine you're a parent planning that long-awaited family vacation. You've been saving up for months, carefully budgeting every dollar to ensure your trip is memorable. You want to create those special moments with your kids - building sandcastles on the beach, exploring new places together, and enjoying dinners where everyone is laughing and relaxed. But as you start booking your flights, the anxiety kicks in. You know that airlines often surprise you with hidden fees, especially when it comes to checked baggage. Those extra costs could throw off your entire budget, turning what should be a joyful experience into a stressful one.

Then you come across Southwest Airlines. They don't charge for your first two checked bags. At first, this seems like just a nice bonus, a feature that might save you a little money. Most brands and sellers would stop right there, expecting you to connect the dots yourself. They'd tell you, "We don't charge for bags, so you save money." That's a feature and an advantage. While it's a good start, it's not enough. It assumes that you, the customer, will automatically understand and feel the benefit. That assumption is a mistake.

Because saving money alone isn't what truly resonates with Southwest customers, it's what those savings represent: fewer surprises, less stress, and greater confidence in sticking to a budget.

Sales leaders must empower their reps to go beyond the surface-level features and advantages to explicitly craft messaging around the benefit. That's where the magic happens. That's where we connect with what really matters to our customers.

By being explicit about the benefit, Southwest is doing something that most brands don't. They're not leaving it up to the customer to figure out why their offer is valuable. They're making it crystal clear how their service improves your life in a way that's deeply relevant to the customer's needs and desires.

Since the writing of this book, bags no longer fly free on Southwest. It has become a perfect case study in how a brand isn't only removing a feature, "free bags," but they've compromised their brand identity and the trust they'd built with their customers. The policy change

Feature: Southwest Airlines doesn't charge for checked bags.

Advantage: This saves you money - money other airlines would take from you through hidden fees.

Here's where we take it a step further:

Benefit: The true benefit is peace of mind and the ability to focus on what's most important to you. When Southwest says, "Your bags fly free," they're not just talking about saving a few dollars. They're talking about freeing you from the stress of unexpected costs. They're giving you the confidence to plan your vacation without worrying about hidden fees that might spoil your carefully laid plans. They're telling you that the money you saved can now be used to enhance your experience, whether that's treating your family to a special dinner, booking an extra activity, or simply enjoying your trip without financial stress hanging over your head.

sparked significant backlash from long-time customers who expressed feelings of betrayal. *

This is a crucial lesson for anyone crafting and communicating a value proposition. If you leave the benefit unstated, you risk missing the opportunity to connect with your prospect on an emotional level, and risk your solution being seen as just another option.

Southwest's messaging resonates because it leads with benefits – the feeling of being understood, the ease of travel, and the confidence of no surprise fees. The emotional payoff is what drives customer choice.

Your job is to ensure your team understands how to spotlight benefits clearly and consistently. You're not selling a product; you're offering a better outcome. When your message shows how life gets easier, better, or more fulfilling, you don't only earn attention – you earn trust, action, and the ability to build a durable pipeline.

Access the free downloadable Guide to Micro-Campaigns at www.salesledgtm.com/value or use the QR code and walk through an exercise to help you build an ICP segment and matching value proposition.

---

*Author's Note

CHAPTER 10

Developing a Micro-Campaign Strategy

"Everyone is not your customer." –Seth Godin

Kevin had made huge progress. He knew exactly who his best prospects were, and he'd spent a lot of time personalizing all of this sales outreach. Despite all this hard work, he was still struggling to consistently get responses. Frustrated, Kevin reached out to his sales leader, Emily, for advice.

"I don't get it," Kevin admitted. "I did the segmentation exercise. I thought I'd built clear value propositions for every group we identified. But when I send out emails, I hardly get replies. It feels like I'm still doing something wrong."

Emily nodded sympathetically. "You've done great work, Kevin. Your segments and value propositions keep getting better, but I noticed your emails still have a lot of generic contact-level personalization, like congratulating someone on their Series A funding or mentioning their new VP title. How is that type of personalization helping you?"

Kevin hesitated. "I guess it's not really working. I thought doing that type of personalization for every prospect was important, but now it feels forced. Most of the details I include don't even connect to the reason I'm reaching out."

"That's exactly the problem," Emily explained. "At our average deal size of $22,000, you don't need to waste time with superficial, contact-level personalization. It usually comes off as irrelevant or worse, disingenuous."

Kevin looked uncertain. "But isn't congratulating someone on their Series A a polite way to get their attention?"

Emily shook her head gently. "Not if your message has nothing to do with their funding. Think about it from their perspective. They get an email that says, 'Congrats on your Series A,' and the rest of your email is completely unrelated to how they plan to spend that funding or grow their business. It doesn't build trust; it actually hurts your credibility."

Kevin nodded, absorbing what Emily was saying. "I see your point, and I suppose saying 'I see you're the VP at XYZ company' doesn't add much value either."

"Bingo!" Emily confirmed, "Reading a prospect's CV back to them isn't meaningful personalization. They already know their own job title. It's wasted real estate that could have been used to show you understand their challenges and how your solution helps them succeed."

"So instead," Kevin summarized, "You're saying I need to keep working on my segment-specific value propositions, so I use more relevant personalization and outcome-centric messaging?"

"Exactly," Emily smiled. "We call those micro-campaigns, and they are how you scale personalization. By creating messaging that resonates deeply with each ICP segment, you communicate real relevance at scale, without wasting time trying to include contact-level personalization in every single message."

Kevin finally understood what Emily had been emphasizing. Personalization wasn't about randomly congratulating people on job titles or funding rounds. It was about using carefully crafted value propositions to deliver relevant messages to every lead in each targeted segment.

Emily continued, driving her point home. "Remember Kevin, micro-campaigns aren't just efficient, they're effective. They let you speak to exactly what each segment cares most about, and that's what earns buyer attention and trust at scale."

With Emily's guidance, Kevin learned how to turn his hard work on segmentation and value propositions into scalable success. Instead of chasing superficial personalization, he would leverage relevant insights and outcome-centric value in his micro-campaigns.

Personalization that matters is about relevance. It's about showing the prospect that you understand their world, their industry, their company's current situation, and their unique role within that company.

MICRO-CAMPAIGN DEFINITION

Micro-campaigns are highly targeted sales initiatives designed for specific segments within your Ideal Customer Profile. Built from your value-based segmentation work, micro-campaigns use tailored messaging that directly addresses the distinct problems, goals, or needs of each segment.

Precision Through Segmentation

When you stack ICP buyer groups, Value-Based Segmentation, and segment-specific value propositions together, you get micro-campaigns. Micro-campaigns allow you to focus your personalization efforts on the highest-potential leads, identified through layered criteria like firmographics, demographics, psychographics, internal data, and signals. This depth of segmentation ensures that your messages are finely tuned to resonate deeply with the recipient without having to ask about their recent family vacation to Disney.

This approach increases the likelihood of reaching enough of the right prospects with the right message at the right time to ensure you have a full profit generating pipeline. When you tailor your message to the realities the prospect is dealing with *right now*, it signals that you're paying attention and that your outreach isn't generic.

Three science-backed reasons why relevant specificity is critical to writing great sales copy:

1. **Cognitive Engagement and Memory Encoding**: The Encoding Specificity Principle suggests that information is more easily recalled when the context at the time of encoding matches the context at the time of retrieval. Specific details provide richer context, creating more cues for memory retrieval. This means that highly specific information is more likely to be remembered because it is encoded with more context, making it easier for the prospect to recall your message.

2. **Emotional Resonance**: Specific details can evoke stronger emotional responses. When your message includes vivid descriptions, it is more likely to engage the reader's emotions, making the message more persuasive and memorable. Emotionally charged content is far more likely to be remembered and believed because it creates a personal connection with the reader.

3. **Neurological Activation and Credibility**: Studies have shown that concrete details in messages can influence brain activity related to credibility evaluation. When the brain processes precise information, it activates cognitive areas associated with believability, making the message seem more credible. When your communication includes specific details, it signals that you've done your research and that you have a deeper understanding of the prospect's needs. This fosters trust and makes your message more believable.

*You do not, and in my opinion, should not need to use contact-level hyper-personalization in all of your sales messaging to earn your prospect's attention. I am not suggesting that you should never use contact-level personalization, but if you are over-reliant on it, you're sabotaging your ability to scale. ***

The majority of sales leaders are running outbound sales motions that require them to balance quantity and quality outreach. The reality is that having enough "at-bats" (quantity) still matters. However, quantity without quality is SPAM. Quality without some ability to scale is a recipe for missed revenue goals. A super low-volume, contact-level hyper-personalization campaign (quality) doesn't work in most B2B organizations, which, like Emily & Kevin's, have an average contract value (ACV) between $22,000 and $40,000 USD[7].

Micro-campaigns are the key to unlocking relevant personalization at scale.

---

[7] Nick Perry, "What Is the Average Deal Size for Private SaaS Companies?" *SaaS Capital*, November 21, 2024, https://www.saas-capital.com/blog-posts/what-is-the-average-deal-size-for-private-saas-companies/.

---

*Author's Note

Specificity Makes All the Difference

The power of relevant personalization in sales copy is directly linked to how specific you can be. Specificity enhances believability and memorability due to several psychological and neurological factors. The more specific you can be, the more your message will stand out.

Generic copy tends to get ignored because it feels like it could have been sent to anyone. Personalized copy that references priorities, challenges, or opportunities and illustrates how it's connected to the outcomes you offer shows that your outreach is thoughtful and targeted. This creates an immediate connection, making the recipient more likely to engage.

For example, using Value-Based Segmentation, let's say you sell a recruiting solution and you're reaching out to SaaS companies that have grown their customer base by 20% or more in the six months and are hiring for multiple senior-level customer success (CS) roles. Most sales messaging stops at mentioning features and maybe a reference to saving time and money. You've connected the dots about the challenges that segment is facing based on the signals you uncovered. A segment-specific message might say:

"Hi John - Scaling CS during high-growth periods often puts a strain on SaaS orgs.

New customers expect an exceptional onboarding experience, but CS teams are maxed out. This leads to a poor onboarding experience & delayed time-to-value.

We've helped orgs like [lookalike company] & [lookalike company] leverage temp workers while filling full-time roles.

Worth learning more?"

This approach is relevant to what they're dealing with at this moment, tailored to their needs, and requires no contact-level personalization.

Personalization at Scale: The Role of Artificial Intelligence

Many sales reps hesitate to personalize their outreach because they worry it will take too much time. Alternatively, salespeople waste hours of their day obsessing over the personalization of an email that never gets read.

Micro-campaigns provide the right balance of quantity and quality, allowing reps to reach more prospects with targeted and useful messaging. After nearly twenty years of testing ways to balance quantity and quality in outbound, this is the only method I believe allows teams to personalize at scale effectively.

Personalization at scale shows prospects that you've put in the effort to connect your solution to their unique context. It builds trust and opens the door for further conversation.

Artificial Intelligence (AI) and automation can help you get there faster, but they can't replace your judgment. Tools like AI agents, lead scoring platforms, email sequencers, and predictive analytics can all support a targeted, strategic outbound strategy if used correctly. You can use AI to build smarter lists, surface relevant signals, uncover persona-based insights, and even generate first drafts of outreach copy. But none of that matters if the message isn't relevant, and that's where AI falls short today.

Most teams are experimenting with AI, but few are being trained on how to use it well. Sales leaders can't just roll out AI tools and hope for the best. You need to teach your team how to prompt, how to edit, and how to use their judgment. That means teaching your reps what good looks like, reviewing examples together, and creating a repeatable workflow for using AI as part of outbound. Teams that skip this step will move fast but create junk. Teams that get it right will move faster and win more.

AI cannot fix a broken outbound motion. If your segments are vague or your messaging is weak, AI isn't the answer. Before using AI or automation to scale, make sure you have your strategy locked in and your reps trained on how to appropriately incorporate AI into their work. The goal isn't to take reps out of the process. It's to give them better tools so they can focus more on the parts of selling that require judgment, creativity, and connection.

I've reviewed dozens of AI email tools, and none of them get it 100% right. Large language models are trained on past data. They can't generate original insight or identify new patterns in buyer behavior. That's why AI-generated copy is easy to detect. Plus, when your competitors are all using the same tools, everybody's copy sounds the same.

At the time of writing this book, my recommendation is that every email should still be reviewed by a human before it's sent. Your message should sound like it was written by a person, not a robot obsessed with being a game-changer in today's landscape.

The good news is that once you've done the work of building a segmented territory and writing value propositions for each segment, you can use automation to scale your outreach.

Micro-campaigns make this easy. Instead of rewriting every email from scratch, your team can automate much of the messaging while still delivering personalized, relevant outreach. This frees up time for the activities that actually move deals forward, like connecting with prospects in real life, picking up the phone, and building relationships on social. With the right balance of AI support and human oversight, your outbound strategy becomes both efficient and effective.

AI Harms: The Cost of Generic Outreach

In Chapter 8, we talked about the real financial impact of damaging your brand reputation. Remember, the cost of using AI to scale bad messaging is greater than getting ignored. I caution you not to follow a shiny object AI strategy that will damage long-term revenue potential.

Generic outreach harms your chances of building a connection. Prospects sense when they're on the receiving end of a templated message, and it signals that you haven't invested the time to understand their needs. It can leave the impression that your solution is too broad or not suited to their specific circumstances. Worse, it can get your email and organization blocked or reported as spam. We live in a world of information overload. Only highly relevant and personalized messages have a chance of cutting through the noise.

A major barrier to clarity is ambiguity - using vague or generic language that leaves prospects unsure about the exact benefit or solution being offered. To avoid this, your sales copy should clearly articulate the specific problems you solve and exactly how you solve them. Don't just say you "improve efficiency," state precisely what aspect of efficiency you improve and how measurable the improvement will be. AI will struggle with this because its training data doesn't reflect the nuanced, forward-looking thinking required to sell complex solutions. That's why your reps - not the AI - need to own the final message.

Territory Management: Stacking Segments, Value Propositions, and Micro-Campaigns

Even as an individual contributor, understanding how to manage a territory can be the difference between hitting your targets, maybe even exceeding them, and missing quota.

In a previous Head of Sales role, I started in a player/coach position, so I also acted as the company's first AE in North America. They had an established system for grading accounts from A to F, with the expectation that A-grade accounts would yield the best results. My Chief Revenue Officer (CRO) wanted me to focus exclusively on top-tier accounts in industries like consumer-packaged goods (CPG) and pharmaceutical manufacturing, which the company believed would deliver the highest returns.

I followed these guidelines for the first few months, but it didn't take long to realize that the application of account grades did not translate well to the North American market. While I did close significant deals with Grade A & B accounts—think logos like Kraft Heinz and Mars Wrigley—the Grade A accounts were slow-moving, tough negotiators, and ultimately closed at lower price points. The territory strategy I was prescribed wasn't holding up in practice.

Before the start of the next year, I decided to take a different approach. I presented a North American go-to-market (GTM) strategy aimed at quadrupling revenue in the region, and it focused on a different segment altogether - financial services organizations with revenue over $6 billion. This wasn't in line with the global grading formula, but my pipeline data validated that it was a pivot worth exploring. I found that large financial institutions not only moved faster but also closed at higher price points, with less time spent on red lines and contract negotiation.

My CRO trusted my instincts and data-driven approach enough to support me, even though it diverged from the company's established playbook. The results spoke for themselves: I personally closed 20+ new logos, including heavyweights like Visa, Vanguard, Goldman Sachs, Blackstone, and American Express. This strategic shift didn't just boost sales; it transformed our entire approach to the US market.

In less than 18 months, I had added well over $1 million in year one annualized contract value (ACV), including over 16 Fortune 500 logos, all because I didn't accept the grading system as gospel. Instead, I used Value-Based Segmentation to identify the segments where I could close deals faster and at higher price points by understanding what outcomes drove their decision-making. Once I had a few financial services logos closed, my segment-specific value propositions were made even stronger by the use of industry knowledge and social proof. At the end of my second year in seat, the sales cycle had decreased by 22 days, the ACV increased by over $10,000, and we maintained a renewal rate over 96%.

This anecdote underscores the importance of strategic territory management. It's an opportunity to drive outsized revenue impact by focusing on the right accounts.

From Mass Outreach to Micro-Strategy

Imagine you're a sales leader, and your founder has declared that the next big push is into the CPG space. The old way would be to dump a list of every CPG company into your CRM and start dialing. Now, with Value-Based Segmentation in your toolbox, you might narrow that list down to companies between $6-10 billion in revenue, then further refine it to focus on the food and beverage (F&B) sector within CPG. You continue to segment by only targeting F&B companies in the Northeast, where you already have a strong foothold.

I'm sure you can imagine the difference between giving your reps a list of 5,000 CPG accounts and hoping you can get traction with enough of them to fill your pipeline versus trimming that list of accounts into segments to take a more strategic approach. Starting with a smaller list of only $6-10 billion revenue F&B accounts in the Northeast sets you up to gain better momentum.

You may end up reaching out to all 5,000 accounts over time, but you're starting with the segment that is most likely to pay attention to your sales messaging and ultimately buy. You're no longer calling down a list; you're executing a micro-campaign strategy, and that's what drives results.

Take this example of a company selling labeling solutions to industries like CPG, electronics, pharmaceutical manufacturers, and others. If a seller attempted to write sales messaging that applied to prospects in all those industries who may buy their solution, the messaging would be generic. It would be difficult, if not impossible, to give the prospect a compelling reason to buy from them. However, by applying filters and signals to segment your territory, you create a list of accounts matched to a specific reason for outreach.

The outcome might look something like this:

VALUE BASED SEGMENT STACK
Example for a Packaging and Labeling Vendor

SUB-INDUSTRY:	Pet Products (CPG)
GEOGRAPHY:	United States
REVENUE:	$30-50 M Annual Revenue
JOB TITLE:	Chief Financial Officer
SIGNAL:	Recently announced FDA pet-food regulations

This segment stack allows you to create a micro-campaign about the impact of recently announced FDA pet food regulations, rather than talking about the cost or quality of labels. Putting yourself in the prospect's shoes: Which type of message would you be more likely to respond to?

The ability to focus on the most promising leads is one of the most significant advantages of value-based segmentation. As noted in the ViB Tech article titled *The Only Guide You Need to B2B Customer Segmentation*, "Value-based segmentation helps you figure out who your best customers are, what their unique challenges and needs are, and how to create more personalized experiences for these customers."[8]

Sales resources are limited, and you can't afford to waste them on low-value leads. A micro-campaign approach ensures that you're not only targeting the right accounts but also doing so in a cost-effective manner, maximizing the return on your outbound efforts.

Coaching to the Data: Teaching Reps Where They Win

Strategic sales leaders help their teams take ownership of their territories and drive better results using Value-Based Segmentation. A key pivot is to stop relying solely on companywide averages and start coaching your salespeople to dig into their own performance data. Their personal data will reveal where they win the fastest, with the least resistance, and the most consistency.

For example, encourage your Sales Development Representatives (SDRs) to analyze which account types require the fewest touchpoints to secure meetings. That insight can help them focus on segments where their outreach is most effective. Instead of spreading effort too thin across the entire territory, they can work with precision.

For your AEs, coach them to look at which industries most readily move from the discovery meeting into the qualified pipeline. That helps reps

---

[8] VIB, "The Only Guide You Need to B2B Customer Segmentation," *VIB*, accessed May 23, 2025, https://vib.tech/resources/marketing-blogs/the-only-guide-you-need-to-b2b-customer-segmentation/.

refine their pipeline and focus on the verticals where they're most likely to gain momentum and close with efficiency.

Too often, reps look at a territory and ask, "How can I quickly get in front of everyone on this list?" Your job is to help them reframe that thinking. The better question is, "Where am I most effective, and how can I spend more time there?"

When you guide your team to integrate ICP or Value-Based Segmentation into their territory planning, you're helping them work smarter, not just harder. You're enabling them to prioritize the accounts that are most likely to convert and deliver meaningful revenue, all while using their time and resources more effectively.

Rolling Out a Micro-Campaign Strategy

To start, you need a clear, structured approach that's rooted in the data available and aligned with how your buyers actually behave. This is not about complexity for complexity's sake. It's about helping your team work smarter by identifying which accounts are most likely to convert, and when.

As we discussed in Chapter 8, building a high-quality list requires layering multiple types of data - demographic, psychographic, and firmographic. We've also emphasized that true clarity comes when you narrow your focus from a broad TAM to the specific segments that represent real opportunity. The next step is knowing when those accounts are most likely to be receptive to outreach.

That's where signal-based data comes in. These signals are your reps' cue that *now* is the right time to reach out. At the account level, that could include things like head count growth, a recent funding round, a new executive hire, a shift in strategic priorities, or a product launch. These are signs of movement. They indicate that change is happening and that priorities may be evolving. When change is happening, buyers are more open to hearing new ideas. Signal data can also come from an activity you're already tracking. Has someone at the account downloaded a resource, registered for a webinar, or interacted with one of your sellers on LinkedIn? Those are engagement signals. When layered onto your segmentation criteria, they help your team focus their time on accounts that aren't just a good fit but are also showing signs of intent.

When this type of segmentation work is done well, it changes the conversation. Instead of "I need more accounts in my territory?" your reps start asking "Where am I most effective?" and "Which accounts are most ready to hear from me now?" That shift is what drives better performance across outbound teams. It builds focus and intention into prospecting, and it ensures that the outreach happening across your team is aligned with real opportunities instead of just activity for activity's sake.

Segmentation is only the first half of the equation. Once your team knows which accounts to prioritize and when, they need to know what to say. That's where relevance becomes critical. When a segment values speed, the message should speak to fast implementation and how the saved time will impact the outcome. When a segment is driven by risk avoidance, the message should lead with compliance, control, and business continuity. When your team pairs Value-Based Segmentation with messaging that aligns with those priorities, the result is a more effective outbound strategy and a more confident sales team.

We'll take these concepts further in the next two chapters. You'll see how to use what you've built through this segmentation process to write messages that resonate with each segment and drive stronger engagement across your pipeline.

The CEO Mindset: Teaching Your Salespeople to Own Their Territory

By rejecting the "boil the ocean" approach, you can optimize your territory management strategy, close deals faster, and ultimately drive greater revenue for your business.

When deploying a territory management strategy, it's easy to have siloed thinking about what the best accounts are. A common mistake is assuming that big accounts are better. It may be the case that you work at an early-stage start up trying to penetrate the enterprise, so closing a huge logo is an essential growth milestone. However, I more often see salespeople spend an inordinate amount of time chasing well-known logos that are harder to reach and tend to close more slowly, because they are driven by ego. Everybody wants to close the biggest accounts, but big doesn't equal most valuable.

To help avoid blind spots and pitfalls like this one, get clear with your sellers about the company's goals and how they are used to inform the territory strategy. You can reference the examples of non-obvious reasons an account may be ideal that I shared in Chapter 8 to help illustrate this point. Without that transparency, it can be difficult for sellers to understand the logic behind your territory strategy.

Once your sellers are bought into the validity of the territory management strategy, they can effectively build their own micro-campaigns.

I've worked with dozens of sales leaders and trained thousands of reps. In doing so, I've found that sales leaders struggle less with deciding which sellers will get which accounts and more so in empowering the sales team to take ownership of their territory. The best results come from encouraging each rep to behave like the CEO of their own business.

One of your most important roles is to instill a sense of ownership in your team. Each rep should see their territory not as a list of accounts, but as their personal business - something they are responsible for growing, nurturing, and optimizing. The mindset shift can significantly elevate performance and drive better results.

To foster this ownership, it's crucial to encourage your reps to deeply understand their territory, not only in terms of the accounts they manage but also in the broader market dynamics at play. This involves teaching them to analyze the potential within their territory, identify key opportunities, and develop a strategic plan that aligns with both their personal goals and the company's objectives. Equip your team with the tools and data they need to make informed decisions. Encourage them to use data-driven insights to prioritize accounts, focus on high-potential opportunities, and allocate their time and resources effectively. By giving them some autonomy to make these decisions, you empower them to take charge of their success, turning their territory into a thriving business unit.

To help your team adopt the CEO mindset, you need to provide them with a clear framework and the right support. One of the most effective strategies is to train your team to assess their territory based on market potential. This requires you to share what you've learned about ICP iden-tification, Value-Based Segmentation, and micro-campaigns, making the ideas accessible to your team. As a sales leader, it's likely that you assign territories and help craft messaging. I'm not suggesting reps own the strategy, but I believe helping reps understand and embrace the logic behind it improves their ownership.

To start instilling the CEO of Territory Mindset, I've had the best success with giving reps specific direction on exactly how to use VBS to create a sub-segment of their territory. Encourage your salespeople to consider one of these three segmentation techniques when deciding how to create a territory plan: personal passion, firmographics, and account triggers (signals).

These easy-to-understand segmentation techniques help create lists with a clear entry point for conversations, increasing the likelihood of engagement.

Personal passion plays a crucial role in how a rep approaches their terri-tory. When a rep is passionate about a particular industry or cause, their enthusiasm can translate into more engaging and authentic outreach. For example, a rep who is passionate about sustainability might prior-itize accounts focused on clean water technology, emission reduction, or renewable energy. This passion-driven approach not only makes outreach more genuine but also increases the likelihood of success because the rep is deeply invested in the subject matter.

Encourage your team to identify what excites them within their terri-tory and to focus on accounts that align with these interests. Whether it's a passion for technology, finance, healthcare, or any other sector, leveraging personal passion can drive higher engagement and better outcomes. This enthusiasm can also help salespeople overcome chal-lenges and maintain motivation, as they are more likely to stay commit-ted to accounts and industries they care about deeply.

Account triggers (also referred to as intent data or signal-based selling) are the specific reasons that justify reaching out to a particular account. These triggers could include changes in legislation or compliance regulations, an increase in IT department head count, the opening of a new office, or a recent security breach. Other triggers might involve the company winning a relevant award, securing new funding, undergoing acquisitions or mergers, or issuing a request for proposal (RFP). Account triggers provide a timely and relevant reason to initiate contact, making the outreach more pertinent and increasing the chances of a positive response.

Your team should be trained to monitor their accounts for these triggers, ensuring that their outreach is aligned with current events and developments within the target organization. By staying attuned to these triggers, reps can position themselves as proactive and informed partners who understand the specific needs and timing of their prospects, which can significantly enhance the quality of their interactions and the likelihood of advancing the sales process.

Firmographics refer to organizational attributes that define the business entity. This includes data such as the industry sector, revenue band, employee count, and geography. Firmographics help sellers segment their territory more effectively by focusing on accounts that share similar characteristics with their most successful clients.

For example, if a rep has historically closed deals with midsized tech companies based in Canada, they should prioritize similar firms within their territory. Additionally, firmographics can help reps identify industries with the highest win rates or companies within a specific revenue range that are more likely to engage. Layering these firmographic insights with personal passion and account triggers empowers your team to create a highly targeted and strategic territory plan.

I am a huge fan of demographic and psychographic filters as well, but I've found that when rolling out a new territory planning strategy, it is best to start with firmographics because they overlap with the most readily available CRM fields. When reps can easily understand and apply filters, they are more likely to use them.

Leveraging these three segmentation techniques introduces your sales team to the habit of approaching their territory with a strategic lens. This strategic approach allows your team to focus their efforts on the segments of the market where they are most likely to succeed, optimizing their time and increasing their chances of closing deals.

Building a Repeatable and Scalable Territory Plan

Another key aspect of strategic territory management is helping your team build a plan that focuses on repeatability. Encourage reps to create habits and processes that focus on consistent, high-quality outreach at scale.

Set clear objectives for what success looks like in their territory, and ensure they have a plan that enables them to repeat their successes monthly or quarterly. Implementing a 30 to 90-day planning cycle where each rep creates a proposal that outlines their target accounts, key objectives, and specific outreach strategies can be incredibly effective. This plan should be revisited and adjusted based on performance metrics and market changes, ensuring it remains relevant and aligned with both individual and company goals.

Managing account load is another critical component. Research suggests that an SDR can effectively work 40 to 205 accounts per month, depending on the level of multi-threading and the complexity of the sales process.[9] Work with your reps to determine the optimal number of accounts they can manage effectively, recognizing that this will vary based on their skill level, the complexity of the sales process, and the level of engagement required. For example, if a rep is managing complex midmarket accounts, they may need to focus on fewer accounts to ensure each one is properly worked on. Alongside this, train reps on how to refresh their lead lists regularly to ensure they are always working on the most relevant and high-potential accounts. This might involve using tools like CRM analytics to identify accounts that have gone cold or to discover new opportunities within their territory.

Rolling Out a CEO of Territory Mindset

Providing your team with the technology and training that enables their success is a non-negotiable. Your CRM system should be set up to support the CEO mindset, enabling reps to easily create filtered lists, track engagement, and incorporate triggers. This ensures each rep is enabled to align their passions, firmographics, and account triggers to build a robust territory plan.

---

[9] "Leaders in Driving Recurring Revenue Growth." Winning by Design. https://www.winningbydesign.com/.

Case Study: Gartner's Targeted Outbound Strategy in Action

Gartner, a global leader in research and advisory services, demonstrates exactly how powerful a targeted, segmented outbound sales strategy can be. At the heart of their success is a concept discussed throughout this book - leveraging precise segmentation and creating highly relevant, persona-based messaging through micro-campaigns.

Gartner's sales approach begins with careful segmentation. They understand that trying to sell to every qualified lead in their market won't yield the best results. Instead, their teams apply detailed segmentation criteria such as industry specifics, seniority levels, strategic initiatives, and readiness to engage. This allows them to narrow their list to high-value accounts. These prospects are not only most likely to convert but also likely to generate significant long-term revenue.

Once these ideal segments are identified, Gartner creates micro-campaigns tailored specifically to each audience's unique context. Let's take a closer look at how this works in practice:

In one highly successful campaign, Gartner targeted a Fortune 500 company undergoing a large-scale digital transformation. Rather than sending generic messaging about Gartner's services, the sales team conducted extensive research into the company's recent announcements, strategic objectives, and competitive landscape. They discovered the company faced specific challenges around IT modernization, including integration of new technologies, data management, and operational efficiency.

Leveraging this knowledge, Gartner created a micro-campaign built entirely around the unique pain points this specific segment of senior executives was experiencing. Gartner didn't waste time sending irrelevant personalization such as "Congratulations on your latest funding round." Instead, their outreach included detailed, customized research reports highlighting the exact issues the company faced and offering actionable recommendations. This demonstrated real value, immediately earning the prospect's attention and trust.

The results speak for themselves. This approach led to several high-level executive meetings and ultimately resulted in a multimillion-dollar consulting agreement. Gartner's ability to deliver highly targeted, research-driven insights established their position as a trusted advisor rather than just another sales rep competing for attention.

Gartner's EVP of Products and Services, Ken Davis, explains this clearly: "Selling isn't just about closing deals; it's about providing insights that challenge the status quo and help clients see opportunities they might have missed." Gartner's sales reps embody this philosophy by turning outbound interactions into educational, consultative experiences. Instead of pitching features or generic product messaging, Gartner's reps provide value first, building credibility and making prospects eager to continue the conversation.

To scale this strategy, Gartner uses multi-channel micro-campaigns, coordinating messaging across email, LinkedIn, and direct calls. Each channel reinforces the same focused message, aligned precisely with the segment-specific value proposition. By creating a cohesive narrative tailored specifically to each targeted group, Gartner ensures maximum impact with minimal wasted effort.

Another critical aspect is Gartner's intentional focus on senior-level decision-makers like CIOs and CFOs. Because Gartner understands the strategic priorities of these executives, such as reducing costs, accelerating innovation, or managing risk, they can customize their micro-campaigns to address these goals directly. Gartner's sales outreach is not about reading a prospect's résumé back to them or congratulating them on irrelevant achievements. It is about connecting directly to the outcomes executives care deeply about.

As Whitney Bouck, former EVP at Box, noted: "The value Gartner brought to our decision-making process was immense. Their consultative approach made it feel less like being sold and more like gaining a trusted advisor." Gartner does not rely on surface-level personalization; they rely on precise segmentation, value-based messaging, and strategic relevance, exactly what we are learning to replicate throughout this book.

Continuous improvement and adaptation are core to Gartner's outbound sales culture. Their reps regularly analyze what messaging works best and why, sharing this knowledge internally to refine their segmentation and micro-campaign strategies even further. This ensures their outreach consistently evolves to match shifting market conditions and buyer expectations.

In summary, Gartner's case study underscores several key lessons:

- **Precise Segmentation is Essential:** Gartner doesn't sell to everyone. They focus deeply on the segments that align best with their strengths and value propositions.

- **Micro-Campaigns Create Relevance at Scale:** By carefully crafting campaigns tailored to each segment's specific needs, Gartner achieves personalization at scale without irrelevant, generic touches.

- **Value-Based Messaging Drives Engagement:** Gartner's approach leads with relevant insights, strategic recommendations, and tailored content, instantly earning the prospect's attention and trust.

- **Continuous Adaptation Ensures Long-term Success:** Gartner's culture of constant learning ensures their strategy stays fresh, relevant, and impactful.

Gartner's sophisticated approach to outbound sales perfectly illustrates the principles of targeted segmentation, value-based messaging, and micro-campaigns that we have explored in this book. It is a real-world blueprint of how sales teams can achieve extraordinary outcomes by focusing on relevance, credibility, and precision in every outreach effort.

The most difficult part of rolling out the CEO Mindset is change management. Expect your team to be resistant to change. Be prepared with a strong narrative about the value of change as well as a series of trainings to support a new approach to territory management. Start with an interactive workshop that introduces territory management and what it means to take ownership and practice ranking accounts or building ICP segments together. Use real-life examples and case studies to demonstrate how this approach has driven success. This includes role-playing scenarios where reps can practice identifying account triggers, segmenting their territory, and creating segment-specific value propositions. That type of hands-on training will help solidify these concepts and give them practical experience.

Following this, conduct personalized territory planning sessions with each rep. In these sessions, work through the territory account planning framework, helping each rep align their passions, firmographics, and account triggers to build a robust territory plan. The 30 to 90-day planning framework will be instrumental in helping reps set clear, actionable goals and ensure they have a structured approach to their territory management. While you're transitioning to a CEO Mindset culture, that strategy needs to be supported with repeatable processes.

Regular check-ins are essential to review progress and make necessary adjustments. Encourage your team to advocate for their territory plans by bringing data and insights to these meetings, fostering a culture of continuous improvement. Use these sessions to troubleshoot challenges and celebrate wins, ensuring that reps stay motivated and on track. Providing continuous learning opportunities, such as access to industry webinars, workshops, and courses, will keep your team informed about market trends and best practices in territory management.

Finally, it's important to recognize and reward wins that come from successful territory management. Celebrating successes and highlighting the achievements of those who exemplify the CEO mindset will reinforce the behavior you want to see across the team. Recognition and rewards not only motivate individual salespeople but also set a standard for the entire team, encouraging everyone to strive for excellence in their territory management efforts.

The Role of Territory Management in Long-Term Success

Empowering your team to take ownership of their territories sets them up for long-term success. When sellers think and act like the CEO of their territory, they become more invested in their work, more proactive in seeking out opportunities, and more committed to achieving their goals. When salespeople think like CEOs, they stop chasing accounts and start building pipelines.

Giving sales reps autonomy and ownership over their work leads to higher job satisfaction, motivation, and engagement. Your team will be happier, more likely to succeed, and more likely to stick around. Remember, this isn't a simple ask to follow a new process. You are asking your team to build new skill sets and embrace a new mindset.

A 2022 meta-analysis in the *Journal of the Academy of Marketing Science* concluded that intrinsic motivation—driven by autonomy, purpose, and self-direction—has a stronger positive impact on salesperson performance than extrinsic motivators like commissions or bonuses.[10] When salespeople are trusted to shape their own path to a goal, their engagement and consistency increase.

Research published in the *Journal of Organizational Behavior* found that an employee's sense of psychological ownership was defined by feeling a personal stake in their success, and it is positively linked to both job satisfaction and job performance.[11] Employees who can claim ownership over ideas, initiatives, or projects demonstrate greater satisfaction and initiative.

It's essential to provide the guidance, support, and resources they need to thrive in this role. By teaching them to approach territory management strategically and with a sense of ownership, you're helping them

---

[10] Ahmed, Sabih. "Why Giving Sales Reps Ownership Is the Smartest Move for Driving Performance: Blog." SalesScreen, May 13, 2025. https://www.salesscreen.com/blog/sales-goal-tracking-and-autonomy/.

[11] Cameron, K., Mora, C., Leutscher, T., & Calarco, M. (2011). Effects of Positive Practices on Organizational Effectiveness. *The Journal of Applied Behavioral Science*, 47(3), 266-308. https://doi.org/10.1177/0021886310395514 (Original work published 2011)

build the skills and the mindset needed to succeed in B2B sales and to drive sustained growth for your organization.

We don't have space in this book to discuss sales compensation in a meaningful way, but as you design a territory strategy to support revenue goals, I caution you to ensure your compensation plan incentivizes the right behaviors. We can acknowledge that money may not be a salesperson's top motivation, but paying sellers for activity that is most closely linked to building a profit generating pipeline is critical.[*]

This comprehensive approach to territory management, combining strategic planning with tactical execution, ensures that your team is not just covering their territory but truly owning it. The result is a more motivated, engaged, and successful sales team, ready to drive growth and deliver exceptional results.

The Case for Account & Contact-Based Personalization

Account-Based Marketing (ABM) is a term coined by the Information Technology Services Marketing Association in 2004. While the concept of ABM had been popular for decades, it was a strategy siloed to marketing efforts, especially agency work. After Sara Sheppard published the first in-depth study titled "Account-Based Marketing: The New Frontier," we saw that the idea of ABM had started to bleed into sales practices.

A cornerstone of the success of my career has been blurring the lines between demand generation and lead generation, or between activities historically siloed to marketing and those siloed to sales. Creating a buyer-centric revenue strategy that aligns sales and marketing is the dream for many CROs, one that I've been lucky enough to see play out more than once.

While I do believe the process of segmenting your territory to create persona-based value propositions that can be used to run micro-campaigns is the answer for most B2B sales outbound motions, I must acknowledge the value of ABM. Throughout this book, we follow Emily

---

[*]Author's Note

and Kevin, who have an average deal size of $22,000 and a large address-able market. A full-blown ABM strategy would not provide appropriate return on investment (ROI), meaning the cost of customer acquisition (CAC) would be extremely high, and it would be difficult to ensure pipeline coverage.

If you are working on an especially high-dollar sale or in an especially small TAM, you may want to incorporate all or some elements of ABM. While I am not an ABM expert, I came across this case study from Gartner while researching *Profit Generating Pipeline*. I think it illustrates a great blend of ABM tenets with what I am endeavoring to teach you throughout this book.

Micro-Campaigns: The Answer to Personalization at Scale

This chapter introduced a powerful approach to achieve relevance at scale: micro-campaigns. A micro-campaign is messaging built around highly segmented lists, each crafted specifically around the priorities of a clearly defined group of prospects. By doing deep up-front work - segmenting territories, building specific persona-based value propositions, and creating outreach tailored to each segment - you can eliminate the need for superficial, contact-level personalization.

This method of personalization at scale has proven highly effective. Consider Gartner's success targeting senior decision-makers at a Fortune 500 company undergoing digital transformation. Gartner didn't waste time on generic personalization. Instead, they researched the company's strategic challenges deeply, using tailored insights to connect their outreach directly to the client's needs around IT modernization. The result: Gartner positioned themselves as trusted advisors rather than sellers, earning a multi-million-dollar consulting engagement.

I've come back to this strategy throughout my career. From four to six-figure deal sizes and small business owners to Fortune 250 C-suite executives, this path to relevance at scale works.

By bringing this strategic vision into your sales organization, you teach the team that successful reps don't attempt to contact every name in their CRM. They leverage their own historical data, identify segments with the highest potential, and build outbound strategies around those opportunities. This shift from broad outreach to strategic, data-driven engagement leads to faster deal cycles, higher close rates, and stronger long-term relationships.

By stacking together what we've covered in Chapters 8, 9, and 10, you can confidently help your team identify who to reach out to and what to say to them. Together, these techniques create more effective, personalized outreach. In the next chapter, we'll build on this foundation to craft sales messaging that drives real pipeline.

CHAPTER 11

Writing Sales Copy That Generates Pipeline

"Always lead with insight that is relevant to the recipient. Make sure your email teaches them something they didn't know before and connects that insight directly to a problem they care about."
—Jen Allen-Knuth

Sales copywriting is more than putting words on a page; it's about creating messages that resonate, engage, and inspire action. In B2B sales, where decision-making is complex and prospects are often overwhelmed with information, effective copy is key to generating pipeline and moving prospects forward in their buying journey.

At its core, sales copywriting is about communication. Every email, LinkedIn message, cold call, and voicemail is a chance to connect with a prospect in a meaningful way. But with limited time and attention from prospects, the window to make that connection is small. Well-crafted copy acts as a bridge between your solution and the prospect's pain points or needs. It's not just about getting a response - it's about getting the *right* response from the *right* person.

To build a profit generating pipeline, you must compete for your prospect's attention and time. Every word of your sales copy must earn the right to both. Your copy should promise value, not just ask for it.

This means writing with precision, crafting copy that is easy to digest, and delivering content that feels valuable at first glance. Prospects need to feel that their time spent engaging with you will be worth it.

This means the structure (format) of your message is just as important as its content. Each element should be designed to get the prospect interested enough to spend their limited time reading further or responding.

This single chapter is 15% of the total book. That is how important and nuanced sales copywriting is. Because this chapter is so lengthy, I encourage you to take breaks to apply what you're learning. To ensure that you absorb as much of this chapter as possible, stop to audit your sales copy by applying the techniques as you learn them.

Your prospect has a shorter atten tion span than a goldfish.

Connecting Copy to Prospect Behavior and Brain Science

To truly understand why effective sales copywriting matters, we need to look at how the brain processes information. Research has shown that the average attention span is roughly eight seconds, which means your prospect has a shorter attention span than a goldfish. Your copy needs to make an impression in those critical first moments to avoid being dismissed.

Here are four cognitive phenomena that you need to know:

- Cognitive Overload: When people are exposed to too much information, their brains become overwhelmed. This overload makes it more likely that they'll ignore or discard what they see. Simplifying your message and focusing on clear benefits reduces cognitive load and increases retention.
- The Primacy Effect: This psychological principle suggests that people are more likely to remember the first few pieces of information they encounter. This is why your opening line in any sales copy mat-

---

*Author's Note

ters. It must be strong, relevant, and benefit-driven to maximize recall and engagement.

- Decision Fatigue: The more decisions prospects make throughout
  the day, the less likely they are to engage with complex or unclear
  sales copy. To overcome decision-fatigue, make your copy easy to
  digest, with a clear call to action that guides the reader toward one
  simple next step.
- Pattern Recognition: The human brain is wired to recognize and respond to patterns. If your copy follows a logical flow that prospects
  expect, like problem, solution, benefit, it will be easier for them to
  process and respond. Alternatively, commonly taught tactics like
  the "quick question" subject line train your prospects to recognize a
  pattern used heavily in sales, which immediately triggers their mental spam filters.

By tailoring your sales copy to align with these cognitive principles,
your reps can significantly increase their chances of getting prospects
to engage.

Setting the Foundation for Impactful Sales Messaging

It's a common misconception that good sales copywriting is an inherent talent. The truth is that sales copywriting is a learned skill - one that
evolves with practice, guidance, and incorporating data-backed techniques. Most sales reps, even experienced ones, are not naturally gifted
copywriters. This is why it's critical for sales leaders to not only value
but also *teach* this skill. Even if your salespeople are strong writers, it
doesn't mean they know how to write a technically optimized and properly structured, outcome-based cold sales email.

Expecting reps to be masters of sales copywriting from day one sets them
up for failure. Like any skill, it requires continuous feedback, structured
training, and a deep understanding of what works and why. Investing
time in teaching your team how to write effective sales copy isn't just
valuable, it's essential. Without this foundation, your reps risk sending
out messages that are easy to ignore or fail to resonate with prospects,
leaving valuable pipeline-building opportunities on the table.

As a sales leader, it's your responsibility to ensure your team has the
right tools and knowledge to succeed. Building a strong copywriting

skill set is part of that. When taught correctly, it empowers your team to communicate clearly, create urgency, and ultimately drive meaningful results for your organization.

Stop Getting Ignored: Avoid These Four Common Sales Copywriting Mistakes

Even well-intentioned sales messages can miss the mark if they repeat these common missteps. These mistakes can prevent your team from building meaningful connections with prospects, ultimately reducing the effectiveness of their outreach and the chances of generating pipeline.

Focusing Too Much on Yourself, Your Product, and Your Company

One of the most prevalent mistakes in sales copywriting is focusing too much on the product or service itself. When the copy is centered on what the seller is offering rather than what the prospect needs, it risks sounding self-serving and irrelevant.

When scanning recent cold emails that I've received, 87% began with "I." Common, but ineffective cold email phrases often include "I just noticed," "our product, "I'd love to," and "we do." This type of seller-centric language does not earn the right to your prospect's attention. If you're writing copy like this, an easy audit to perform is reviewing your copy words like "I," "we," "our," or "my." By pivoting to more "you," "your," "their" language, you ensure your copy stays clearly focused on the prospect. Writing from their viewpoint allows you to highlight what they genuinely care about, showing you understand their situation.

Rather than describing product features, clearly articulate the problems they face or the outcomes they want. When your messaging reflects buyer challenges or goals, it becomes far more compelling. Your goal is to help prospects quickly recognize themselves in your copy and feel that exploring solutions with you is worth their time.

Prospects don't care about product features unless those features solve a specific problem they're facing. You're not selling a product; you're selling a solution to the prospect's unique problems.

*We've covered how to identify benefits in the FAB's material, so please reference that material to ensure your copywriting stays problem-focused or outcome-focused. **

Using Jargon and Complex Language

Sales reps often fall into the trap of using jargon or overly technical language, especially when they're deeply familiar with the industry. What feels natural, or perhaps represents their idea of a professional email, may be confusing or meaningless to the prospect.

Complex language creates barriers. It confuses the prospect, makes your message harder to digest, and causes frustration or disengagement. Clear, simple copy helps prospects quickly grasp your message. Clarity is what drives action.

Always prioritize straightforward, conversational language over complex terms or industry jargon. Use words your prospect can easily understand at first glance. Make your message so clear that prospects immediately understand the benefits and value you're offering and feel confident taking the next step - no extra explanation needed.

Information Overload = Cognitive Overload

Another common mistake is cramming too much information into one message. While it may seem logical to provide as many details as possible up front, in reality, this overwhelms the prospect. A long, information-heavy script or message demands too much cognitive effort from the reader.

For text, the reader is quickly scanning. When a prospect sees a large block of text or too many ideas in one message, their brain often tunes out. It's easier for them to ignore the message than to sift through the information to figure out if they should care. This approach also leaves no room for curiosity or engagement, as the prospect feels they've been given everything up front without a clear next step. Sales reps often treat sales messaging like a marketing pamphlet with a goal of

---

*Author's Note

comprehensive information delivery. Overloading a message can lead the prospect to disregard the outreach entirely, meaning the opportunity to spark a conversation is lost.

Instead, keep cold outreach concise and focused on a single clear idea or compelling insight. Your messages should be easy to scan, quickly digestible, and highlight one relevant benefit or intriguing question. Remember, the goal of cold sales outreach isn't to educate the prospect on everything – it's to start a conversation.

> *"In sales copywriting, simple stands out."*

Take the pressure to write a perfect email off of yourself and your salespeople. In sales copywriting, simple stands out.

Over-Indexing on Personal Preferences

Many sellers mistakenly write sales copy based on the type of message they think they would like to receive, focusing too much on their own communication style or preferences. They have never faced an inbox flooded with hundreds of emails a day, so they don't fully understand the cognitive overload that many of their prospects struggle with. As a result, they rely on gut feelings rather than cognitive principles and data-driven insights.

I didn't fully grasp this until I got my first Director title six years into my sales career. Overnight, my inbox exploded from 100 emails a day to nearly 400. When I scanned my inbox, I wasn't looking for emails that would give me more to do. I looked for emails I could delete immediately. My goal was to eliminate as many emails and tasks as quickly as possible. Your prospects are doing the same.

Your team may believe their messages are compelling, but without understanding how overwhelmed decision-makers process information, they are likely missing the mark.

To correct this, sales reps need to shift their perspective. It's not about what *they* would respond to – it's about what immediately captures your buyer's attention. Effective sales copy is built on what consistently drives engagement across audiences, not personal preference. Coach your salespeople to use proven frameworks, templates, or guidelines to balance a desire to infuse their personality into outreach with what actually generates engagement with your target audience.

Remind them to step into the prospect's shoes, considering the mental load and inbox noise decision-makers experience daily. When sellers understand what drives real responses rather than relying on gut instinct, their outreach becomes significantly more effective.

Messaging Precision: Inspiration from Real Brands

Take a page from some of the most successful marketing campaigns that have mastered the art of clear, concise messaging. Their slogans are more than words; they're synonymous with the brands themselves, instantly recognizable and powerful because of their simplicity. I acknowledge that marketing slogans cannot be dragged and dropped into sales copy, but I believe they show that simplicity is memorable, which is a critical point.

By keeping your messaging clear, concise, and benefit-focused, you increase the chances that your message will resonate, be remembered, and ultimately lead to action. Just like the iconic slogans from Nike, M&M's, the US Marines, and Las Vegas Tourism, your sales copy

Nike: "Just Do It."

Nike's slogan is a masterclass in concise messaging. In just three words, it delivers a statement that is not only instantly recognizable but also motivating and empowering. It doesn't need further explanation. Whether you're a professional athlete or just starting to exercise, the message resonates. This level of clarity in messaging allows Nike to connect emotionally with their audience, and that connection is what makes the message unforgettable.

Lesson: In sales copy, the same principle applies: the simpler and more direct your message, the easier it is for prospects to absorb and remember.

M&M's: "Melts in your mouth, not in your hand."

This classic tagline demonstrates how a clear, benefit-driven message can become a signature for a brand. It's short, sweet (literally), and addresses a common concern–chocolate melting in your hand. Without diving into the details of how the candy is made, the message reassures the customer that M&M's are different.

Lesson: In B2B sales, the same approach works - when your message is concise and focused on a specific benefit, it sticks with the prospect long after they've seen it.

U.S. Marines: "The Few. The Proud. The Marines."

This iconic line is a perfect example of how simplicity can evoke deep emotional resonance. The message speaks to the qualities the Marines want to be associated with–pride, exclusivity, and honor. There's no need for a lengthy explanation because the message is so clear and powerful that it stands on its own.

can become a powerful tool for attention, interest, and desire.

Understanding the Prospect's Attention Span

Competition for attention is at an all-time high, and most prospects are already stretched thin. Even well-written sales copy can be overlooked – not because it's irrelevant, but because buyers simply don't have the bandwidth to notice it. Over the past 25 years, the average attention span of a person has shrunk by about one-third, largely due to the pervasive influence of digital technology and the increasing pace of modern life. [12]

The limited nature of a prospect's attention span directly affects whether or not your message will get through. And it's shrinking rapidly. Prospects make split-second decisions about whether or not to engage with sales outreach. If the copy isn't designed to grab attention immediately, your message can get lost. Attention spans are shorter than ever, so your message needs to grab

---

[12] Diena, Yitz. "Average Human Attention Span Statistics." Ambitions, May 24, 2023. https://www.ambitionsaba.com/resources/average-human-attention-span-statistics.

attention quickly and make it clear why it's worth their time.

Every word must add impact. If you miss the window to connect in those first few moments, you lose the chance to get your prospect to consider your solution, no matter how valuable it is.

When people become overwhelmed with messages or decisions, they naturally start filtering out information to protect their mental energy. That's why if your outreach feels complicated, generic, or too long, it's likely to get skipped.

In short, your copy has to feel easy for the prospect to engage with. This isn't about dumbing down your message; it's about respecting their time and mental space. Your prospect will only give you their attention if they believe that your message will be worth the effort to read or listen to.

Lesson: In sales, when your copy is as concise and impactful as this, it elevates your brand, making it easy for prospects to associate your message with your company's values and strengths.

Las Vegas Tourism: "What happens here, stays here."

With just five words, Las Vegas has managed to convey a sense of adventure, secrecy, and excitement. This tagline is memorable because it taps into a universal desire for escapism and fun, while also being incredibly easy to understand.

Lesson: For sales teams, this is a valuable lesson: when your messaging is this clear, it's not only attention-grabbing, it's something your audience can't forget.

Most sales copy fails because it's written with the assumption that the prospect will automatically care about what you have to say. The reality is, they don't. Prospects care about solving their problems and achieving their goals. Effective copy starts by focusing on what your audience cares about, not your brand's agenda.

This requires shifting your perspective. Your goal isn't just to tell the prospect what you're offering; it's to show them why they should care. Every piece of copy should answer the question, "Why is this worth my time?" If your script or copy doesn't make that clear within the first few seconds, it's unlikely your prospect will stick around to find out more.

Your prospect is operating with a limited ability to absorb additional information. Effective sales copy:

- Respects the prospect's time by being concise and getting to the point.
- Speaks directly to their needs or pain points, showing you understand what matters to them.
- Guides them toward the next step without overwhelming them with information.

These principles are vital because they work with, not against, how the human brain processes information. Your prospect is operating with a limited ability to absorb information. By making your copy easy to understand and immediately relevant, you reduce the mental effort they need to consume your message and increase the likelihood that they will engage.

THE 1-10-100 RULE

- 1 Clear, concise CTA
- Optimize the first 10 words
- Keep it under 100 words

Simple framework. Huge results.

Adjusting Your Approach to Compensate for Short Attention Spans

Now that you understand how limited attention spans affect sales copy effectiveness, the next step is to adjust your approach. You must craft every word with intention, knowing that even a few seconds of lost attention can cost you a potential lead.

To compensate for short attention spans, you need to:

- **Lead with relevance and value**: The first sentence of your message should immediately convey why it's worth the prospect's time. Lead with problem versus product-centric messaging.
- **Keep it simple**: Cognitive overload happens when information feels too complex. Clear, concise copy that focuses on one key message or idea is much more likely to be absorbed. Cut out any unnecessary words or fluff.
- **Make it scannable**: Prospects don't read every word of your message. They scan it to decide if it's worth further attention. Use short, simple sentences to make your message easy to digest at a glance.
- **Follow the 1, 10, 100 Rule**: Include one clear, concise call to action per email. Optimize for the first 10 words of your emails so that the reader is inclined to want to open the email to see more. Keep your email under 100 words in total.

When you write sales copy with these principles in mind, you're not just sending a message, you're earning the right to your prospect's attention.

Data-Backed Best Practices: Understanding What Good Looks Like

We've already established the importance of clarity, relevance, and brevity. Now, let's turn that insight into action.

Sales copywriting, whether for emails, phone call scripts, social media, or direct mail, should start with strategies proven to work across the majority of situations. These general best practices offer a foundation that sales leaders can use to begin building their outreach strategies. It's important to note that these practices are based on research and data that suggest what works for the greatest number of prospects. While individual results may vary based on industry or audience, this baseline is critical for establishing what works.

Once you've established a baseline, you'll have a clearer idea of what resonates with your audience. From there, you can begin experimenting with A/B testing to refine your messaging even further, but the key is starting with what is already known to work.

If you don't know what good looks like, it's almost impossible to iterate productively. Whether you're tracking email open rates, response rates, or engagement with social posts, having clear data allows you to understand how well your current messaging is performing. Data also informs you about what to cut and where to test new strategies like subject lines, call-to-action styles, or even the tone of your messaging. The key is starting with what is already proven to work and - *I cannot emphasize enough* – collecting data before iterating.

When taking a data-driven approach, you're no longer reliant on outdated methods, instinct, or guesswork. You're making informed decisions that can steadily improve your outreach results. This is the key to crafting sales copy that not only captures attention but also drives meaningful engagement with prospects.

Technical Mastery Email Copywriting to Reduce Mental Overload

The following best practices, backed by data and research, will help you write technically proficient emails formatted to capture your prospect's attention.

Optimize Subject Lines and Preview Text to Maximize Opens

The subject line has traditionally been viewed as the key to getting your email opened. It's often the first text a recipient sees in their inbox, and the assumption has been that if it's catchy enough, the email will get opened. However, this focus on the subject line overlooks a crucial element - preview text. Subject lines get your foot in the door, but preview text is what gets you through it.

Preview text is usually defined as the snippet that appears next to or below the subject line in the inbox. Applying the 1, 10, 100 rule, think of the preview text of the first 10 words of your email, including the subject line. Preview text is the total text your prospect can see before they open your email. It is the text they use to decide if they want to open your email to continue reading. It carries more weight than sales teams realize. Think of it this way: no matter how compelling the subject line is, if the full preview text falls flat, you risk losing the prospect's attention before they even get a chance to open your message.

Too often, sales teams craft a catchy subject line, only to follow it with generic and uninspired preview text like "I hope you're well" or "Just checking in." For a busy executive, that's an instant delete.

When prospects are bombarded with emails, preview text becomes your best tool to earn enough attention that the prospect clicks "see more" by opening your email.

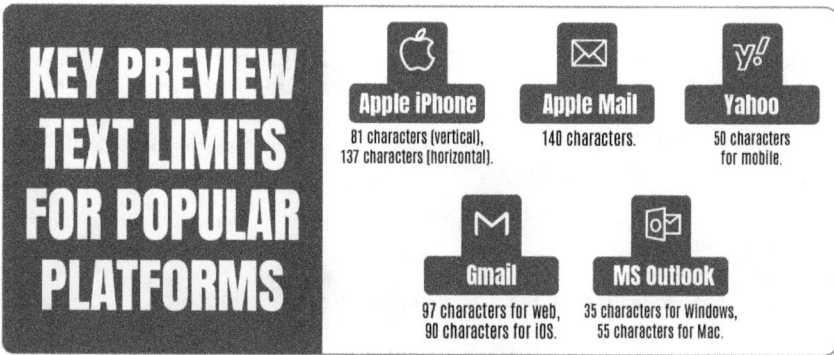

KEY PREVIEW TEXT LIMITS FOR POPULAR PLATFORMS

Apple iPhone — 81 characters (vertical), 137 characters (horizontal).

Apple Mail — 140 characters.

Yahoo — 50 characters for mobile.

Gmail — 97 characters for web, 90 characters for iOS.

MS Outlook — 35 characters for Windows, 55 characters for Mac.

Given that, depending on industry, an average of 46% - 78% of emails are first opened on mobile devices [13] it's crucial to keep your preview text concise and punchy. [14] Mobile users tend to scan especially fast, and you don't have the luxury of extra characters to grab their attention.

Train your team to write preview text that complements the subject line and gives a compelling reason to open the email. By treating the preview text as a core part of your email copy rather than an afterthought, your team can significantly improve the performance of their cold email campaigns.

---

[13] HubSpot, "Mobile Email Optimization: A 5-Step Guide," *HubSpot Blog*, accessed May 24, 2025, https://blog.hubspot.com/marketing/optimize-email-mobile-list.
[14] Jordie van Rijn, "The Ultimate Mobile Email Statistics Overview," *Emailmonday*, last updated May 2025, https://www.emailmonday.com/mobile-email-usage-statistics/.

Application: Editing to Reduce Cognitive Load

Making only minor changes to this email, I want to illustrate how important editing to reduce cognitive load is.

I am not suggesting that you send the After Email Example, but I hope this illustrates how much seller and product centric an average sales email is. Over 80% of the sales emails that hit my own inbox are full of fluff just like this example.

Before Email:

Subject Line:

Increase your revenue by 20%

Hi [First Name],

My name is Alex, and I'm reaching out from [Company Name].

We help business owners like you boost revenue, save time, and streamline operations. We know that protecting your bottom line is important to business owners and you want to do it without having to spend extra hours working. Our best-in-class software helps with that. Our clients typically see revenue growth of at least 20% after working with us.

I'd love to schedule a quick 15-minute chat to show you exactly how we help businesses like yours.

Are you open to learning about how our software can help you?

Looking forward to hearing from you!

Best,
Alex
Account Executive
[Company Name] | [Website URL]
[Phone Number] | [LinkedIn URL]

Example of Edited Email:
Subject Line:

~~Increase~~ your revenue ~~by 20%~~

Hi [First Name],

~~My name is Alex, and I'm reaching out from [Company Name].~~

~~We help business owners like you boost revenue, save time, and streamline operations. We know that~~ protecting your bottom line is important to business owners and you want to do it without having to spend extra hours working. ~~Our~~

~~best-in-class software helps with that.~~ Our clients typically see revenue growth of at least 20% after working with us.

~~I'd love to schedule a quick 15-minute chat to show you exactly how we help businesses like yours.~~

Are you open to learning ~~about~~ how ~~our software can help you~~?

~~Looking forward to hearing from you!~~

Best,
Alex
Account Executive
[Company Name] | ~~[Website URL]~~
[Phone Number] | ~~[LinkedIn URL]~~

After Email:
Subject Line:
Your Revenue
Hi [First Name],

Protecting your bottom line is important. You deserve to do it without spending extra hours working.

Our clients typically see revenue growth of at least 20% after working with us.

Are you open to learning how?

Best,
Alex
Account Executive
[Company Name]
[Phone Number]

As a long-time user of Regie.ai and similar software that analyzes the probability an email will get a response, I couldn't resist checking the scores for both sets of copy. Before scored a 71 out of 100. After scored a 96 out of 100.*

Best Practice for Email Length

The length of an email plays a crucial role in determining whether it captures attention and generates a response. In an information-saturated environment, the cognitive load you place on your recipient can directly influence their willingness to engage. Cognitive load refers to the mental effort required to process information. The higher the cognitive load, the

---

*Author's note

more taxing the task becomes, which often leads to email deletion or being ignored.

It's important to remember that emails are not being read in the traditional sense—they are being scanned. Whether you're teaching your team how to write or writing the emails yourself, email content must be designed for brevity and quick digestion. Your prospects are not reading every word; they are skimming for relevance, value, and clarity.

Studies show that prospects scan emails for less than 9 seconds. [15] Executives, in particular, spend an average of just 3-4 seconds scanning an email before deciding whether to engage with it or delete it. This brief window of attention emphasizes the need for concise and impactful messaging. Emails that are too long or unfocused create a heavier cognitive load, increasing the likelihood that the recipient will abandon them entirely.

Brevity is notoriously difficult to master. Some of the greatest writers and thinkers have commented on the challenge of being concise without losing meaning. Friedrich Nietzsche once said, "It is my ambition to say in ten sentences what others say in a whole book," while Mark Twain famously remarked, "I didn't have time to write a short letter, so I wrote a long one instead." These quotes have become legendary because they capture a truth that sales professionals must embrace - getting to the point quickly without losing substance takes real skill.

The same principle applies when writing sales copy. It's not about writing long, detailed messages that drown the reader in information. It's about delivering high-value, actionable insights in as few words as possible, respecting your prospect's limited attention span. This requires careful editing, a clear understanding of what matters most to the reader, and an ability to craft messaging that cuts straight to the core of the value you offer.

The Challenge of Brevity: Hemingway's Lesson

"You know you're writing well when you're throwing good stuff into the wastebasket" is one of the many famous quotes from Ernest Hemingway

---

[15] Litmus, "Trends in Email Engagement," *Litmus*, accessed May 24, 2025, https://www.litmus.com/resources/trends-in-email-engagement.

about the difficulty of brevity in writing. Another favorite is, "The first draft of anything is shit." And he wasn't kidding. Hemingway famously rewrote the first part of *A Farewell to Arms* over 50 times, and there are 47 different endings to that novel, all written by hand.

When asked what stumped him so much about the book, Hemingway responded simply: "Getting the words right." It took him page after page of cutting and editing to distill those final moments of *A Farewell to Arms* down to one stark, simple sentence: "After a while, I went out and left the hospital and walked back to the hotel in the rain."

That's the magic of Hemingway's writing - his ability to say more with less. It's one of the reasons I've devoured everything he's ever written. For years, *The Sun Also Rises* was my favorite book, mainly because Hemingway's writing made it easy to imagine myself on those European adventures. Hemingway's gift was in his ability to transport readers with short, direct sentences. He made every word count. And when it comes to crafting sales emails, the lesson is the same: it's harder to write less, but it's also more effective.

I had further refined this skill when I started creating content for LinkedIn. Writing in a way that made a point quickly, while staying relevant to people scrolling through a fast-paced newsfeed, was a challenge. But learning to be brief while still delivering a powerful message has paid off, just as it does in sales copy.

The art of simplicity in writing isn't just about saying less; it's about saying the right thing in the fewest words possible. Just like Hemingway stripped away everything that wasn't necessary to get to the heart of his story, you should do the same with your sales emails.

Core to Hemingway's writing style are simple sentences. You can use the same formula to coach your team to write between a grade three and an eighth level of comprehension. I personally aim to write emails at a fifth-grade comprehension level. Writing at a fifth-grade reading level isn't childish, and it doesn't mean you are talking down to the reader. It means using clear language that's easy to understand, even if someone's skimming on their phone.

Boomerang's data revealed that emails written at a third-grade reading level receive 36% higher response rates than those with more complex language. [16] The simpler and clearer your message, the more likely it is to be understood and acted upon.

In the end, writing simply is harder than it sounds, but the payoff is clear. Sales professionals, like great writers, must edit ruthlessly and focus on delivering value in as few words as possible. Your goal isn't just to write, it's to communicate something meaningful, quickly, and efficiently, to earn the right to your prospect's attention.

Writing: Art Meets Science

Research consistently supports the idea that shorter emails yield better results. An analysis of over 40 million emails revealed that the optimal length for a cold outbound email is between 50 and 125 words. [17] When emails fall below or above this length, response rates begin to decline.

Similarly, a study by Constant Contact analyzing over 2.1 million marketing emails found that emails containing approximately 20 lines of text (about 200 words) achieve the highest click-through rates (CTR). [18] I've found that emails up to 200 words work better for follow-ups or newsletters where more detail is necessary. However, for cold outbound emails, it's crucial to stick to a shorter word count.

Regie.ai's research showed that emails between 16 and 68 words sparked maximum engagement and response rates. This concise length strikes a

[16] Alex Moore, "7 Tips for Getting More Responses to Your Emails (With Data!)," *The Boomerang Blog*, February 12, 2016, https://blog.boomerangapp.com/2016/02/7-tips-for-getting-more-responses-to-your-emails-with-data/.

[17] Alex Moore, "7 Tips for Getting More Responses to Your Emails (With Data!)," *The Boomerang Blog*, February 12, 2016, https://blog.boomerangapp.com/2016/02/7-tips-for-getting-more-responses-to-your-emails-with-data/.

[18] Dave Charest, "What's the Best Length for My Email Newsletter?" *Constant Contact Blog*, June 21, 2024, https://www.constantcontact.com/blog/best-length-email-newsletter/.

balance between being brief enough to respect the recipient's time and long enough to clearly communicate the message and call to action. [19]

While brevity is essential, going too short can be detrimental. According to data from HubSpot, emails with fewer than 10 words saw significantly lower response rates compared to those in the 50–125-word range. [20] Sending a message that's too brief risks coming across as thoughtless or irrelevant, as it often lacks the necessary context to engage the prospect. The goal is to make sure that your message length provides enough value while respecting the reader's limited time.

Data sources vary, but nearly 20 years of sending cold outbound emails combined with averages of current data lead me to believe the sweet spot for B2B sales emails is 25–100 words. That length strikes a balance between brevity and meaningful content.

As you experiment with email length, I recommend that you start by getting a baseline for engagement using emails

Data-Backed Recommendations

- Boomerang's study found that response rates peak for emails that are 75-100 words, making this the ideal range for B2B sales emails.
- Regie.ai found that cold outbound introduction emails between 16-68 words had the highest response rates.
- Avoid extremely short emails, as fewer than 10 words significantly decreases your chances of a response, according to HubSpot.
- I developed the 1-10-100 Rule based on nearly two decades of experience sending sales emails. The rule recommends that cold sales emails should not exceed 100 total words.

---

[19] Regie.ai, "The Power of Readability: 9 Ways to Write Simple, Clear Emails That Get Results," *Regie.ai Blog*, accessed May 24, 2025, https://www.regie.ai/blog/how-to-write-readable-sales-emails-that-get-results

[20] Mike Renahan, "The Ideal Length of a Sales Email, Based on 40 Million Emails," *HubSpot Sales Blog*, February 19, 2016, https://blog.hubspot.com/sales/ideal-length-sales-email.

between 25 and 100 words. Once you have the engagement data using the best practice email length, you can experiment with shorter or longer emails.

Sales leaders must train their teams to embrace brevity in sales copy without sacrificing the necessary information that leads to conversions. The key is to make every word count, ensuring that each message feels purposeful, clear, and easy to digest for a busy prospect. Your emails get one glance, use it well.

Let Your Message Breathe: Why White Space Matters

A significant benefit to writing shorter, mobile-optimized emails is that it allows you to incorporate white space.

Formatting plays a crucial role in how emails are perceived and read. Dense blocks of text can overwhelm busy prospects, making it difficult to scan for key information. The use of white space helps break up the text, improving readability and engagement. White space provides breathing room for your message and prevents the email from looking cluttered.

According to HubSpot, emails with shorter paragraphs are more likely to be read and absorbed than those with dense text. I aim for one to two sentence paragraphs in my email copy and only one short sentence per paragraph in messages being sent on social media.

Considering our goal of decreasing the cognitive load for the reader, it's easy to understand why sub-100-word emails with plenty of white space get higher engagement.

How to Drive Engagement Using Calls to Action

Now that we're writing emails that are getting opened and read, we need to get replies. The most important rule to apply to drive engagement using calls to action (CTAs) is to have one clear, concise CTA. A call to action is a clear prompt that tells your audience exactly what to do next. One of my favorite CTA techniques to use in email copy is low-pressure asks in your initial emails. The two highest performing low-pressure CTAs are:

- Yes/no questions like "Does this resonate with your team?"
- Deposits or non-sales resources like a short video, a checklist, or an article that offer value up front.

The goal of a deposit CTA is to give before asking to receive. The idea is that you're making a deposit before you try to make a withdrawal in the form of a bigger ask for their time. For instance, invite them to check out a relevant piece of content, watch a brief video, or respond with their thoughts on a particular challenge. This simple question invites the prospect to engage without feeling like they're being pulled into a heavy sales process right away.

We visited some of the most iconic CTAs in history when looking at famous marketing slogans. They reinforce how clarity drives action. The US Army's "I Want You" poster made the next step obvious and specific. Nike's "Just Do It" inspired action without pressure. While these aren't sales CTAs, they demonstrate how direct, memorable asks work.

Instead of overwhelming the prospect early in your outreach with a high-pressure request, such as a hard push for an in-person meeting or a sales call, opt for a CTA that feels light and easy to engage with. A low-pressure ask creates a sense of ease and increases the likelihood that they'll follow through.

The clearer and more actionable your CTA is, the better. Prospects shouldn't have to guess what to do next. Whether it's clicking through to an article or replying with a quick answer, make the action you want them to take obvious and straightforward. In fact, data from HubSpot shows that emails with a single CTA significantly outperform those with multiple CTAs. Multiple asks can introduce friction, reduce clarity, and lead to inaction. A well-crafted CTA eliminates ambiguity, making it easier for prospects to engage and continue the conversation.

For instance, at the point in your outreach when it's appropriate to ask to book a time for a deeper discussion, your CTA should reflect that, but in a way that feels natural. Rather than "When are you available to discuss?" you might say, "Would a 30-minute call next week work to discuss how we could solve X problem together?" The more specific and clear the next step, the easier it is for the prospect to take action.

In the next chapter, we'll talk about the value of sequences. One powerful concept to keep in mind when we start talking about outreach sequences is the idea of escalating CTAs. As your sequence progresses and you provide more value, you earn the right to be more direct in your requests. Early on, your CTAs should be low-pressure, focused on engagement. As you demonstrate relevance and build trust over multiple touchpoints, you can escalate your ask to something more direct, like the example above, asking to schedule a call.

This concept of escalating CTAs aligns with the broader idea of earning the right to the prospect's time. By adding relevance and value at each touchpoint, you increase your credibility and make the prospect more comfortable engaging with a more significant ask, like a meeting or demo. Gradual escalation respects the prospect's autonomy and builds trust and value before making bigger asks. [21]

We'll dive deeper into how to manage this in the next chapter, but it's important to introduce it here as a guiding principle for your sequence strategy.

In the preliminary stages of your outreach, it's about earning trust, building recognition, and nurturing the relationship. The more you can shift the focus away from pushing your sales agenda and toward simply getting the prospect to take incremental steps, the stronger your foundation for a future close will be. The aim is to build a sense of trust and to position yourself as someone who is genuinely interested in solving the prospect's problems. When your focus is on the next step rather than the end goal, prospects feel less pressure and are more likely to engage.

Crafting Winning Messaging: Attention to Action

Now that we've explored the technical foundations of effective email formatting, clarity, and readability—it's time to focus on the messaging itself. Research from ZeroBounce shows that while 66% of consumers prefer short

---

[21] "Psychological Reactance: Neuromarketing and Behavioral Economics - Psychology Corner." PSYCHOLOGY CORNER - Everyday Psychology. Critical Thinking and Skepticism. https://psychologycorner.com/neuromarketing-and-be havioral-economics/psychological-reactance/.

emails, 28% are indifferent to length, as long as the content is highly relevant to their needs.[22] So, yes, brevity is key, but relevance is nonnegotiable.

In this section, we'll cover how to craft outreach that not only captures attention but also compels action. You'll learn how to use ROI and cost of inaction (COI) language to create urgency, open calls with relevance and confidence, structure conversations that earn attention, and leverage scripts and voicemails that actually drive results.

Create a Sense of Urgency Using ROI and COI Messaging

Sales pressure is often misunderstood and misused. Sales reps apply sales pressure to create artificial deadlines or constraints to push the prospect into action. These tactics might work in Business-to-Consumer (B2C) or transactional environments, but they tend to backfire when targeting B2B decision-makers. You've likely encountered messages that rely on phrases like "Only 8 seats left" or "This deal ends at 5 p.m. today." These strategies can feel manipulative, and in a buyer-driven market, they often erode trust before a prospect even has a chance to get curious about your offer.

In cold outreach, especially when you're trying to build trust with a high-level decision-maker, you need to move away from these outdated methods. Instead of relying on external sales pressure that puts force on the buyer, focus on creating internal urgency. Internal urgency is a more sophisticated and authentic way to prompt action. It comes from the buyer's own recognition that taking action is important because of what they stand to gain or what they risk by staying the same.

Sales pressure, in the traditional sense, is an external force imposed by the seller. It focuses on the seller's agenda, trying to force a quick decision by introducing a sense of scarcity. I'm not suggesting that these strategies don't work – they do, but this approach often leads to buyer's remorse. I caution you to be wary. Increasingly, savvy buyers see through these tactics, and when sales pressure is overplayed, it can feel desperate, leading to skepticism and a reluctance to engage.

---

[22] ZeroBounce, "Into the Inbox: Email Statistics Report for 2025," ZeroBounce, accessed May 24, 2025, https://www.zerobounce.net/email-statistics-report/.

Urgency, on the other hand, is an internal force. It's what the buyer feels when they recognize the value in what you're offering and realize that delaying a decision could cost them. This type of urgency is not something you impose. It's something the buyer creates within themselves. Rather than pushing them into a decision, you guide them toward seeing the value in taking action.

Sellers cannot manufacture urgency. Too often, teams try to move at their desired pace, rather than the pace of trust. Urgency can only be generated by understanding what outcomes your prospects are most motivated to achieve today.

This is where ROI and COI come in. When crafting cold outbound sales emails, knowing when to use ROI and COI language is key to creating internal urgency without feeling manipulative. Both strategies have their place in your outreach sequence, but the key is to use them at the right time and in the right context.

ROI language is about highlighting the potential gains your prospect will experience by engaging with your solution and is the default in the majority of sales emails. It speaks directly to their desire for growth, efficiency, or profitability. However, research from Gong Labs analyzed over 132,000 cold emails and found that using ROI language too early in the sales process can actually decrease success rates by up to 15%.[23] This is because ROI claims, in the initial stages, often lack the necessary context for the buyer to see their relevance. If a prospect doesn't yet understand how your solution solves their problem, numbers and claims of return feel empty.

ROI language is most effective after you've established some level of rapport or credibility, or when the prospect has shown interest in exploring new opportunities. For example, once a prospect understands the value of your offer, you can highlight how your solution will increase productivity or save costs, factors that align with their goals. In this stage, you can say something like:

---

[23] Jonathan Costet, "Before You Hit Send: 7 Sales Email Statistics To Boost Your Email Game," Gong Blog, December 14, 2021, https://www.gong.io/blog/sales-email-statistics/.

"Our platform has helped [lookalike company] save 17% in operational costs.

The result was a 2% uptick in EBITDA. Is now the right time for us to explore how you can achieve the same results?"

COI language, on the other hand, is often a better strategy in the early stages of cold outreach. COI focuses on the risks or costs of doing nothing. Rather than appealing to a potential benefit, COI language highlights the potential pain points, inefficiencies, or losses a prospect will face if they continue with the status quo. This taps into the psychological principle of loss aversion, which states that people are generally more motivated to avoid losses than to seek gains. Forrester's research, highlighted in a blog titled, *Are B2B Buyers Cowards?*, found that B2B buyers are highly risk-averse and that only one in 10 salespeople are effective at communicating true value. [24] Which means there is a misalignment between what we believe the prospect's value is and what they actually find compelling. I believe an overreliance on ROI language causes this gap. When you highlight the consequences of inaction using COI, it creates internal urgency that nudges the prospect toward making a change.

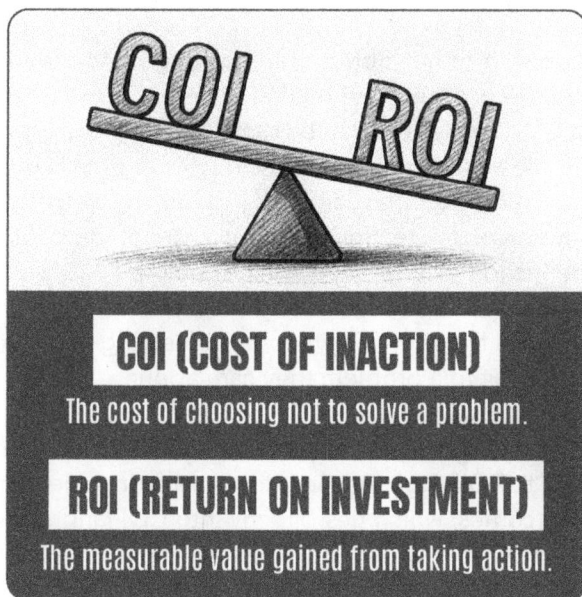

COI (COST OF INACTION)
The cost of choosing not to solve a problem.

ROI (RETURN ON INVESTMENT)
The measurable value gained from taking action.

---

[24] Ian Bruce and Zachary E. Stone, "Are B2B Buyers Cowards?" *Forrester*, January 24, 2024, https://www.forrester.com/blogs/are-b2b-buyers-cowards/.

A COI-focused email might look like this:

"Multi-national FinTech firms without sub-tier supplier tracking lose 2-7% on their margins annually. That level of leakage erodes enterprise value.

How are you monitoring supplier margins?"

This creates urgency and action not through artificial deadlines or promises of ROI, but by making the buyer realize the tangible consequences of not acting.

Blending both ROI and COI language throughout your outreach sequence ensures you're engaging prospects from multiple angles. Some buyers are motivated by the excitement of growth (ROI), while others are more focused on avoiding negative outcomes (COI). Value-Based Segmentation can help you identify which motivator is likely to resonate more with each group, allowing you to tailor your language accordingly. By matching your message to what your segment values most, you're not just creating urgency—you're speaking their language. Incorporating both strategies, you increase your chances of capturing the attention of different buyer personas.

This dual approach is not about manipulating or fearmongering; it's about helping the prospect see the full picture. Let me take a moment to clarify that COI language is not the same as telling a prospect they are bad at their job. Personally, anybody who DMs or emails me and leads by telling me that I'm doing a really bad job with my website/Instagram/SEO is an immediate delete. Because I am aware of the gaps. I've strategically deprioritized those projects, which could be easily uncovered in an email that led with curiosity or insight rather than an attack. The way to earn attention is to teach the prospect something they don't already know and connect it to a problem they care about.

When teaching the FABs approach, it's important to clarify that benefits aren't exclusive to ROI language. Benefits can also include the avoidance of negative outcomes, which ties directly into COI language. A benefit doesn't always have to be about gaining something. It can also be about avoiding something detrimental. For example, while an ROI-focused benefit might highlight how your solution increases efficiency by 20%, a COI-focused benefit could emphasize the risk of continuing with outdated processes that lead to wasted resources or declining results. Both approaches answer the critical question of "Why act now?" but they appeal to different decision-making motivators.

By highlighting both the rewards of taking action (ROI) and the risks of inaction (COI), you empower them to make a more informed decision - one that feels both urgent and valuable.

Using both ROI and COI in your messaging, you provide a fuller picture of the value your solution offers. You're giving them the tools to justify their decision both emotionally and logically. They need to see the potential upside of working with you while also understanding the risks of standing still. Together, these approaches create a more complete and compelling message that resonates with a wider range of prospects.

TRY THESE 4 COLD EMAIL TEMPLATES

Pain Point Pitch
Pain point, solution, relevant solution

Same, Same but Different
Call out comparison, illustrate preference, confirm value

Answered Assumption
Relevant assumption, expert recommendation, answer

Learn-it-All Approach
Problem statement question, inquisitive question, advice question

Want to test different applications of ROI and COI copy? Try four of my favorite cold email templates:

Visit www.salesledgtm.com/value or scan the QR code to download these four email templates and sample copy that you can use as inspiration for your team's sales emails.

Create Curiosity and Build FOMO

Your ultimate goal in early-stage sales outreach is to get the prospect interested enough to engage with your message. One of the most effective ways to do this is by creating curiosity. Instead of overwhelming the prospect with too much information up front, give them just enough to pique their interest. You are not aiming to fully explain your product or service in one go. You are offering a glimpse into something valuable that they'll want to learn more about. This is why long sales emails written like newsletters or marketing pamphlets don't start conversations. It's also why generic messaging falls flat – you've not said something worth being curious about.

The most effective sales copy is often the one that leaves something unsaid. It offers a teaser, a hook, or a question that makes the prospect curious enough to continue the conversation.

A powerful way to create curiosity is by leveraging the fear of missing out (FOMO) and social proof. When prospects see that others like them are benefiting from something they're not yet part of, it creates a sense of urgency and desire to engage. For example, a newsletter sign-up message could say: "Join the 6,212 other sellers getting my weekly newsletter full of tips to close more deals." This statement doesn't just inform the prospect. It highlights that others in their space are already benefiting, subtly implying that they're missing out if they don't join in.

Netflix is an expert at using curiosity-driven social proof. When promoting new shows, Netflix often uses copy like, "Everyone's talking about [new show]. Find out why." This piques viewers' curiosity without giving away too much, drawing them in to explore the show for themselves. Netflix also uses social proof through their "Top 10" list of shows and movies, signaling to viewers that these titles are what everyone is watching. As humans, we are naturally inclined to try something if it feels like everyone else is doing it. This taps into our fear of being left out or missing something culturally relevant, increasing the likelihood that we'll engage.

In sales, this same principle applies. Mentioning how your solution has helped a competitor or peer in the industry can create a powerful motivator for the prospect to engage. For example, when selling to Coke, you might say: "We've helped Pepsi streamline their operations by 15%."

By showing that a competitor is already seeing results, you build curiosity and urgency, making the prospect more likely to engage.

Four Types of Social Proof That You Can Try

There are several ways to leverage social proof effectively. Here are four that I've used in cold sales outreach to drive engagement:

- Expert social proof involves citing respected authorities or industry analysts to reinforce credibility. For example, referencing Gartner's recognition or a respected industry publication can instantly increase your credibility in the eyes of prospects.
- Celebrity social proof leverages the influence of well-known figures in your industry. In B2B sales, this might include respected industry leaders or executives who have endorsed your product or highlighted your company publicly. Such endorsements can create immediate trust and spark interest.
- User social proof is drawn directly from satisfied customers or clients. Real testimonials or case studies demonstrating tangible outcomes resonate strongly because prospects see real results achieved by similar companies. Using specific customers' names and company names gets the best results when applying user social proof. However, anonymized social proof is still compelling. For instance, sharing that "Over 500 B2B SaaS companies increased their close rates by 20% after implementing our sales sequence framework" makes your claims both credible and relatable.
- Wisdom of the crowd uses the sheer number of users or customers to suggest quality and reliability. This is exactly what the earlier newsletter example demonstrates. Another example is: "5,384 sellers are already applying what they learned during Leslie's Masterclass. Join them." The specific number provides immediate credibility, implying widespread adoption and satisfaction.

When leveraging social proof, authenticity is nonnegotiable. Exaggerated or misleading claims can erode trust quickly. Prospects are quick to sense fake sales pressure and dishonesty, and once trust is broken, engagement plummets. My experience is that it is best to lead with transparency.

Social proof and FOMO work because of a basic human instinct: we want to belong, and we fear missing out, especially when our peers or competitors are involved. By carefully choosing credible examples and truthful statements, you can tap into your prospect's psychological motivation to avoid loss or exclusion, making them more likely to engage with your outreach.

Sales Scriptwriting for Cold Calling and Voicemail

Why It's Important to Work from a Script

Working from a script is critical in cold calling and voicemail outreach, especially for sales reps who are starting a new job or selling a new product. A well-prepared script ensures consistency across calls and helps maintain professionalism, no matter the skill level or confidence of the salesperson. Data from organizations like HubSpot and Cognism has shown that structured scripts lead to more successful calls, increasing conversion rates by 28%[25] and 10%[26], respectively. By eliminating guesswork, you can help your sellers ensure key talking points are always hit.

Starting from a script doesn't mean rigidly following a formula without adapting to the flow of conversation. Rather, a script serves as a foundation. Outside of practicing and role-playing, you should coach your salespeople to a point where they do not need to read a script word for word as fast as possible.

At that point, the script becomes their road map, ensuring that even in the midst of interruptions or difficult responses, the main points stay on track. As sellers gain confidence and experience, they can inject more flexibility and personalization into the conversation, but the script remains a key framework. Scripts help salespeople to clearly communicate value, address objections more effectively, and avoid long, meandering conversations that fail to provide value.

---

[25] Daisy Shevlin, "The Top Cold Calling Success Rates for 2025 Explained," *Cognism*, March 18, 2025, https://www.cognism.com/blog/cold-calling-success-rates.Cognism

[26] "7 Winning Scripts for Cold Calling Success in 2025," *Call Criteria*, March 13, 2025, https://callcriteria.com/scripts-for-cold-calling/?utm_source=chatgpt.com.Call Criteria+1Call Criteria+1

Call Openers: How to Capture Attention in the First Few Seconds

In cold calling, the first few seconds are the most crucial. According to research from Orum, SalesLoft, and others, you have less than 10 seconds to capture your prospect's attention and make a positive impression. [27] Nook's data shows that sellers who use an opener that identifies a pain point or frustration are 6.3 times more likely to book a meeting.[28] The goal during this brief window is to pique the prospect's interest and motivate them to stay on the line long enough for you to demonstrate value. This moment can make or break the call because a well-crafted opener sets the tone for the entire conversation.

The best openers are relevant and straightforward, instantly connecting your reason for the call to the prospect's specific business challenges or industry. The opener should never feel forced or scripted; instead, it should flow naturally and show that you've done your research. Starting with the prospect's name and immediately referencing a relevant pain point or goal will ensure that your opener feels genuine and professional.

When I teach sales reps how to master cold calls, I emphasize the importance of using a *relevant reason for the call* opener. This approach works because it respects the prospect's time while also demonstrating that you've come prepared. You aren't asking for permission to explain why you're calling; you're confidently delivering a reason that directly ties into their business, which builds trust from the outset. For example:

"Hi [Prospect], this is [Your Name] from [Your Company]. I noticed that your team has been focused on expanding [specific area] this quarter. We helped [lookalike company] [ROI or COI-based outcome] when they were expanding."

---

[27] "30 Minutes to President's Club Tips to Cold Calling with Orum." Orum. Accessed June 20, 2025. https://www.orum.com/reports-and-guides/30mpc-cold-calling?utm_source=chatgpt.com.

[28] "Three Unexpected Ways to Book Way More Meetings in 2025." Nooks Blog. Accessed June 20, 2025. https://www.nooks.ai/blog-posts/three-unexpected-ways-to-book-way-more-meetings-in-2025.

Unlike permission-based openers, which rely on awkward and often ineffective scripts, *relevant reason for the call* openers immediately show value. A permission-based opener (PBO), like "Can I have 30 seconds to explain why I'm calling?" does nothing to demonstrate relevance or value and only forces the prospect to decide whether they want to take a gamble on an unknown call with zero context. Most often, they'll say no. While asking for permission is perfectly fine, it should always come *after* you've provided something that matters to the prospect, not before.

Additionally, *relevant reason for the call* is a better strategy because it's naturally iterative. Your opener can and should evolve as you learn more about the segment of the territory you're contacting. Your opener can always be updated to stay relevant and current. This flexibility ensures that your approach stays fresh, whereas *permission-based openers* tend to be static and generic. As a result, these generic openers become ineffective over time.

Examples of PBOs like, "Do you want to roll the dice and see why I've called?" (which I'm not convinced ever worked) or the once-popular "Did I catch you at a bad time?" opener, which is now 40% less likely to book a meeting compared to the baseline success rate[29] are still recommended by sales 'gurus." These PBOs trigger mental spam filters, causing psychological reluctance and increasing early call hang-ups. Earlier, we talked about pattern recognition. Buyers are quick to recognize a sales call when the opener sounds more like a punchline than how any human would speak.

By using a *relevant reason for the call* opener, you avoid these traps. Your opener adapts to the prospect, keeping the conversation valuable and timely, rather than falling into the common pitfalls of stale and predictable scripts. This adaptability is key to maintaining credibility and engagement with your prospects.

Tips for Crafting an Engaging Opener

The more relevant your opener is to your prospect's specific situation, the more likely they'll stay engaged in the conversation. However, this

---

[29] Jonathan Costet, "The 3-Point Framework To Overcome Cold Call Objections," *Gong Blog*, November 22, 2021, https://www.gong.io/blog/cold-call-objections/.

doesn't mean requiring sellers to perform detailed research on every individual contact before each call. That approach simply isn't scalable. Instead, leverage the thoughtful segmentation and targeting you've already established.

Each campaign identifies common pain points, priorities, or industry-specific trends that resonate broadly with every account in the segment. Your team's opening lines should directly reference these targeted, persona, or account-level insights to demonstrate that your salespeople understand the challenges and opportunities relevant to that segment. This approach builds instant credibility without sacrificing efficiency.

Prospects want context quickly. They want to know why this conversation deserves their attention. As discussed, one of the most effective ways to provide immediate context is through social proof. Encourage your salespeople to mention the specific, lookalike organizations facing comparable challenges. Prospects naturally pay attention when they realize others in their industry or role have already seen success through your solution.

Application: Leslie's Favorite Cold Call Opener

Template:
"Hi [prospect name] – Calling because we've worked with [lookalike company] & [lookalike company] on [common industry pain point]. Usually [assumption about why the pain point occurs]. Wondering if that's the same for you?"

Example:
"Hi Alice – Calling because we've worked with ABC Fencing & DEF Gutters on getting jobs booked from website leads. Usually, small businesses are too busy delivering work for their customers to take full advantage of their websites. Wondering if that's the same for you?"

Leveraging social proof validates the relevance of your outreach while creating urgency and interest. Prospects don't want to miss out on opportunities their peers are already benefiting from, and highlighting this early in the conversation makes them far more likely to engage. It is important not to name-drop at random. If your prospect doesn't care about the company you name-drop, the social proof can do more harm than good.

Successful openers immediately highlight the specific value you offer. Instead of generic introductions or begging for 30 seconds, your sales reps should confidently state how your solution addresses identified issues or opportunities relevant to your targeted micro-segment. Establishing value up front is critical because prospects are inundated with calls and messages daily. If your team doesn't clearly communicate how the conversation will add immediate value, prospects will simply disengage and move on. Ensure your opening messages are crisp, clear, and directly connected to the core value your solution delivers.

Structuring a Cold Call to Capture Attention

After your opening, keep the conversation moving by introducing an impact statement – one that concisely communicates the value of your offer, tied to the prospect's goal. The best impact statements are concise, outcome-focused, and centered on what matters most to the buyer, not just what your product does.

Here's an example of an impact statement:

"We recently worked with a company in [prospect's industry], and they saw a 15% reduction in downtime after implementing our solution. I believe we could deliver similar results for you, especially considering the challenges [prospect's company] is facing with [specific pain point]. [Verify prospect wants to continue the conversation]"

The role of the impact statement is to establish relevance and to earn the right to keep the conversation going. Without it, prospects may not see the need to invest more time in the call, especially if they don't immediately connect your product to their specific situation.

The impact statement is often a seamless continuation of the relevant reason for the call opener. When I am helping sales teams structure cold call scripts, I think of each part of the script as working to earn them the right to a little more attention. The first 10 seconds are the call opener, which earns you the right to another 30-45 seconds where you continue with an impact statement.

Once you've established surface-level relevance and rapport, you may already be a minute into the dialogue. At this point, you need to pivot to a more conversational tone. I've audited thousands of cold calls during my career, and one of the biggest mistakes that I see is sales leaders giving their team scripts that make them sound like a walking billboard. While I am an advocate of scripts, that does not mean you should ask your salespeople to memorize and regurgitate a lengthy advertisement for your company features. That is a fast path to hang-ups.

Instead, give them language that helps them lead with relevance and transition quickly to thoughtful (non-qualifying) questions. Preparing five questions that allow your reps to start a process of discovery without making the conversation feel like an interrogation is essential to leading successful cold calls. As Kevin Dorsey shares, "On a cold call, you get four or five questions before the person tells you they have to go." Meaning you need to make every question count.

Assuming you've been able to effectively leverage your four to five questions in a way that sparked enough interest that the prospect has agreed to continue the conversation, the final step of the cold call is to establish a mutually agreed-upon next step. Ideally, that is a calendared meeting.

Application: The Six-Minute Call Structure

Step 1: State a relevant reason for the call.

Step 2: Deliver an impact statement.

Step 3: Verify the prospect's interest in continuing the call.

Step 4: Be prepared with five outcome-based questions.

Step 5: Set specific, mutually agreed-upon next steps.

Step 6: Ask essential qualifying questions.

Step 7: End call by confirming the agreed-upon next steps.

According to new data from Orum, the average cold call lasts approximately 52 seconds. However, calls that result in a booked meeting tend to be significantly longer, averaging around six minutes.[30] This data highlights how essential it is to use the first 60 seconds of your call to establish enough value that you earn the right to your prospect's additional attention.

The Role of Tone and Confidence

While the words you choose are important, the way you deliver them is just as critical. Decades of communication research suggest that when someone can't see you, how you say something often carries more weight than what you say. Your tone, pacing, and confidence shape how your message is received, especially in the first few seconds of a cold call. When you sound confident, enthusiastic, and genuinely interested in the prospect, you're more likely to hold their attention. That's why I teach sales reps to practice their call scripts and especially their call openers until they feel comfortable delivering them with confidence, whether it's the exact script or a variation that feels natural to them.

However, tone without substance falls flat. A strong opener earns attention when it sounds confident and delivers immediate value to the prospect. This combination of tone and relevance is what makes a *relevant reason for the call* opener the most effective strategy for cold calling. It shows that you respect the prospect's time, builds trust quickly, and sets the stage for a meaningful conversation.

Voicemail Scripts: Make Every Message Count

We will get specific about how to incorporate voicemails into your sequences in the following chapter, but it's important that we talk about voicemail messaging here. Leaving a voicemail can often feel like a wasted effort, but when done correctly, voicemails will be an effective part of your outreach strategy.

---

[30] Adam Sockel, "Cold Calling Tips for 2025," *Orum Blog*, accessed May 24, 2025, https://www.orum.com/blog/cold-call-success.

If you think the only reason to leave a voicemail is to get a call back, you're missing the point. If you think that pitching your product on the voicemail may get a prospect interested, you're turning off the very prospects you want to attract.

Voicemails should be designed to provide value and leave a memorable impression. Some industries still respond to a request for a returned call, but I've most often used voicemails to guide the prospect to engage with another touchpoint in your sequence. Using voicemails correctly, you can build interest and move the conversation forward, even if you never get a call back.

If you're ready for a deep dive on how to strategically leverage voice-mails, visit www.salesledgtm.com/value or use the QR code to down-load my free Strategic Guide to Voicemails.

For now, here are four of my favorite tips to help you create voicemail scripts that help you earn your prospect's attention.

Keep It Short and Impactful

One of the primary rules for voicemail is brevity. Voicemails should be short, value-focused, and clear about the next step. According to research from Sales Hacker, the optimal voicemail length is around 20–30 seconds.[31] Anything longer risks losing the prospect's attention, while shorter messages may lack the information necessary to spur a callback.

Prospects are busy, and their attention spans are short. To maximize impact, ensure that your message gets straight to the point. Sellers need to avoid the temptation to talk about themselves and their company first.

---

[31] Jake Dunlap, "Best Practices to Turn Those Leads into Sales Meetings," *GTMnow*, June 4, 2014, https://gtmnow.com/best-practices-to-turn-those-leads-into-meetings/.

Instead, focus on delivering value immediately. This approach hooks the listener, making it more likely that they'll stay engaged.

Optimize for Visual Voicemail

Many prospects read their voicemail messages through visual voicemail transcription rather than listening to them. Therefore, it's important to optimize the voicemail script for easy readability as well as clear verbal communication. Your script should be simple, clear, and free from jargon. This increases the likelihood that even if the prospect reads the message, it resonates and prompts further action.

I coach sales leaders to write voicemail scripts that read more like a 3-4 sentence cold email rather than a meandering voice note. As with all cold sales interactions, getting to the point is paramount.

Leverage the Human Voice for Emotional Impact

Voicemail offers a unique opportunity to create an emotional connection, as your tone and delivery can communicate more than just words. As we've discussed, your tone is just as important—if not more important—than what you say. Use your voice to convey enthusiasm, urgency, or sincerity, depending on the message, and make sure that emotion is appropriate to the context of the call. Tone can make your message more memorable than a simple text or email.

Don't Default to Asking for a Call Back

Using a voicemail to ask for a direct call back is often ineffective. This varies by industry, but my teams and clients have seen better results from voicemail scripts that encourage engagement on other channels like email or LinkedIn. For instance, you might direct the prospect to look for a specific subject line in their inbox or accept your LinkedIn connection request. As a good rule of thumb, save asking for a call back when reaching out to prospects who work exclusively in an office, like dentists, or those who heavily use the phone themselves, like realtors. This approach increases your chances of getting a response by meeting the prospect where they're most comfortable communicating.

By following these principles, you can craft voicemail scripts that not only increase engagement but also complement your broader outreach strategy.

Writing Skills Are Essential for Sales Success

Sales copywriting and scriptwriting are critical skills that directly impact your team's ability to generate pipeline. As a sales leader, it's essential to help your team understand why mastering this skill is key to their success.

By training your team to avoid common mistakes like focusing too much on the product or using jargon, you'll ensure their outreach is relevant, clear, and value-driven. Encourage your team to craft messages that are simple, benefit-focused, and easy for prospects to digest. Every touch-point, whether an email, LinkedIn message, or voicemail, should be designed to build trust and move the conversation forward.

The goal is to help your salespeople earn the right to your prospects' attention and keep them engaged. When done correctly, strong copy will consistently help your team build meaningful connections and generate the pipeline needed for sustained growth.

CHAPTER 12

Optimizing and Managing Outreach Channels

> *"A successful outbound strategy is built on understanding your buyer's journey and aligning your approach accordingly."* —Jill Konrath

Multi-Channel Mastery: The Strategy Behind AND1's Rise

AND1's rise to becoming a mega-brand in basketball culture is a testament to the power of creative, multichannel execution. Unlike most sportswear companies that leaned on polished ads and big-name endorsements, AND1 understood that their ideal customer wasn't being reached through traditional means. Their audience wasn't spending their time flipping through magazines or watching TV commercials. They were on the blacktops in city parks and streetball tournaments, immersed in a culture that lived outside the mainstream.

Instead of forcing their message through the same old channels, AND1 met their audience where they actually were.

One of the most iconic pieces of their strategy was the AND1 Mixtapes. Mixtapes were first distributed by VHS, and those tapes became coveted. They weren't commercials, they were full-length highlight reels showcasing the kind of raw, unfiltered talent that couldn't be contained in an arena. The footage featured real players in real neighborhoods, putting on off-the-cuff, unapologetic shows of streetball creativity. The Mixtapes worked because they were an unforgettable pattern interrupt. They had cultural currency.

The brand became something people could touch, experience, and belong to. Soon after, AND1 products started hitting store shelves at Foot Locker and other major retailers. For some customers, the first brand interaction came through lacing up a new pair of sneakers. For others, it was catching a mixtape or watching a local tournament. Every experience was different, but it all felt connected. It all felt intentional.

AND1 didn't rely on a single channel to reach their fans. They understood that different segments of their audience needed to be reached in diverse ways. The key to their growth was their ability to use multiple, complementary channels to reach and connect with the people they most wanted to engage. Their strategy was to choose the right message for the right person delivered through the right channel.

That's exactly the shift I am inviting you to make in this chapter. By taking a multi-channel approach to your outreach, you acknowledge that prospects have varied communication preferences. Using a multichannel approach optimizes the chance to reach a prospect on their channel of choice (CoC), which increases the chance for engagement.

Choose Your Channels: Turn Your Micro-Campaigns Into High-Performing Sequences

This chapter is where strategy turns into execution. In earlier chapters, you learned how to build micro-campaigns by identifying a segment of your territory, figuring out what matters most to those buyers, and crafting segment-specific value propositions that speak directly to their priorities. Now it's time to put that work into motion.

Before you start creating micro-campaign-based sequences, you'll need to decide which channels to use. Taking a multichannel approach asks you to consider every channel at your disposal to ensure you utilize the best-fit channels. That means deciding which channels - like email, phone, LinkedIn, historically marketing-led channels like events, or under-utilized sales outreach channels like direct mail – you will deploy. When you focus on understanding where your buyers are most likely to engage (their CoC), you increase the probability of earning their attention.

Optimizing and managing outreach channels requires you to stack appropriate channels together to get your message seen, read, and acted on. CoC, a phrase popularized by top LinkedIn sales creator Melissa Gaglione, is simply defined as the channel your prospect is most comfortable using for sales communications. The goal is to use multichannel sequences to tell your buyer a compelling story about the outcomes that matter most to them over a series of messages on a variety of mediums.

Channel of Choice: Meet Your Buyers Where They Are

Mary Meeker, a venture capitalist known for tracking technology and buyer trends, once said, "You have to be where your customers are, and if you're not, you will lose out." That's exactly what CoC is about.

Meeker's research is important because she showed that when you follow your buyers to the platforms they already use, you gain an edge. Buyer behavior shifts fast, and the companies that adapted gained a massive competitive advantage. When you don't, you fall behind.

If you design every outbound campaign to include a minimum of three channels, you give yourself more chances to reach the right person on their CoC. AND1's story reminds us that when you meet people where they are instead of where it's convenient for you, you earn attention and trust.

Consumers choose when, where, and how they engage. The goal of your outbound strategy cannot just be more activity. More is not a strategy. You need to be more intentional and impactful with every touchpoint by creating a GTM motion that incorporates an understanding of CoC. Meeker's trends research makes it clear that you can't expect results if you're not showing up in the right places.

> *"The goal of your outbound strategy cannot just be more activity. More is not a strategy."*

Profit Generating Pipeline

The Business Case for Multi-Channel Outreach

A multichannel approach allows sales teams to reach their audience through a variety of touchpoints, creating multiple opportunities for engagement. According to Mailchimp, companies that leverage three or more channels in their outbound sales strategies experience a 287% higher purchase rate compared to those that rely on just one.[32] La Growth Machine reports that implementing multichannel sequences has been proven to boost response rates by over 250%.

These astounding results prove that by using multiple approach paths, you increase the chances of catching your prospect's attention where they're most comfortable. Too often, sellers lean heavily on their preferred channels, ignoring the preferences of their prospects. This CoC approach encourages sellers to acknowledge that while some prospects may respond better to a personalized email, others are more active on LinkedIn or would only respond to a phone call.

ZoomInfo found that companies using a multichannel approach see 23 times higher customer satisfaction, proving that engaging prospects across multiple platforms leads to deeper relationships and improved outcomes.[33] When your team meets prospects on the channels they use most, it shows that you're attuned to their behaviors and preferences.

The Pedowitz Group further highlights the advantage of this strategy by showing that organizations with strong multichannel engagement are 50% more likely to hit their financial targets. The modern buyer takes a non-linear path to purchase. They research, engage, and make decisions across multiple platforms, often combining online and offline interactions.

A multichannel approach caters to the different ways your prospect might approach a buying decision. For example, the head of IT might prefer engaging via email at their own pace, a CFO might prefer the speed and directness of a phone call, or a marketing manager may only

---

[32] Mailchimp, "Omnichannel Marketing," *Mailchimp Marketing Glossary*, accessed May 24, 2025, https://mailchimp.com/marketing-glossary/omnichannel-marketing.
[33] ZoomInfo, "Multichannel Marketing Statistics," *Pipeline by ZoomInfo*, accessed May 24, 2025, https://pipeline.zoominfo.com/multichannel-marketing-statistics.

174

engage on social channels. Covering multiple channels means you're more likely to reach every key stakeholder in the buying decision.

On top of that, companies that embrace a multichannel approach also benefit from actionable analytics and insights. By tracking how prospects interact with emails, phone calls, social media, events, and direct mail, you gain valuable data on which channels perform best for different segments of your audience. This allows sales teams to refine their strategies, optimizing outreach efforts based on what's working. Without the data from a multichannel approach, you're flying blind and missing key opportunities to tweak and improve your process.

Furthermore, relying on just one or two channels exposes your business to unnecessary risk. Channels can become oversaturated, leading to diminishing returns. The Pedowitz Group points out that 46% of organizations deliver poor customer experiences because they fail to integrate multiple touchpoints into a seamless journey.[34] Without diversifying your outreach, you risk becoming irrelevant or invisible to prospects who've grown numb to a single form of communication. In contrast, multichannel strategies mitigate this risk by creating multiple ways to engage, ensuring that prospects are constantly reminded of your value in a way that feels natural rather than forced.

It's also important to note that B2B buyers today are spending less time interacting directly with sales reps, which makes each point of contact even more valuable. According to Gartner, B2B buyers spend less than 20% of their buying journey speaking with potential suppliers.[35] That means the majority of their decision-making happens online or via indirect interactions, and if your team is not present across multiple channels, you're missing a huge portion of the buying process. Prospects are researching on their own terms - through social media, content marketing, emails, and peer recommendations. A multichannel approach gives

---

[34] Majda Anwar, "Omni-Channel Marketing: Statistics to Know and Key Differences from Multi-Channel," *The Pedowitz Group*, May 15, 2025, https://www.pedowitz-group.com/blog/26-statistics-on-why-you-should-consider-omni-channel-marketing.

[35] Gartner. "The B2B Buying Journey: Key Stages and How to Optimize Them." Gartner, 2025. https://www.gartner.com/en/sales/insights/b2b-buying-journey. Gartner

you more opportunities to influence their journey, even before you've had a direct conversation.

The impact of a well-executed multichannel strategy is clear in its financial benefits. Companies that integrate multiple channels effectively see a 9.5% year-over-year increase in revenue compared to a mere 3.4% for companies with weak multichannel engagement, according to Aberdeen Group.[36] This significant difference shows that a multichannel approach not only boosts short-term engagement but also drives long-term growth and profitability. As buyer journeys become increasingly complex and fragmented, the ability to maintain a consistent presence across channels is key to staying top-of-mind and closing more deals.

A single-channel approach is simply no longer viable. If you're limiting your sales efforts to just one or two channels, you're leaving money on the table. A multichannel strategy gives you the flexibility, data, and reach you need to build lasting relationships with prospects, engage decision-makers where they are, and drive higher conversion rates. To build a resilient, scalable sales strategy, your team must be present on the channels where your prospects spend their time, ensuring that your message gets heard loud and clear across platforms.

Incorporating Demand Generation Practices Into Lead Generation

In B2B outbound sales, email, phone, and LinkedIn remain the foundational channels that every sales leader must master. Each has unique strengths, but it's the combination of these channels - and how they integrate with your broader strategy - that leads to successful outreach. Here, we explore how to use each effectively while blurring the lines between demand generation and lead generation to build a cohesive, impactful strategy.

Traditionally, demand generation, focused on creating awareness and interest, was assigned to marketing, while lead generation, the task of

---

[36] Lee, Sarah. "8 Proven Strategies for Effective CX in Retail & E-commerce." *Number Analytics*, March 27, 2025. https://www.numberanalytics.com/blog/proven-strategies-effective-cx-retail-ecommerce.

identifying and contacting potential buyers, was siloed to sales. Blending demand generation and lead generation strategies has been a hallmark of my success and the success of my revenue organizations.

Fights between marketing and sales about attribution are a waste of time and money. Successful outreach requires connecting the dots between these functions, ensuring that your team is not only pushing prospects toward a purchase but guiding them with messaging that sparks interest, builds relationships, and moves them smoothly through their buyer's journey.

My Journey with Cold Calling and Why It Still Works

Despite the rise of digital channels, phone outreach remains a powerful, direct way to engage prospects. Cold calling, when executed well, can cut through the digital noise and create meaningful connections, particularly when combined with other channels like email and social media.

Cold calling has been the backbone of my career in sales, and the lessons I've learned from dialing those numbers are invaluable. The teams I've managed and trained have made well over 10 million cold calls. Personally, I've made over 250,000 cold calls, and during that time, I've experienced everything from immediate hang-ups to career-changing connections. From my high school days calling community members to support a local school lobby to convincing Fortune 500 executives to invest in a research platform, I've witnessed how cold calling cuts through noise and opens doors.

In the beginning, I cut my teeth on some of the toughest calls imaginable. Early in my career, I called people who had defaulted on loans, informing them their property faced foreclosure. These weren't friendly conversations. I was yelled at, cursed out, and hung up on countless times. But these challenging interactions shaped my resilience. They taught me that cold calling is more than handling rejection; it's about persistence, adaptability, and, most importantly, learning how to genuinely connect with people.

In college, I took a few telemarketing jobs - telemarketing for the university's fundraising department, calling alums to request donations, and another doing B2C cold calls from a grey, windowless office, which I quit the moment my first paycheck cleared the bank.

My first "real" sales role involved cold-calling construction and engineering SMBs in Montana, asking them to pool resources for international projects. It was an unconventional ask. I had to bring together competitors who saw no reason to collaborate. Despite the challenges, I learned the critical importance of positioning and relevance. This role showed me clearly that cold calling is the fastest way to start meaningful conversations and quickly demonstrate value.

The beauty of phone calls is the direct, personal connection they offer. In an era where inboxes overflow with emails, notifications, and automated messages, a phone call cuts straight through the clutter, creating space for real human interaction. Throughout my career, I've made cold calls to buyers in every field imaginable - from Chicagoland small businesses to power plant managers, even chief procurement officers navigating global crises.

Reaching Decision-Makers and Cutting Through Digital Noise

Business communication has become increasingly crowded. Decision-makers receive endless emails, LinkedIn messages, Slack notifications, and more. I've seen this firsthand during economic crises, like the 2008-2009 financial collapse. I was cold-calling CFOs to invite them to business intelligence events in Las Vegas, and emails alone couldn't cut it. Only by picking up the phone could I get their attention. Even if they didn't immediately accept my offer, cold calling allowed me to stay top-of-mind.

Studies confirm that nearly 70% of buyers still accept cold calls, and research shows that 57% of C-level executives still prefer business conversations via phone.[37] I've experienced this repeatedly: even when emails went unanswered, a timely cold call could initiate productive dialogue.

---

[37] Shevlin, Daisy. "The Top Cold Calling Success Rates for 2025 Explained." *Cognism*, March 18, 2025. https://www.cognism.com/blog/cold-calling-success-rates.

Cold calling lets you jump to the front of the line, bypassing gatekeepers and distractions. Once, I had to convince hospitality manufacturers to invest marketing budgets in an unproven minimum viable product (MVP). It was an unproven solution in a crowded market, and the future of the startup depended on my success. These were high-stakes, high-pressure conversations. Cold calls allowed me to personally make my case, and as a result, I secured 21 new logos within nine months of post-launch.

Immediate Feedback and Adaptability: Real-Time Advantage

One unique advantage of cold calling is real-time feedback. On the phone, you immediately sense a prospect's reactions—hesitation, excitement, or doubt. This allows instant adaptability. Emails or LinkedIn messages might go unanswered for days, but cold calls provide direct opportunities to adjust your approach in the moment.

I'll never forget cold-calling power plant managers who were convinced my product would flop. They'd never seen it done before and were resistant to the idea that I'd be the first. Because I had them on the phone, I addressed their concerns immediately. I could pivot my pitch in real time, turning skepticism into enthusiasm. By year-end, the product became a million-dollar revenue stream. Without cold calls, I don't believe that the product would have thrived.

Research confirms this adaptability advantage.[38] People who can adjust their approaches, strategies, and behaviors in response to changing conditions outperform those who remain static—sales reps who adjust in real-time increase their success rates. Cold calling uniquely offers this flexibility, making it indispensable.

Strategic Persistence: Always #EarntheRight

If there's one overarching lesson from my quarter-million cold calls, it's that persistence is strategic. Cold calling isn't about a single perfect

---

[38] Reeves, Martin, and Mike Deimler. "Adaptability: The New Competitive Advantage." Harvard Business Review, July 1, 2011. https://hbr.org/2011/07/adaptability-the-new-competitive-advantage.

call - it's hundreds or thousands of calls, knowing many won't connect immediately. While I've had more one-call closes than the average seller, 99.9% of the time, a call doesn't result in a close. I had to persist, leave voicemails, send follow-up texts, and incorporate additional channels. Ultimately, this persistence led to successful outcomes.

Organizations that neglect cold calling experience significantly less growth, up to 42% less, according to some studies. I've seen this reality consistently throughout my roles as ISR, AE, player/coach, and senior leader. Yes, cold calling is challenging. In 2024, success rates average around 5%.[39] But when combined thoughtfully with layered outreach - texts, voicemails, social selling, and emails - cold calling becomes incredibly powerful.

The mistake organizations often make is treating cold calling in isolation. The true power lies in leveraging the phone as a channel. This means taking a strategic approach to voicemails and also looking at texting and voice notes as mediums.

Texting: The Personal and Immediate Layer Within the Phone Channel

Texting adds a powerful dimension to your cold outreach. People are constantly connected to their phones, and well-timed text messages can reach prospects that other mediums miss.

Texts boast a staggering 98% open rate, 90% within three minutes of receipt, far surpassing cold B2B email open rates, which average 15%,[40] up to 25% on the high end.[41] This immediacy makes SMS incredibly valuable. After important calls or voicemails, I use personalized texts as gentle nudges, reminding prospects to check emails or call back. The

[39] Raval, Binal. "The State of Cold Calling 2024 Report." Cognism, March 18, 2025. https://www.cognism.com/state-of-cold-calling.

[40] Borysov, Petro. "B2B Email Marketing Statistics: Insights to Shape Your 2025 Strategy." Stripo.email, June 20, 2025. https://stripo.email/blog/b2b-email-marketing-statistics -insights-to-shape-your-2025-strategy/.

[41] Kaur, Falak Preet. "20+ Cold Email Statistics and Insights You Should Know." Mailmodo, May 20, 2025. https://www.mailmodo.com/guides/cold-email-statistics/.

informal nature of texting fosters genuine connections, enhancing your personal touch.

In a layered multichannel strategy, texting complements and rein- forces cold calls and voicemails within the same channel. Texting never replaces calling - it strengthens it. This approach ensures you meet pros- pects through their CoC, optimizing chances for response.

*Please check your local regulations to ensure full legal use of texting in your sales outreach.**

Voicemail Strategy: Reinforcing Calls Through Layered Outreach

Today, voicemails play a crucial role in phone-based outreach. Even if prospects don't answer, voicemails provide valuable opportunities to connect. Your voice conveys emotion, urgency, and sincerity in ways emails or texts cannot, humanizing your outreach and reinforcing mes- sages left on other channels.

Effective voicemails are brief, value-focused, and personalized. Reference specific pain points and end with clear, actionable next steps. For instance, when calling CFOs during the Great Recession, my concise, specific voicemails referencing their pressing concerns substantially improved callback rates.

As I shared in Chapter 11, I do not believe that defaulting to an ask for a call back is the best use of a voicemail in most sequences. You'll need to A/B test to discover how to best leverage voicemails in your sequences.

Please download my Strategic Guide to Voicemails at www.salesledgtm. com/value for more information.

By layering voicemails with texts or emails, you create continuity across outreach efforts, increasing your chances for engagement. This cohe- sive flow demonstrates intentionality and earns the right for continued conversations.

---

*Author's note

Outbound Email Is Dead (Just Kidding)

Email has long been a cornerstone of outbound sales, but many teams still struggle with how to personalize without wasting hours of effort. The balance lies in crafting relevant, meaningful emails that address prospects' needs without over-investing in unnecessary, disconnected details.

Rather than spending time on contact-level hyper-personalization, focus on building templates that feel tailored. Use industry pain points, recent trends, or company-specific challenges to highlight the benefits of your product or service. As Kevin learned, disingenuous personalization didn't win attention, but relevance did.

As sales teams fight for space in the inbox, it is extremely tempting to feel like the answer to getting more replies is more emails. Sales email tools, usually bolstered by AI and promises of awe-inducing ROI, feel like a sensible answer. In reality, most are being used to send really bad emails at scale.

My thoughts on how AI is being leveraged in B2B sales are constantly evolving because the technology moves quickly. As I shared, as of today, I don't think a tool exists that is writing and sending exceptional sales emails that replace humans. That may change. If you'd like to get my up-to-date takes, please follow me on LinkedIn at www.linkedin.com/in/leslievenetz. *

Since we covered how to write great emails extensively in Chapter 11 and how to figure out what is worth writing about in Chapter 9, I have instead shared a few random thoughts about email that didn't seem to fit elsewhere in the book, or I felt were worth repeating.

- Email is not dead, but relying solely on sales emails to generate leads sure is.
- Relevance is more important than contact-level hyper-personalization.
- I adore a reply email, so if you've written an email that you're confident speaks to an outcome the recipient cares about, it's okay to

---

*Author's Note

talk about that outcome in one additional email using a reply. After that, you need to move on to other talking points.

- I despise "Thoughts?" emails. They do not work because they are good emails; they work because most salespeople give up on their sequences too early. If you're going to send a "Thoughts?" email, I beg of you, remind your prospect what you would like their thoughts about. For example, "Hi Katie – What are your thoughts about [problem-centric ROI or COI statement]?"
- Always start your sequences with at least a double tap.
- Always include an email on day one of your sequence as part of a double to quadruple tap. Yes, I said quad-tap, which would look like LinkedIn InMail, LinkedIn Connect Message, Email, and Cold Call.
- My default is to stack emails three days apart, and I will increase the space between emails based on the type of sequence or the seniority of the recipient. Data from companies like Outreach backs up the 3-day default,[42] but once you have a baseline, please A/B test.
- Except for nurture sequences, I cap my sales outreach at eight emails. The majority of my top-performing sequences are five to seven emails. Data from Lemlist shows that sending more than nine emails is usually a waste of time and increases your chance of getting flagged as SPAM.[43]
- Sales leaders love obsessing about the perfect time of day or day of the week to send emails. 90% of the time, the obsession over optimizing emails is a worthless distraction because the emails that are being sent are not making it to the primary, are not getting engagement, and are not driving profit generating pipeline. Before you get distracted by the nuances, master the foundations of good email.

I'm sure there are more random thoughts I could share, but I'll leave you with these nine.

---

[42] "Outbound Sales Sequences That Actually Convert." Outreach. Accessed June 20, 2025. https://www.outreach.io/resources/blog/how-we-create-outbound-sales-sequences-that-convert.

[43] Team, Lemlist. "How Many Cold Email Follow-Ups Should You Send to Increase Your Replies?" lemlist Blog, May 26, 2025. https://www.lemlist.com/blog/how-many-cold-email-follow-ups.

LinkedIn Selling: Build Trust Before You Sell

LinkedIn has become a cornerstone of modern B2B sales, offering unique opportunities for social selling. It allows sales teams to not only connect with prospects but also build credibility, establish thought leadership, and nurture relationships in a more casual and engaging manner.

There are a lot of ways to "sell" on LinkedIn. They include hosting LinkedIn Lives to attract inbound leads, building a Founder-led brand, and interacting with the content prospects are posting. The more active your prospects are on LinkedIn, the more powerful it can be as a channel. I've seen that firsthand after pivoting from selling to Fortune 500 executives to selling sales consulting to salespeople (salespeople love LinkedIn).

Right now, I do zero outbound on LinkedIn, but it is my primary source of inbound leads. I consider that demand generation, not lead generation, through social selling. In my opinion, social selling is using LinkedIn to actively reach out to prospects via direct messages (DMs) and Sales Navigator InMail. If you have the capacity to leverage the platform further, I highly recommend it, but don't let the fact that your prospects aren't posting or engaging with content on LinkedIn stop you from using it as a channel.

Pulling on what we learned in Chapter 11, all LinkedIn outreach messages need to be extremely short, relevant, and respectful of the fact that you're asking for attention on a prospect's personal social media. Before you start leveraging LinkedIn as a channel, you must spend some time on your profile. Profiles that are complete, up-to-date, and include a professional picture. There are multiple references on LinkedIn's Blog [44] about the impact of a well-rounded profile, including more views, more messages, and a higher connection acceptance rate.

For most B2B sales teams, especially those with a freemium SaaS offer, I suggest that you help sellers professionalize their LinkedIn profiles and

---

[44] "Our Best Linkedin Profile Photo Tips for Salespeople." LinkedIn. Accessed June 20, 2025. https://www.linkedin.com/business/sales/blog/b2b-sales/picture-perfect--make-a-great-first-impression-with-your-linkedi.

then master social selling. Once they've figured out repeatable outreach on LinkedIn, it's worth investing in Creator-led strategies.

Here are a few of my favorite ways to integrate LinkedIn as a channel without creating any content on the platform:

- Using InMail to send an attachment early in the sequence. To avoid email spam triggers, I use LinkedIn to send videos, documents, or images to prospects where they have a higher probability of reaching the prospect.
- Using Smart Links to share content with a single, trackable link. This feature only exists within some Sales Navigator accounts, but Smart Links get high open rates, and it allows you to see how long the document was viewed for, as well as who the prospect shared it with in real-time.
- Leveraging LinkedIn InMail and a connect request double tap. I use InMail to share a deposit and mention that I also sent a connection request. I use the connection request to point to the deposit in the InMail. It increases engagement for both touchpoints.
- I am personally not a fan of a "profile view" as a touch point unless it can be fully automated. If you've tested it and it works, keep doing it.
- 95% of the connection requests that I send are blank, but that's unlikely to be the best strategy for leveraging LinkedIn as a channel because every touch point needs to build awareness, interest, and trust. However, a blank request will always be better than a vague or salesy message.
- Never, and I mean never, connect with a prospect and immediately start hard selling them in the DMs. A connection acceptance is not an invitation to pitch.

Social selling on LinkedIn is about starting relationships, not just pushing a sale. Lead with value and curiosity. Encouraging your team to embrace the platform fully, through content, comments, and conversations, helps build social proof, but make sure the basics are repeatable before expanding.

Sales-Led Motions on Marketing-Led Channels

All sales leaders should be using at least three channels in their cold sales outreach. My advice is to master email and the phone first. Then add social media—probably LinkedIn, but it may be a different platform depending on who you sell to. Beyond that, you should look at taking a sales-led approach to channels that have historically been owned by marketing, like events or direct mail.

Sales-led motions work best when these channels are used to create conversations, not just impressions. If your salespeople are the ones sending the gift or extending the event invite, they are building awareness and a sense of reciprocity. It also ensure these activities are not being done in a silo. When sellers own the timing, the message, and the follow-up, it creates continuity in the buying experience.

This is an opportunity to learn from and partner with marketing. It's about sales activating high-impact plays at the individual level. To be sure you're not stirring up a new fight over attribution, sales and marketing need to be aligned on when and how these channels get used. It's an opportunity to thoughtfully add in additional channels to best reach specific ICP segments or invest more in high-converting intent signals. If you're not ready to partner with marketing, an easy way to test adding a new channel is sending handwritten notes to key prospects. I've used handwritten notes to drive pipeline for nearly two decades; they are one play that never goes out of style.

Ultimately, your focus needs to be centered on how you can best reach your prospects on their CoC.

A Layered Multichannel Approach: Maximizing Impact

The most effective outreach combines multiple channels (phone, email, social) and layers multiple uses of each channel. Each interaction strengthens others, increasing overall impact. Cold calling alone is powerful, but paired with voicemails and texts, it gains momentum. LinkedIn is incredible for DMs, but posting, hosting LinkedIn Lives, and tagging prospects on relevant posts amplify the impact. If you have the resources, blend demand generation with lead generation by having your sales team own in-person events or a gifting strategy to create opportunities for even greater channel diversity. This layered approach lets you strategically engage prospects across their preferred communication methods, or CoC, enhancing results.

Turning Outreach Into Outcomes

This chapter illustrates that effective outbound sales isn't about relying on one perfect message or a single channel. It's about executing a layered, multichannel strategy that aligns with how your prospects want to engage. When you meet buyers where they are and vary your approach within each channel, you create more opportunities to earn their attention. When you commit to showing up with consistency and creativity, just like AND1 did, your message doesn't just land - it resonates.

Some channels will miss. Others will connect. Together, they expand your reach, boost engagement, and give your team more opportunities to win.

This strategy works because it gives prospects the chance to engage on their CoC. But it's not just about which channels you use - it's how you use them. Stay flexible, keep testing, and lead with relevance. When every touchpoint is intentional and aligned to how your buyer wants to engage, your outreach turns into a real pipeline.

Deliverability: Technical Considerations

I am not an email deliverability expert. However, I would be remiss not to spend a few paragraphs highlighting the importance of domain reputation as it pertains to cold email deliverability.

Even well-written emails will be routed to junk if you are sending them from a domain with a poor reputation. This can severely hurt your chances of getting your emails read and replied to, and of converting leads into opportunities. One of the most crucial factors in ensuring your cold emails reach the inbox is maintaining a good domain reputation.

Domain reputation isn't just a technical concern for marketing or IT; it's a core part of your sales infrastructure. If your emails aren't being delivered, even the strongest message won't make an impact. That's why sales leaders must take ownership of email deliverability. Your team's ability to build pipeline depends on it.

In simple terms, domain reputation is the trust score that email service providers (like Gmail and Outlook) assign to the domain from which your emails are sent (e.g., yourcompany.com). A strong reputation helps your emails land in the primary inbox, while a poor one can bury them in spam folders, no matter how valuable the content.

Your domain reputation is affected by several factors, including how frequently you send emails, whether your emails are opened and engaged with, and whether recipients flag your messages as spam. Deliverability doesn't end at setup. It's dynamic, and it's constantly impacted by the behavior of the recipients. Low reply rates, high bounce rates, or high deletion rates without responses all signal to providers that your messages may be unwanted. Over time, these behaviors degrade your domain's reputation. That's why your team can't just "set and forget" their messaging. You need ongoing testing, feedback loops, and continuous improvement to keep inbox placement high.

Tools like SPF (Sender Policy Framework), DKIM (DomainKeys Identified Mail), and DMARC (Domain-based Message Authentication, Reporting & Conformance) are essential in maintaining a positive reputation, as they verify the legitimacy of your emails and ensure they aren't being tampered with during delivery.

Why Domain Reputation Matters in Cold Outreach

In cold emailing, where you're often reaching out to people who haven't interacted with your brand before, the stakes are even higher. Many of your prospects are seeing your email for the first time, and the competition to get into their inboxes is fierce.

Email filters are increasingly robust, designed to block spam and unwanted messages from reaching the inbox. However, legitimate emails often get caught in these filters as well. Cold emails, in particular, can be misinterpreted as spam if they don't follow best practices for deliverability, resulting in missed opportunities and wasted effort. By understanding and actively managing your domain reputation, you can significantly increase your cold email deliverability rates and improve your chances of landing in the primary inbox.

Deliverability testing should become a regular part of your sales process. While domain reputation management may seem like a complex process,

I offer three key steps you and your sales team can take to ensure your emails have the best possible chance of reaching prospects.

Use Multiple Domains and Inboxes

In cold emailing, especially at scale, using multiple domains and inboxes is necessary. For example, instead of sending all emails from "yourcompany.com," consider using variants like "gosalesyourcompany.com" or "tryyourcompany.com." This approach, as Clay points out, is known as inbox rotation and helps protect your main domain from being tarnished if one of your inboxes gets flagged as spam. [45]

Never send cold emails from the same domain you use for marketing newsletters, customer service responses, or executive communications. Separating cold outbound from your primary domain protects your core business functions. If your cold outreach gets flagged or throttled, you want that risk to be isolated to a separate domain. This approach is especially important for companies running large-scale outbound motions.

Implement SPF, DKIM, and DMARC Authentication

Setting up these email authentication protocols ensures that your emails are verified as legitimate by email providers. According to Clay and Pedowitz Group, these protocols authenticate the origin of your emails, helping to establish trust with email services like Google and Outlook. Failing to implement these protocols can result in your emails being rejected or marked as suspicious.

Warm Up Your Email Accounts

When using a new domain or inbox, it's important to gradually build up your sending volume. This is a process known as warming up an inbox. As Clay explains, sending too many emails from a new domain or inbox too quickly can trigger spam filters. By starting with a small number of emails and gradually increasing volume, you give email providers time to trust your domain.

Ultimately, even the most carefully written email is worthless if it doesn't land in your prospect's inbox. By focusing on improving and maintaining a strong domain reputation through these simple steps, you'll give

---

[45] Clay, "21 Cold Email Deliverability Best Practices for 2024," *The GTM with Clay Blog*, accessed May 25, 2025, https://www.clay.com/blog/b2b-cold-email-deliverability.

your cold emails a much better chance of reaching the primary inbox and maximizing the effectiveness of your outbound sequences. The investment in getting deliverability right will pay off in higher open rates, better engagement, and more opportunities to drive pipeline growth.

Keep Your Emails Out of Spam: Triggers to Watch Out For

While sales leaders may not always have control over their company's domain reputation, they can still play a critical role in protecting and enhancing it. The marketing team might be sending thousands of emails every day, and IT may need to set up multiple domains to manage outbound efforts effectively. Still, the actions of your sales team will have a direct impact on whether your emails make it to your prospect's inbox or get dumped into spam. One of the simplest and most effective steps your team can take is avoiding common spam triggers.

Spam filters protect email users by identifying patterns that suggest unwanted or suspicious emails. Over time, they've evolved to evaluate multiple factors – from language and formatting to links and attachments – and assign a "spam score" to each message. If your email exceeds a certain threshold, it's flagged and rerouted to the spam folder.

When this happens, it's not just a missed opportunity – it also harms your domain reputation, making future emails more likely to be filtered out. Left unchecked, this can lead to a sharp drop in overall deliverability.

Let's take a look at key elements that raise your spam score and why they should be avoided.

> *"Salesy language is one of the quickest ways to get your email flagged. Over time, spammers have relied on these phrases to catch the reader's attention, but they've also become synonymous with pushy, unsolicited sales pitches."*

The Risk of Spammy Words

Salesy language is one of the quickest ways to get your email flagged. Words like "Buy now," "Free trial," or "Guaranteed" are classic examples of phrases that spam filters are trained to look for. Over time, spammers have relied on these phrases to catch the reader's attention, but they've also become synonymous with pushy, unsolicited sales pitches. As a result, email filters now treat these words with extreme caution.

When you include overly promotional language in your cold email, you risk being lumped in with the masses of unsolicited offers that hit inboxes every day. Your email might get flagged even before the recipient has a chance to see it, severely limiting your outreach efforts. Remember, cold emails are about building trust and starting a conversation, not pushing for a sale in the first message. To avoid being seen as just another spammy salesperson, focus on genuine value and relevance rather than flashy promises.

The Pitfalls of Rich Text, Images, and HTML

Rich text and images might make your email look more polished, but they also make it more likely to end up in the spam folder. Spam filters are designed to detect emails that resemble promotional materials. Think marketing blasts filled with glossy images and heavy HTML formatting because they mimic the formatting used in many mass-marketing or malicious campaigns.

Personal, one-to-one messages rarely include such elements. That's why emails with excessive visuals or formatting raise flags: spammers often use them to mask harmful content or manipulate recipients. Even if your content is completely legitimate, spam filters err on the side of caution and block messages that contain these elements.

In short, simplicity is key. Stripping away unnecessary images and formatting helps your emails avoid the spam folder because they look like a real conversation rather than a marketing ploy.

The Dangers of Links and Attachments

Including links or attachments in your initial cold email is another major red flag for spam filters. Because spammers often use these elements to deliver malware or direct recipients to phishing sites, email providers treat them with heightened suspicion, especially when the sender is unknown.

Even a simple tracking link can trigger a spam filter. While tracking opens and clicks can provide valuable insights, they can also trigger spam filters that flag embedded tracking code as a potential threat, particularly in bulk sends.

Attachments are even riskier. Whether it's a PDF, an image, or any other file, sending attachments is commonly blocked in cold outreach due to their association with viruses. Including one in your first email can dramatically reduce your chances of landing in the inbox.

The Hidden Spam Trigger: Fancy Signatures

Of all the spam triggers out there, one of the most overlooked is the email signature. After auditing thousands of cold emails, I can confidently say that one of the quickest ways to hurt your deliverability is by including a fancy, image-heavy signature in your emails. It's something sales teams don't often think about, but it can have a massive impact.

Many teams spend hours perfecting the email's content, making sure the subject line is compelling, the message is clear, and the spammy words are nowhere to be found. But all of that hard work is wasted if the signature includes a headshot, a company logo, or a link to your website. Often, these signatures are packed full of images and links, which immediately set off alarm bells for spam filters.

When sending cold emails, you need to think of your signature as part of the email itself, not as an afterthought. A simple HTML signature with no links or images is the way to go. The goal is to keep your email looking like a genuine, personal outreach, not a marketing blast. Fancy signatures belong in later-stage conversations, not in cold emails where trust hasn't yet been established.

By stripping down your signature and focusing on a clean, straightforward format, you reduce the chances of your email being flagged as spam. This small adjustment can make an enormous difference in your deliverability rates and help you build a stronger connection with your prospects.

Getting Into the Primary

Channel of Choice ensures you deliver your message where your buyer prefers to engage. For many prospects, that means email, making deliverability a critical part of your CoC strategy.

Focusing on deliverability ensures your emails land in the primary inbox, not lost in spam or buried in promotions. Optimizing email as a channel is pointless if the message never arrives.

Sales leaders must master both the strategy of CoC and the technology of deliverability to make sure outreach is seen, opened, and acted on.

CHAPTER 13

Building and Maintaining Effective Sales Sequences

"If you want to build trust, be trustworthy. And one of the best ways to do that is through consistency." –Stephen Covey

It's time to turn strategy into structure. In this chapter, you'll learn how to design sequences that align with the prospect's buying journey, build trust over time, and consistently drive your leads closer to conversion. You'll learn how to use sequences to create consistency without rigidity, and how to create visibility into what's working so you can do more of it.

If you want a pipeline you can count on, you need a process you can count on - that starts with sequences.

Rockefeller as a Sales Role Model

Building and maintaining effective sales sequences isn't rocket science, but crafting them with skill and refining them to maximize impact is a true art. John D. Rockefeller Jr. captured this mindset when he said, "The secret of success is to do the common thing uncommonly well." Rockefeller's success came not from flash or novelty, but from his ability to standardize and perfect his operations, a lesson that applies to sales leaders looking to build high-impact, adaptable sequences.

Rockefeller was known for his meticulous approach to standardization, focusing on creating uniform processes that could be replicated across his entire business. He famously insisted on controlling even the smallest details, understanding that quality, efficiency, and profitability could be exponentially improved with consistent, refined processes. For example, Rockefeller was relentless about standardizing barrel production, setting precise requirements for the size, strength, and material of each barrel. This approach not only ensured quality but also cut costs by enabling bulk orders and efficient, repeatable assembly.

Rockefeller's standardization also extended to production methods. He identified inefficiencies in common practices and streamlined them, ensuring that every step in the process was predictable, measurable, and cost-effective. He required his employees to measure each component and follow specific protocols so that every part of the process could be optimized for maximum output and minimum waste. This attention to uniformity resulted in fewer errors, consistent quality, and a reputation that prospects could trust.

This approach is a powerful analogy for building sales sequences. Like Rockefeller's operations, a well-designed sales sequence requires precise attention to each touchpoint. For sales leaders, this means guiding your team to set specific standards for each interaction within the sequence - whether it's a carefully crafted email template, a strategically timed phone follow-up, or an engagement-building LinkedIn message. Each touchpoint should be intentional, consistent, and designed to reinforce your messaging.

Furthermore, Rockefeller's commitment to monitoring and refining each part of his operation speaks to the ongoing nature of effective sales sequences. He would analyze data from each production phase, identify areas for improvement, and continually adjust and refine the process. Similarly, sales sequences should be treated as living, adaptable processes. By tracking engagement data - open rates, reply rates, conversions - you can make informed decisions about which touchpoints resonate most effectively with your prospects and adjust sequences accordingly.

Rockefeller's approach teaches us that success in sales sequences doesn't come from complexity but from the disciplined execution of each step. By setting high standards, refining processes, and measuring results, you create sequences that provide value and stay top-of-mind for prospects. Like Rockefeller's standardized methods, a meticulously crafted sales sequence builds trust, projects reliability, and earns the right to win business.

If your salespeople are reaching out to prospects without structured sequences, you're not running a repeatable sales process. You're letting randomness rule your pipeline.

Sequencing = Strategy in Action

Every technique you've learned in this book works best when it's deployed inside a sequence.

We've already walked through how to segment your territory into ICP segments, so your team isn't wasting time on the wrong leads. We've talked about how to build buyer-centric value propositions that speak to the specific needs of each segment. We've explored how to write messaging that is clear, relevant, and rooted in problem-solving instead of product pitching. We've also shown how a multi-channel CoC strategy increases engagement by meeting buyers where they are already.

Each of these steps matters. But none of them work in isolation.

Great copy gets ignored if it's only sent once. Channel diversity doesn't matter if there's no strategy guiding the order and timing. Personalization efforts go to waste if your team doesn't know when or how to follow up. Micro-campaigns lose their value if there's no way to measure which message or touchpoint actually drove the conversion.

That's why sequences are so important. They are what bring structure to your strategy. Sequences are how you map the message, the moment, and the medium, and make it repeatable. They ensure that your best thinking gets executed consistently across your team. They are how you build momentum across touches and channels. They are how you generate data that you can learn from.

> *"Sequences are how you map the message, the moment, and the medium, and make it repeatable. They ensure that your best thinking gets executed consistently across your team."*

Consistency over Chaos

Without sequences, you can't measure performance, you can't optimize timing, and you can't scale what works. But with them, outbound becomes easier to execute, to coach, and to refine.

Sequences don't limit creativity; they make it safer and more valuable. When your team isn't guessing what to do next, they can focus on how to show up with relevance, precision, and value.

When you provide your sales team with carefully designed sequences, you set them up to engage prospects meaningfully and move them forward to conversion. Sales sequences create repeatability and sustainability in your sales approach. By connecting every touchpoint thoughtfully, you ensure each interaction feels relevant and valuable, helping prospects trust your outreach and respond positively. This chapter will guide you through creating, refining, and maintaining sales sequences that consistently generate profit for your pipeline.

At the core of effective sales sequences is purposeful sequence design. Each interaction within a sequence needs a clear objective. Without purpose behind every message, your outreach will seem scattered and random to your prospects, reducing engagement. You must coach your team to clarify the specific outcome they expect from each sequence.

For instance, a sequence designed to earn the attention of an MQL with strong intent data might span two weeks and include eight touches across multiple channels. It could start with a personalized LinkedIn connection request to establish familiarity, followed by a phone call and email the next day. You'd want to stack touch points close together and make cold calls early in the sequence to help reach the prospect quickly.

Alternatively, a nurture sequence might stretch over many weeks, spreading touchpoints out. It may rely more heavily on easy-to-automate channels with a goal of staying top-of-mind without pushing immediate action.

Each sequence and step has a defined purpose, either to educate, build trust, or encourage action, ultimately guiding the prospect toward engaging in a meaningful conversation about their needs.

As we've discussed in the previous chapter, layering channels and even different applications of each channel isn't about redundancy – it's about resonance. Building upon purposeful sequence design, varying your format and timing keeps the prospect engaged without overwhelming them. Instead of relying on one touch or even one channel to do all the work, smart sequencing allows each message to play a specific role in a larger conversation, building familiarity and trust over time.

Throughout this chapter, I'll use the terms sequence and cadence interchangeably. For clarity, when I think of a sequence, it's the exact structure of steps in sales outreach. When I think of cadence, it's the timing or pace of those steps. As you build sequences, please keep in mind that the number of steps, channels selected, order of steps, and cadence of steps all matter.

Multi-Channel or Bust

At risk of belaboring the point, if you're not ready to use multichannel sequences, you're probably not ready for this book. Single-channel outreach (which is almost always blasting out generic emails) is ineffective and, I'd argue, not even a sales activity.

The data underscores this point powerfully. Salesloft reports that leveraging multichannel cadences increases engagement by up to 4.7x compared to single-channel outreach. When executed effectively, this integrated approach can lead to a 77% to 91% increase in response rates. Similarly, research from Outreach highlights that companies utilizing three or more channels report a remarkable 287% higher purchase rate compared to teams relying solely on one channel.[46] These statistics confirm the necessity of consistent, thoughtful touchpoints across various platforms. Sales leaders should encourage their teams to consistently maintain interactions across multiple channels, as this sustained visibility significantly boosts the probability that prospects will engage with your messaging and move closer to a purchasing decision.

---

[46] Salesloft. "2021 State of Multichannel Sales Engagement." Salesloft, 2021. https://www.salesloft.com/resources/reports/2021-state-of-multichannel-sales-engagement.

Core Elements of a Strong Sequence

To implement multichannel outreach successfully, your sequences must include several core elements: value-driven messaging, balanced cadence, and clear calls-to-action.

Value-Driven Messaging

As previously detailed in Chapter 9, value-driven messaging ensures every message in your sequence adds meaningful value, positioning your solution directly against the prospect's challenges and opportunities. Coach your team to understand the prospect's pains and goals deeply and reflect that understanding clearly in each message. For instance, Emily, a sales leader coaching Kevin, reminded him that rather than simply describing features, he should frame each message around solving the specific problems their prospects consistently mentioned. Once Kevin shifted to value-driven messaging, prospects began responding at higher rates

Each channel brings unique advantages suited to different messaging needs. Emails allow for detailed explanations and easy tracking of engagement, while phone calls provide immediate, real-time conversations that can swiftly build rapport. Social media, particularly platforms like LinkedIn, fosters ongoing interactions, helping maintain an authentic connection and establishing social proof. Guiding your team to blend these channels strategically means your outreach becomes more effective in moving prospects through their buying journey.

Scripts are powerful tools for helping reps practice and internalize strong outreach and objection-handling techniques – but they should never be read verbatim on live calls. Think of a script as a foundation, not a leash.

Provide fully written examples that model clear, effective language or structure. These show reps what "good" sounds like while giving them room to bring their own tone and personality. The goal is precision, not robotic delivery.

Voicemails are no exception. A solid script ensures clarity and consistency, especially when every second counts. But just like cold call scripts, voicemail scripts should be personalized. Encourage reps to make them their own while staying direct and concise. As covered in the previous chapter, voicemails should be strategic, reinforcing other touches in the sequence and guiding prospects toward meaningful engagement.

Ongoing Sequence Optimization

Maintaining and refining sequences for long-term success involves regular performance reviews and ongoing improvement. Encourage your team to refine their sequences with subject lines, message length, tone, and timing through A/B testing to identify the most effective combinations. Kevin A/B tested subject lines and discovered shorter, more curiosity-driven phrases consistently generated higher open rates. Emily used these insights to standardize effective practices across the team.

Regular updates are also essential, as market and buyer preferences constantly evolve. Emily encouraged Kevin to hold quarterly sequence reviews to refresh value propositions and adjust to emerging trends or shifts in their ICP's needs. Establishing feedback loops allows teams to collectively refine and improve their sequences, ensuring they remain dynamic and effective.

Finally, the concept of stacking touchpoints within sequences strategically

because they felt genuinely understood.

Balanced Cadence

Thoughtful timing helps your sequences maintain steady momentum without overwhelming or losing the prospect's interest. Too frequent outreach causes annoyance, while too infrequent can lead prospects to forget about your offering entirely. Teach your salespeople to review past sequence performance, noting when engagement spikes or falls off. Emily worked with Kevin to identify optimal intervals between touches by evaluating historical data on open rates and replies. They discovered a pattern of three touches per week generated higher response rates for their buyer segment, allowing them to replicate this cadence effectively in new sequences.

Clear Calls to Action

Clear CTAs keep prospects moving forward through your sequences, eliminating ambiguity around next steps. Coach your team to use CTAs strategically. Instead of vague requests like "Let's connect soon," Kevin learned from Emily to specify precise actions like scheduling a call or reviewing a valuable resource. Clear, focused CTAs help prospects quickly understand exactly what to do next, reducing friction and increasing conversion rates.

groups several interactions closely together to build momentum and urgency. Stacking leverages repetition and familiarity, ensuring your message stays top-of-mind.

Emily and Kevin utilized this approach when preparing for a major industry event, strategically stacking LinkedIn outreach, personalized emails, voicemails, event interactions, and timely follow-up communications. This carefully coordinated sequence not only ensured Kevin stood out before and during the event but also significantly boosted the likelihood of post-event engagement.

EVENT-LED OUTBOUND SEQUENCE

Use this sequence to increase your meeting rate with 10-20 key contacts from a live event.

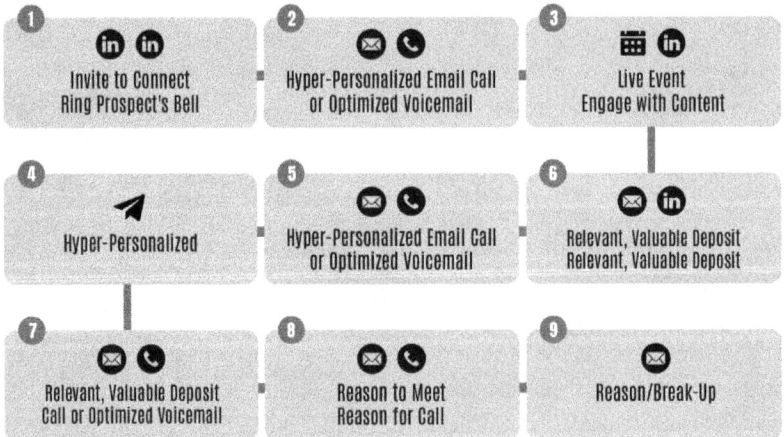

1
Invite to Connect
Ring Prospect's Bell

2
Hyper-Personalized Email Call
or Optimized Voicemail

3
Live Event
Engage with Content

4
Hyper-Personalized

5
Hyper-Personalized Email Call
or Optimized Voicemail

6
Relevant, Valuable Deposit
Relevant, Valuable Deposit

7
Relevant, Valuable Deposit
Call or Optimized Voicemail

8
Reason to Meet
Reason for Call

9
Reason/Break-Up

Application: Sales-Led Live Event Sequence

Emily's decision to send Kevin to an industry event reflected a significant milestone in this growth. Kevin wanted to make the most of this opportunity, so he asked Emily for help building an event-led outbound sequence.

Kevin's sequence was designed to strategically leverage the event as an additional, high-impact channel, significantly boosting the likelihood of securing meetings with top prospects. Rather than waiting until the event itself, Kevin and Emily started outreach two weeks early. This pre-event engagement was essential to establish familiarity and warm prospects, ensuring Kevin wasn't introducing himself cold at the event.

The inclusion of a live event as a fourth channel provided Kevin a unique opportunity to interact face-to-face, adding a powerful layer of personal connection to the sequence. Even prospects he couldn't meet directly experienced his presence through thoughtful LinkedIn engagement, creating deeper credibility. Crucially, the sequence didn't end at the event - it continued afterward to capitalize on the momentum and deepen relationships through timely follow-ups referencing specific event conversations and insights. By planning this comprehensive, event-led sequence, Kevin and Emily ensured that every touchpoint reinforced the last, transforming the event into a powerful driver of pipeline growth.

By integrating purposeful sequence design, layered multichannel interactions, strategic stacking, and continuous refinement, Kevin and Emily successfully transformed a single industry event into an exceptional opportunity. They anticipated converting 80% of their key prospects into booked meetings, proving again that purposeful, structured, and thoughtful sequencing delivers real pipeline growth.

11 Data-Backed Tips to Build Better Sequences

Persistence Pays Off: Expect 8+ Touches
It still takes eight or more touches to earn a response from most prospects. Multiple touches significantly increase the chances of breaking through the noise, with studies indicating that sending multiple messages can double response rates. Creating sequences with at least eight touches helps reps persist without becoming overwhelming, ensuring prospects receive consistent reminders of your message.

Channel of Choice (COC): Use at Least Three Channels
Using three or more outreach channels significantly boosts prospect engagement and response rates. Companies using at least three channels experience a 287% higher purchase rate compared to single-channel outreach. Incorporating multiple channels (phone, email, social, direct mail) allows your reps to meet prospects exactly where they're most likely to engage.

Stacking Matters: Timely, Layered Outreach
Stacking is about timing multiple touchpoints closely together to reinforce your message effectively. Reps should layer outreach steps carefully to build recognition and create urgency. For instance, sending an email, quickly followed by a voicemail referencing that email, reinforces the initial message and increases response likelihood through repeated visibility.

Stack Tighter for Lower-Level Contacts
For lower-level titles or prospects from smaller organizations, stack touchpoints closer together. Lower-level contacts typically receive fewer overall messages and are less likely to be overwhelmed, making tighter stacks effective in maintaining attention and driving quick responses.

Give Breathing Room to Senior Titles
With higher-level executives or contacts at larger organizations, spacing outreach slightly further apart is important. Senior leaders receive significantly higher volumes of email and communication, and a slightly longer interval (3-5 days) gives them enough time to process each touchpoint and respond comfortably, improving overall response rates.

Sequences Prevent Over- or Under-Contact
One primary advantage of using sequences is ensuring that reps consistently follow the optimal cadence without over-contacting or neglecting prospects. By standardizing outreach intervals and touchpoints, sequences provide clarity and structure that helps teams avoid common pitfalls like overwhelming prospects or forgetting key follow-ups.

Data-Driven Iteration Is Key
Sequences also provide invaluable data to improve future outreach efforts. Sales leaders can analyze sequence data, such as which channels perform best, how quickly prospects respond, and at which steps responses typically occur. For

example, noticing prospects rarely respond after the 12th step means you can optimize sequences to end earlier, improving overall efficiency and effectiveness.

Empower Reps to Act Outside the Sequence (Thoughtfully)

While sequences ensure structured outreach, empower your reps to add personalized, out-of-sequence steps when appropriate. If a prospect makes a relevant LinkedIn post, encourage your rep to engage authentically. If your sellers get an autoreply stating the recipient will be on holiday for the next two weeks, ensure they know how to pause outreach. Avoid turning sequences into a check-the-box activity.

Use Nurture Sequences for Future Opportunities

Not every key contact is ready to buy immediately. When high-value prospects indicate that now isn't the right time, move them from direct sales sequences into nurture sequences. These sequences provide consistent, high-value insights without explicitly selling. A thoughtful sales-led nurture approach maintains rapport and positions your team as trusted advisors, significantly increasing future responsiveness when prospects become ready to buy.

Always Begin with a Double or Triple Touch

I always recommend beginning sequences with a double, or even triple, touch to immediately establish visibility and credibility. A double touch could be sending an email containing valuable information, followed closely by a voicemail referencing that email. A triple touch might involve a personalized LinkedIn connection request, supported by an InMail referencing the request, and mirrored by an email. This immediate stacking firmly anchors your outreach in the prospect's awareness and boosts initial engagement.

Creativity Comes After Baselines

Some reps feel constrained by sequence structures, worrying it limits creativity. But sequences aren't designed to stifle creativity; rather, they set a proven baseline. Once you've established solid messaging frameworks, creativity can be thoughtfully applied in A/B tests of email subject lines, length, tone or even get extra creative with elements like memes. Personality shines in live conversations, but sequence emails should remain consistent, clear, and relevant, allowing you to measure precisely how creative adjustments impact results.

Breakup Emails Are Bad Business

Your prospects do not care that you are "breaking up" with them. They probably didn't want to hear from you in the first place, so threatening to withhold that interaction is utterly meaningless, sometimes even a bit laughable.

Bad breakup emails tend to fall into a few categories:

- Threatening to never reach out again.

- Letting them know you are very busy, so have to stop reaching out now, but will try again later.
- Begging for their attention and pleading for a response, so you know the buyer is alive (often in the form of a choose-an-option-style list).

This list is far from comprehensive, but you get the point – your prospect does not care that you are breaking up with them. Best case scenario, they were interested, and now you've turned them off. More likely, they are somewhere on the spectrum of unaware to uninterested, and sending a breakup is a waste of a touchpoint.

That being said, you will still see me include a "breakup" email step in my sequences. Depending on the goal of the sequence, I've found a few ways to use the final email in the sequence to either gather information or share value. Instead of sounding thirsty or threatening, try these "breakup" emails instead:

- Asking for a different point of contact. This works best when you've done the work to identify who the better point of contact is, so you can ask, "Would it be better for me to reach out to [name] or is there somebody else who handles [priority]?"
- Inviting them to subscribe to your newsletter. Getting a prospect to opt in to receiving your newsletter allows your brand to stay top of mind even when the prospect is not enrolled in an active sequence.
- Adding value as a final step by sharing a deposit. This might sound like, "It seems like now is not the best time to discuss [known priority]. No worries at all. This [article, blog post, podcast, etc.] dives into how [lookalike company] is thinking about [priority]. Thought you'd find it interesting."

Just because the sequence the prospect was enrolled in did not allow your team to earn their time, doesn't mean they won't be enrolled in future sequences. Resist adding meaningless breakup emails in favor of emails that set your salespeople up for success with the account in the future.

Sequences as Storytelling Tools

As someone who writes sales emails and sequences for a living, what I love most about sequences is their ability to tell a story across multiple touchpoints and channels. They remove the pressure to make a single email perfect and allow each message to focus on one problem or outcome the prospect actually cares about. This makes the experience feel clear, intentional, and easy to engage with, reducing the risk of cognitive overload.

When I'm auditing emails for sales teams, the urge to include every benefit of their product often shows up in the form of long emails, usually including bullet points. I was a bit devastated when I first saw the data on how much bullet points hurt engagement and replies in cold email. At the time, I was bullet points' biggest fan. However, after testing emails with and without bullet points, it's undeniable that they are a net negative. Data from LinkedIn, SalesFolk, SalesLoft, and Belkins backs up my own A/B tests.[47]

The good news is that if you've written an email using bullet points and you are confident that they represent the outcomes your prospects care about most, you already have the content for an entire sequence. Sequences allow you to tell the story of how you can help prospects achieve those outcomes without feeling the pressure of cramming too much information into a single touch point.

Sequences are most effective when they are purpose-built, structured around buyer-relevant value propositions, and supported by the right cadence. They allow for a layered, multichannel approach, give reps a framework to avoid over- or under-contacting prospects, and give sales leaders a clear way to ensure consistency without sacrificing personalization.

When you roll out micro-campaigns using sequences, you enter the process knowing the story you want to tell. That story unfolds one touch at a time - optimized for clarity, timing, and buyer impact.

Why Multi-Threading Is the New Sales Standard

Integrating multi-threading into your outbound strategy is essential to creating a profitable, sustainable pipeline. Multi-threading means you

---

[47] Heather. "Stop Using Bullets Points in Cold Emails!" SalesFolk, March 11, 2021. https://salesfolk.com/blog/stop-using-bullets-points-cold-emails/.

engage several different people within a single account at the same time. Rather than relying on one contact, your team intentionally reaches out to multiple decision-makers or influencers who hold roles relevant to your solution. Multi-threading is not simply a sales best practice. Gartner predicts that companies adopting multi-threaded strategies will outperform peers by 50% in revenue growth by 2026.[48] That's because engaging multiple stakeholders from the start significantly boosts win rates, shortens sales cycles, and results in larger average deal sizes.

The first significant benefit of outbound multi-threading is increased win rates. Deals today rarely get done by a single decision-maker. Organizations increasingly rely on consensus, especially for larger or strategic investments. When your team reaches out to multiple stakeholders early, they multiply their chances of finding the person who will champion your solution internally. If one stakeholder is hesitant or distracted, another can still advocate for the deal. This redundancy ensures that no single point of failure can derail the entire opportunity. Instead, your salespeople gain multiple pathways to success within each account. It's simple math: more advocates within the account means more potential votes of confidence, which translates directly into more closed deals.

Outbound multi-threading also creates faster sales cycles. Instead of discovering late in the process that key stakeholders haven't been engaged, your team identifies and reaches out to these individuals up front. By proactively establishing relationships with multiple contacts, you reduce friction later in the sales process. Reps no longer have to backtrack or introduce themselves at critical decision points because they've already been building rapport from the earliest stages of outreach. Multi-threaded outreach ensures that your entire deal isn't reliant on a single individual's availability or responsiveness. This approach significantly accelerates the pace at which opportunities move through your pipeline.

---

[48] Egloff, Dave. 2022. "Why Multithreaded Engagements Are the Secret to Accelerating Revenue Growth." *Gartner*. https://www.gartner.com/en/articles/why-multithreaded-engagements-are-the-secret-to-accelerating-revenue-growth.

Finally, effective multi-threading results in larger deal sizes. When your team speaks to different stakeholders within the same account, they uncover varied pain points, needs, and opportunities for value creation. For example, while your messaging to a CFO might highlight financial risk mitigation, your outreach to a Director of Accounting might empha- size enhanced visibility and forecasting accuracy. Each stakeholder understands your solution through the lens of their unique role and challenges, allowing your salespeople to position your offering more comprehensively. When multiple stakeholders see value tailored specif- ically to their own responsibilities, it's easier for them, collectively, to justify larger, more impactful investments.

From Strategy to Structure: Implementing Multi- Threading

Understanding *why* multi-threading matters is just the beginning. The real impact comes when strategy meets execution. Now that you see the benefits – higher win rates, faster cycles, and bigger deals – it's time to build a repeatable structure your team can run with. In this section, we'll walk through exactly how to implement multi-threading in your outbound process.

First, coach your team to proactively identify multiple stakeholders within each target account. Account mapping tools make it easy to under- stand organizational structures and find contacts in key roles. Train your team to identify stakeholders across different departments, roles, and seniority levels, ensuring your outreach covers both users and economic decision-makers.

Next, encourage your team to run multiple sequences in tandem, tailored to specific personas within the same account. Each sequence should reflect distinct persona-level messaging based on that stakeholder's unique priorities. Even within the same company, each role demands its own clearly articulated value proposition. Remember, a CFO cares about different problems than a Director of Accounting. Using targeted micro-campaigns ensures each message feels relevant and personal rather than generic or templated.

Coordinate these parallel sequences carefully. If a prospect refer- ences a colleague who is also being contacted, your sales reps should demonstrate awareness, professionalism, and a cohesive approach. For example, your reps might proactively mention, "I've also reached out to [colleague's name], as we typically find their perspective valuable when organizations consider [specific challenge or solution]." This coordinated effort reinforces your credibility, demonstrating that you've done your homework and understand their internal structure.

Mixmax, citing data from UserGems and LinkedIn, highlights the critical importance of this approach: "78% of reps are still single-threaded in most deals. Multithreading increases win rates by 25%.[49] This highlights the untapped potential of early stakeholder diversification in outbound pipelines."

Finally, embed multi-threading directly into your team's daily outbound process. This isn't a tactic to save until your team is deep into a sales conversation. Instead, multi-threading should be built directly into your initial prospecting sequences. Teach your team to prioritize identifying and reaching multiple contacts simultaneously rather than sequentially. By embedding multi-threading into your standard operating procedures, you ensure your sales pipeline is robust, diversified, and consistently generating high-quality opportunities.

Remember, sequences can be used for awareness only. Your CTAs can be focused on awareness and delivering value. When I sold to Chief Procurement Officers (CPOs), I knew the chance of closing a deal increased significantly if the CFO attended the first sales meeting, so outbound efforts were focused on generating a meeting with the CPO. However, they almost always wanted the opinion of the Category Leads. Instead of waiting to introduce the platform once the buying process was underway, we began to multi-thread Category Leads. The sequences never asked for a meeting. That wasn't the goal and would have likely increased, instead of decreased, the sales cycle.

Instead, we shared valuable insights and free resources. The result was that once I reached a CPO, it was easier to get the attention of and build interest with the Category Leads. They already recognized my company

---

[49] Melkonian, Rita. 2025. "Multithreading Sales: The Ultimate Guide to Win More Deals." *Mixmax.* https://www.mixmax.com/blog/sales-multithreading.

brand and associated it with value because of the awareness sequences we used.

Outbound multi-threading is no longer optional. It's a foundational element of building a profit generating pipeline. By systematically engaging multiple stakeholders up front, your team will see increased win rates, shorter sales cycles, and larger deal sizes—all critical drivers of sustainable revenue growth.

Sequences: The Glue That Holds It All Together

Building effective sales sequences is about turning strategy into structure. Every concept learned so far, from territory segmentation to crafting buyer-centric value propositions and executing multichannel outreach, is amplified when brought together into well-designed, structured sequences. Without sequences, your sales process becomes fragmented, making it a challenge to measure what's working, optimize timing, or scale successful approaches. Sequences transform individual touchpoints into a cohesive, powerful journey that prospects recognize, trust, and respond to positively.

Purposeful sequence design provides clarity and direction, ensuring each interaction aligns with specific outcomes. When your reps understand exactly why they're reaching out, each message carries intention and value. Layering interactions thoughtfully within each channel deepens engagement, giving prospects multiple ways to respond and reinforcing your core message. Integrating multiple channels amplifies reach, placing your message exactly where prospects naturally engage, dramatically increasing your chances of breaking through.

While timing is important, the content and value of your follow-up emails are equally crucial for engagement. Effective sequences depend heavily on value-driven messaging, clear calls-to-action, relevant personalization, and adaptability. These core elements ensure your messaging resonates deeply with each prospect and continuously moves them toward meaningful conversations and conversions.

Consistency, a key insight drawn from Rockefeller's meticulous approach to standardization, plays a critical role in sequence effectiveness. Just as Rockefeller achieved unprecedented success by standardizing even the smallest details, your sequences gain impact through consistent execution. Each touchpoint must consistently deliver quality and clarity. Establishing uniform processes for outreach reduces errors, enhances effectiveness, and builds trust through reliability. When sequences are executed consistently across your team, prospects come to recognize and value your predictable professionalism and precision.

Continuous refinement through regular review and testing makes sequences adaptive and ensures they consistently deliver results. Rockefeller understood the power of refining processes through meticulous tracking and iterative improvement. Similarly, by empowering your team to analyze data, experiment thoughtfully, and share learnings openly, you cultivate a culture of ongoing improvement and strategic growth.

The strategic stacking of touchpoints maximizes sequence effectiveness by compressing outreach efforts into thoughtful bursts, rapidly building familiarity, urgency, and engagement momentum. Kevin and Emily's successful sequence around an industry event illustrated precisely how powerful careful stacking can be. Starting outreach before the event created early familiarity, incorporating the event as an additional high-value channel increased their credibility, and timely follow-ups afterward capitalized on momentum to deepen engagement further. This intentional approach dramatically improved their likelihood of converting prospects into meetings and opportunities.

Multi-threading strategies, integrated early into your sequences, are vital for sustainable pipeline growth. Proactively engaging multiple stakeholders within target accounts increases win rates, accelerates deal cycles, and expands deal sizes by uncovering diverse perspectives and aligning distinct value propositions to specific roles. By embedding multi-threading into your outbound strategy, your team positions itself not just for immediate success but for long-term pipeline health.

Structured, purposeful sales sequences are foundational to a profitable and predictable pipeline. By thoughtfully combining strategy, precision, personalization, multichannel integration, strategic stacking, multi-threading, and disciplined consistency, you ensure your outreach consistently generates meaningful engagement and sustained revenue growth.

CHAPTER 14

Mastering Objections with Curiosity and Confidence

"Curiosity will conquer fear even more than bravery will." –James Stephens

The old ways of handling objections pushed aggressive and dismissive techniques. Sellers were told to crush objections and bulldoze prospects into agreement at any cost. Early in my career, I had a manager go so far as to tell me that if I wasn't willing to talk over prospects and tell them why they were wrong, I didn't deserve a job in sales. This outdated mindset sets sellers up for failure. Nobody wants to deal with a combative sales rep who treats every question like a battle.

Transparently, it took me years of hearing objections and responding to them with a singular goal in mind: to overcome at all costs, before I realized it didn't work that well. By that time, I already knew asking questions was one of my sales superpowers, so I decided to start asking more and better questions after hearing objections. I held myself accountable to not jump immediately into seller mode by offering (what I felt was) a helpful solution. It was difficult to resist the temptation to stop telling and start asking, but I kept practicing and evolving my approach. Ultimately, that became the 3C Mindset Approach I teach today.

In this chapter, you'll see how this 3C approach helps sellers lead with curiosity, opening the door to better outcomes. You'll also see how the 4R Active Listening and the concept of Voice of Customer (VoC) play a crucial role when responding to objections. When sellers share real customer stories instead of pitching through resistance, they create opportunities to talk with their buyers instead of at them.

Finally, I'll introduce two practical frameworks your sellers can immediately use to put these concepts into action: the V Formation Model and the EDICT Framework. These tools help your sellers create objection-handling scripts that prioritize curiosity, drive better conversations, and support your ultimate goal of building a profit generating pipeline.

Your team will be equipped with a positive objection-handling mind-set, proven frameworks, and buyer-centric scripts that enable quality conversations.

Embracing an Attitude of Gratitude

When sellers approach objections with gratitude, they fundamentally change their relationship with the buyer and the sales process itself. Instead of perceiving objections as roadblocks, sellers begin to see them as signposts, pointing toward what truly matters to the buyer. This shift reframes the seller's role from someone whose job is to defend their solution to someone whose purpose is to understand their buyer.

Gratitude also transforms the seller's internal experience of objection handling. Gratitude works because it interrupts the reflex to defend. It calms the emotional reaction that makes sellers want to push back or pitch. When you can respond to an objection with a sincere "thank you," you shift your focus from fixing to understanding. Rather than feeling anxious or defensive when hearing an objection, sellers feel encouraged and empowered.

Research published in *The Journal of Positive Psychology* indicates that daily gratitude practices enhance resilience and social support, which are key factors in overall well-being.[50] By embracing gratitude, sellers can reduce their own stress and become more effective communicators.

Greeting objections with gratitude is step one. That shift matters. Gratitude is the mindset that clears space for curiosity. When sellers feel grounded and not under attack, it becomes easier to get genuinely curious about what the buyer is thinking or feeling. If sellers acknowledge that hearing an objection is always preferable to not hearing it, which means a hang up, a lie, or an emission that gets them ghosted later in the sales process, they will have better conversations more often.

---

[50] Kairong Yang, "Gratitude Predicts Well-Being via Resilience and Social Support in Emerging Adults: A Daily Diary Study," *The Journal of Positive Psychology* 19, no. 2 (2024): 123–135, https://doi.org/10.1080/17439760.2024.2322444.

Curiosity and Conversation: Stop "Handling" Objections – Start Understanding Them

Let me be extremely clear: the only way to respond to an objection is with a question. For decades, sellers have been told to tackle and crush objections, so they go straight into telling and selling without getting curious. But before responding, sellers need to understand *why* the objection is being raised. Digging into the "why" helps uncover underlying issues, doubts, or concerns, and gives your sellers the insights they need to address concerns effectively. The move from gratitude to curiosity should be intentional. Before saying anything, encourage your sellers to pause and ask themselves, "What do I still need to understand?" That one second of reflection is the difference between reacting and responding.

Part of the problem is seeing objections in black-and-white terms: either you overcome the objection, or you fail. This perspective is flawed. The ideal outcome of a sales conversation is to find a positive resolution to an objection, but there are other valuable wins, too.

3C Mindset Approach for Objections:

Step 1: Curiosity
The terminology we use sends the wrong message about how we approach objections. We are told to tackle, crush, and smash objections so sales reps try to jump straight to telling and selling.

Before you can respond to an objection, you need to get curious about why you are hearing the objection.

This applies both to why you hear an objection during a specific conversation and, more generally, if you find you're hearing the same few objections again and again.

Step 2: Conversation
The easiest and best way to explore that curiosity is through conversation.

The only way to have a conversation after a prospect shares an objection is by talking WITH that prospect, not AT them.

Shifting your mindset from overcoming an objection to

continuing the conversation is critical. Stop thinking about solving for the objection as your primary goal. Instead, focus on continuing the conversation.

Step 3: Conclusion

Having your call end in agreed upon next steps is not the only positive outcome you should be seeking. Unfortunately, we are trained that if we don't set the meeting or close the deal, the call is wasted. I call BS.

By leading with curiosity and prioritizing conversation, you will uncover opportunities to learn and help. These are also valuable outcomes.

Whatever the conclusion is, embracing the 3C Approach and finding responses that feel right to you will make cold calling more rewarding and productive.

I teach salespeople that their primary objective should be simply to ask one additional question after hearing an objection. Reframing success as continuing a dialogue rather than crushing an objection creates more positive outcomes for sellers and buyers. Genuine curiosity leads to valuable conversations, and those are more likely to lead to mutually beneficial conclusions.

The old narrative around objections was simple: the moment you hear one, your job is to neutralize it at all costs. This approach creates terrible conversations. It's why so many prospects ghost sellers later in the sales cycle. They never felt safe being honest about their doubts or concerns in the first place. It's why deal win rates are at an all-time low: sellers aren't uncovering the real reasons why prospects don't buy.

"Curiosity and confidence are your greatest tools in overcoming objections," according to Tiffani Bova, Salesforce's former Growth and Innovation Evangelist. As the author of two Wall Street Journal bestsellers, *Growth IQ* and *The Experience Mindset*, she underscores that curiosity and confidence not only help in addressing objections but also in building stronger, more trusting relationships with prospects.

My hope is that all sales professionals will reject that old way of objection handling and replace it with an attitude of gratitude and curiosity so they can lead better conversations. This is why I teach the 3C Mindset Approach. You need to get your sellers to shift their mindset from overcoming an objection to continuing the conversation. Without this shift, your sellers won't get access to critical information that prospects would otherwise withhold, leaving you guessing about what's causing your deals to stall and your forecasts to slip.

Here's the bottom line: your salespeople should understand that after hearing an objection, if they can ask one additional question that moves the conversation forward, they're doing a great job. Instead of being maniacally focused on crushing objections, your salespeople can create space for honest dialogue, leading to more meaningful conversations and better outcomes.

The final step of the 3C Mindset Approach is Conclusion. The ideal outcome of every sales call is securing agreed-upon next steps that move forward a qualified sales conversation, but that's not always possible. Unfortunately, sellers have been trained that if they don't set a meeting or close a deal, the call was wasted.

Your role as a sales leader is to help your sellers recognize that even when they cannot secure next steps, other positive outcomes still exist. Encourage your sellers to ask themselves three powerful questions to uncover value in every call:

- What can you learn?
- What can you teach?
- How can you help?

Your salespeople can learn that they're talking to the wrong person, allowing them to quickly redirect their efforts to a better contact. Perhaps they learn the prospect already has a long-term contract in place with another vendor, and importantly, uncover when internal budget discussions about renewal or vendor replacement begin. These are valuable insights that position your team to win future business.

Other times, the value is internal: sellers might realize they need more practice using objection frameworks like the V-Formation or EDICT, which we'll cover in this chapter. They may reflect and realize it's harder to resist "telling and selling" than they anticipated, prompting them to invest more time practicing active listening.

Your sellers might also find meaningful ways to help the prospect. For example, sellers can validate the way the prospect currently solves a problem and help identify what would need to change to make your product or service a better fit. They might introduce peers in their network dealing with similar issues or recommend resources and communities they've heard other prospects speak positively about.

Not every call ends in a next step toward buying, and that's okay. When "ideal" sales outcomes aren't a possibility, identifying ways to learn, help, and set up for future success makes sales conversations more productive and rewarding.

In the next section, we will dive into specific frameworks and scripts that you can use to respond to objections. These tools will help your team gain the confidence needed to handle any objection effectively. Remember, the key to using these frameworks effectively is to encourage your team to first apply the 3C Mindset Approach so that your prospects feel valued, engaged, and understood throughout the conversation.

Active Listening: Your Sales Superpower

When training sales teams, I always start with a session on active listening. It might not be the most typical sales training topic, like objection handling, negotiation, or needs analysis, but it's the bedrock of doing any of those skills well. If you don't have your active listening skills down, you'll never be good at discovery calls, and you'll surely never be able to master middle or bottom-of-funnel selling.

Active listening helps build trust with your prospects. When they feel heard, they're more likely to share their true needs and concerns. This trust is the foundation of any successful sales relationship. As Kate Murphy states in *You're Not Listening*, "Listening is as powerful a means of communication as talking, if not more so. The best conversationalists are often those who do the least talking... To listen well is to figure out what's on someone's mind and demonstrate that you care enough to want to know."

Dr. Rachel Naomi Remen, author of *Kitchen Table Wisdom*, encapsulates the essence of meaningful connection with this simple truth: "The most basic and powerful way to connect to another person is to listen. Just listen." This idea is fundamental in sales. When sales professionals genuinely listen to their prospects, they demonstrate respect, empathy, and a willingness to understand the prospect's needs. This connection fosters trust and paves the way for deeper engagement. Active listening also enhances your ability to ask better, smarter questions.

You can't handle objections effectively if you don't fully understand them. You can't identify needs if you don't listen to them.

4R ACTIVE LISTENING FRAMEWORK

The path to talking WITH your prospecct instead of AT them.

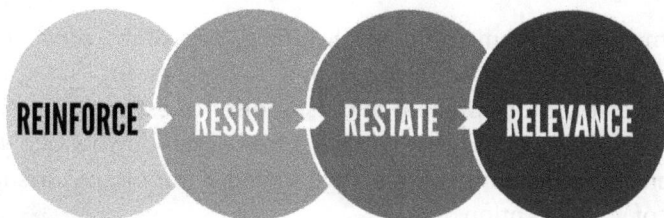

REINFORCE ▸ RESIST ▸ RESTATE ▸ RELEVANCE

REINFORCE:
Verbal and non-verbal cues that encourage the speaker to continue.
RESIST:
Practice listening to understand instead of response.
RESTATE:
Repeat back what you heard to ensure understanding.
RELEVANCE:
Now that you're confident, you can ask relevant questions and share relevant insights, it's time to begin a conversation.

The 4R Active Listening Framework

Active listening is the most important and foundational sales skill. Active listening takes practice, and the goal is to be able to listen to understand, not to respond. When you listen closely, you ask smarter, more targeted questions. This means you can quickly uncover the true needs and timelines of your prospects, helping you position your solution effectively. Active listening also reveals the specific buyer-centric value that motivates prospects to stay engaged during your call and gives them a compelling reason to keep talking to you in the future.

How do you teach listening in a way that actually sticks? Start with the 4Rs of active listening:

Reinforce:
Use verbal and non-verbal cues to show you're listening.

Reinforcing means providing verbal and non-verbal signals that encourage the speaker to keep talking. Direct eye contact, nodding, and mirroring a prospect's posture or emotions are examples of non-verbal cues. Verbal cues like "okay," "gotcha," or "tell me more" show engagement without interrupting.

When I'm training teams on active listening, one of the most common questions I get is, "Is note-taking okay?" I advocate for taking notes if it helps you stay more present and ask better questions. For example, saying, "Jack, I'm going to be jotting a few notes down while we talk. I just want to make sure I don't miss anything important," assures the speaker of your attention.

Your only goal during Reinforce is to keep the speaker speaking. Sellers dominate sales calls, talking up to 75% of the time, so believe me when I say - this step is more difficult than it seems.

Resist:
Avoid the temptation for interruption, judgment, or distraction. Stay focused on the speaker.

Resisting involves avoiding the temptation to interrupt, judge, or shift the conversation focus to yourself. Murphy notes that in our digital age, constant communication can lead to poor listening habits. There are a handful of common ways sellers struggle with listening to understand, not to respond. A few of the behaviors I train teams to resist are:

- The temptation to jump into problem-solving mode too early. Sellers feel like they are ready to help. Buyers feel like they are being hard sold.

- Sellers start thinking about what they want to say next instead of staying focused on the speaker.
- Sharing a relatable story to try to convince the buyer that you understand, instead of doing the hard work to actually understand.

Murphy writes, "Despite living in a world where technology allows constant digital communication and opportunities to connect, it seems no one is really listening or even knows how."

Restate:
Repeat back what you heard to ensure understanding.

According to Kate Murphy, effective listeners make the speaker feel understood and valued, which is central to reinforcing active listening.

Restating involves repeating back what the speaker said to ensure you have understood correctly. This could include paraphrasing their points or summarizing key ideas. For instance, "You told me that reporting is a top priority. Is that the most important thing for you to get right this quarter, or what else is more important?"

Restating shows engagement and helps clarify any misunderstandings. Restating helps overcome this common communication challenge by ensuring clarity and mutual understanding.

Relevance:
When it's your turn to speak, make it count. Don't jump into telling or selling, instead ask probing questions, share insights, and use VoC to tell stories.

When it's your turn to speak, ensure your responses and questions are relevant to what the speaker has shared. Ask probing questions to perform a deeper needs analysis, such as, "What would you expect to happen if you accomplish this goal?" This helps keep the conversation focused on what matters most to the prospect. Further, testing the waters with questions like, "Is making sure that you reduce the number of phishing attacks the right place to focus the rest of our conversation?" ensures alignment with the prospect's priorities.

From Manchester to Mastery: A Crash Course in Listening

In 2015, I joined a company as their first US leadership hire. The company sold extremely high-end audio branding under a subscription model. It was the first time I'd worked in an agency environment, the first time I'd sold a subscription model, and as the first US leadership hire, the first time I'd built a team from employee one.

I was learning a lot, quickly. When I hear the phrase "drinking from a fire hose," this is the role I imagine. I spent the first two weeks in the role onboarding at the company's Manchester office and became close with one of the musicians who created the audio branding. Not surprisingly, they had some gripes that the sales team just didn't "get" the product.

Two months later, in Chicago with a fully onboarded team of 24 sellers, the same musician rang me to ask a question. She shared how impressed she was by how quickly I picked up on the new product and was able to transfer that knowledge to my team with passion and understanding. I said thank you, but didn't think much of it until the next day when one of my reps pulled me aside to ask me how I learned so quickly.

I told them that a previous role required me to manage multiple products that crossed portfolios, so I could be working with Chief Human Resource Officers (CHROs) in the morning, CFOs midday, and wrap up chatting with Private Wealth Managers. I had plenty of practice learning, digesting, and putting that new knowledge to use on the same day.

I followed up with the musician and shared that I learned best by having conversations with prospects - that they taught me more than any product brief ever could. I always knew that I picked up on concepts fast in sales, but I couldn't quite put my finger on why. They said thank you, but seemed unconvinced.

It wasn't until that evening that it hit me - what I was good at was listening. I was MUCH better at listening than my colleagues and I'd known that for a long time. I knew that one of my sales superpowers was listening deeply so I could ask super smart follow-up questions and learn a little bit on each call so that I could be better the next time I talked to a prospect. It was that epiphany moment that led me to this 4R Framework because I realized that salespeople need dedicated training on active listening. Listening is a skill. Just like any skill, we must practice it if we want to be great at it.

Data-Driven Evidence of Active Listening's Impact

Think about a time when you felt truly listened to. The other person made eye contact, stayed focused, and gave you space to speak. You probably walked away feeling valued and understood. Now think about a time when someone interrupted you, seemed distracted, or clearly didn't care what you were saying. You likely felt frustrated or dismissed. Your prospects feel the same way.

Research supports the effectiveness of active listening. According to the research paper, "The Relative Effectiveness of Active Listening in Initial Interactions" in the *International Journal of Listening*, participants reported higher satisfaction in conversations where active listening was applied, with a satisfaction score of 84.3% (mean score: 5.90 out of 7).[51] This data underscores the tangible benefits of implementing active listening techniques in sales interactions.

It's not just academic research that proves this. Sales data consistently backs it up. When sellers let the buyer speak, they gather better information, build stronger rapport, and ultimately close more deals.

By adopting the 4R Framework and understanding the profound impact of active listening, sales teams can significantly enhance their communication skills and build stronger, more meaningful relationships with their prospects.

---

[51] Harry Weger Jr., Gina Castle Bell, Elizabeth M. Minei, and Melissa C. Robinson, "The Relative Effectiveness of Active Listening in Initial Interactions," *International Journal of Listening* 28, no. 1 (2014): 13-31, https://doi.org/10.1080/10904018 .2013.813234.

FEEL FELT FOUND FRAMEWORK

Using Feel Felt Found to practice responding using Voice of the Customer *do not use the exact terms on calls*

FEEL:

I understand how you feel.

FELT:

[Customer] felt the same way.

FOUND:

What they found was...

Why *Feel, Felt, Found* Still Matters

I've called on you to reject old ways of working more than once while reading this book. By this point, you understand that I don't mean reject them so much as I mean reject the really bad ones while appreciating the rest with understanding they almost certainly need to evolve to match the needs of the modern buyer. This brings us to one of my very favorite old-school sales techniques: *Feel, Felt, Found*. It's been around since at least the 1950s–while Zig Ziglar is credited with popularizing it, the exact origins are murky. Still, I teach it to this day, more than 75 years since it hit the scene, because it continues to work.

Feel, Felt, Found is designed to handle objections by empathizing with the customer's concerns, relating those concerns to others' similar experiences, and then demonstrating how those concerns were resolved using the product or service being offered.

The reason I still teach *Feel, Felt, Found* is that it is a brilliant way to practice speaking in the Voice of the Customer (VoC). It is a great exercise to encourage your team to collect a cache of stories that can be used for the Felt and Found steps. I don't actually think we should be using *Feel, Felt, Found* scripting on the phone with our prospects, but the social proof still works because it is human nature to want to reduce risk. We feel a perceived reduction in risk if we know we're not alone and we know how others have acted in the same situation.

VOICE OF THE CUSTOMER (VOC) DEFINITION

The customer's own words describing their needs, problems, priorities, and desired outcomes. Using VoC helps sellers clearly align their messaging and solutions to what truly matters to their buyers.

The Power of the Voice of the Customer

Voice of the Customer in outbound B2B sales means using customer quotes, case studies, testimonials, and even anonymized insights during sales conversations. It allows the seller to pivot from seller-centric language – "I," "we," "my" - to customer-centric language. Using VoC immediately lends the seller credibility because it's customer-centric language that leverages social proof.

Earlier, we talked about how Netflix effectively uses curiosity-driven social proof. When promoting new shows, Netflix often writes copy like, "Everyone's talking about [new show], find out why." They also prominently feature their "Top 10" list of popular titles, tapping into our natural desire to avoid missing out on something culturally relevant. In B2B sales, the same principle applies. When people see that others, particularly their peers, are engaging in a behavior or purchasing a product, it reduces the perceived risk associated with that action.

As noted by HubSpot, "When it comes to harnessing the positive power of social proof, remember that similarity matters. A significant amount of research has disclosed that the impact of social proof is amplified when people from one's own peer group have embraced the idea or behavior. So if you show buyers how others similar to them have purchased your product or service and experienced positive results, they are much more likely to buy it as well."[52]

Humans are inherently social creatures, and our behavior is often influenced by the actions and opinions of others. Faster Capital, the largest online incubator and accelerator supporting over 500 startups, explains that "social proof provides cognitive ease" by offering simple, readily available information that potential customers can use to make decisions. By leveraging social proof, businesses facilitate the decision-making process, leading to increased customer acquisition. The *Feel, Felt, Found* sales technique is timeless because it addresses fundamental human psychology. People want to feel understood. They appreciate knowing they are not alone in their concerns, and they need to see clear, relatable examples of how their problems can be solved.

Real-World Application: Rejection, Recessions, and Reps

Who Keep Going

I started my corporate sales career during the Great Recession cold-calling Fortune 500 CFOs. If you were selling during the most recent market disruptions and following recession due to the pandemic, you got a taste of what selling during the Great Recession was like.

To help you imagine the state of things, I was making 200–250 cold calls a day, every day, without a dialer or a computer at my desk. I was reaching three to four CFOs a day, 75% would respond somewhere on the spectrum of cursing me out to slamming the phone down (yes, these were desk phones, and a slammed phone was a jarring sound). I was lucky to have one conversation a day that didn't drive me to the edge of tears. I'd guess it was hard to sell anything to anybody during those long recession months, but selling to a group who widely reports having post-traumatic stress disorder (PTSD) because of the Great Recession was truly transformational.[53]

---

[52] HubSpot, "How to Use Social Proof to Sell Better and Faster," *HubSpot Blog*, accessed May 25, 2025, https://blog.hubspot.com/sales/social-proof-sales.
[53] Quentin Fottrell, "93% of Financial Advisers Had PTSD After 2008," *MarketWatch*, May 9, 2013, https://www.marketwatch.com/story/93-of-financial-advisers-had-ptsd-after-2008-2013-05-09.

It was a sink-or-swim moment, and it happened in the first months of my sales career. During that time, I was exposed to the *Feel, Felt, Found* sales technique and reveled in the power of social proof. At a time of unprecedented uncertainty, anybody who didn't curse me out or hang up on me was desperately seeking a view on what others were doing. Every CFO felt like they were on an island. Being able to share what their fellow CFOs were talking about was a life raft that I could share to help them stay afloat.

One specific instance comes to mind where this technique led to a breakthrough. I vividly remember a call with a CFO who made it clear from the start that he was skeptical. Given the economic climate, his caution was understandable. Applying the *Feel, Felt, Found* sales technique, I acknowledged that I genuinely understood how vulnerable he felt, especially under intense financial scrutiny. Then I shared the story of another CFO who initially had similar doubts and fears about making the wrong decision. I explained specifically how that peer ultimately found success. In that conversation, the CFO wasn't looking for empty reassurance. He needed clear evidence and a practical path forward.

Approaching his concerns with honesty and empathy shifted his skepticism into trust and allowed us to have the open, productive conversation we both needed. This approach not only kept him on the call but also led to a successful follow-up meeting and, eventually, a deal.

> *"Active listening is the most foundational sales skill. It requires sellers to listen with a goal of understanding rather than responding."*

Given the sheer volume of calls and the minimal engagement rate, I needed to bring my A-game to every single conversation. On a good week, I was making over 1,000 calls and having five to ten meaningful conversations. I needed to leverage every tool in my toolbox to get maximum results from those few interactions. Practicing *Feel, Felt, Found* helped me develop a cache of compelling stories to share. Understanding and leveraging social proof was crucial in these moments, as it provided reassurance and validation to prospects who were looking for guidance during uncertain times. These formidable early career experiences with leveraging social proof in the form of VoC and using *Feel, Felt Found*, led me to develop the Validate, Voice of Customer, Verify framework that I now use and teach.

Writing Mini Case Studies: Using Third Person

Using third-person perspectives makes VoC effective. Research published in the *Journal of Health Communication* shows that "the bystander perspective was more effective for producing persuasive outcomes."[54] Applying this concept to sales, presenting customer experiences from a neutral observer's viewpoint can increase credibility and impact. For example, instead of only sharing internal company views, they include testimonials or case studies from impartial third parties to create a more objective and persuasive narrative. This approach helps prospects view the information as more credible and less biased, enhancing the effectiveness of your message.

Making It a Habit: Collect, Practice, Apply

When preparing to respond to objections using the VoC, start by gathering feedback from your current customers through surveys, interviews, and reviews. Focus on specific pain points and objections they had before choosing your product or service. Develop targeted scripts that address these common objections. For example, if a frequent objection is about implementation time, include a customer quote that reassures prospects about the seamless implementation process.

Practice using VoC in role-playing sessions with your sales team so they get comfortable shifting the focus from your company's perspective to the customers' experiences.

Maintain a database of customer stories and quotes that can be easily referenced during sales calls, ensuring that your responses are not only relevant but also backed by real customer experiences. Regularly

---

[54] Jessie M. Quintero Johnson, Angeline Sangalang, and Sun-Young Park, "First-Person, Third-Person, or Bystander? Exploring the Persuasive Influence of Perspective in Mental Health Narratives," *Journal of Health Communication* 26, no. 4 (2021): 225–238, https://doi.org/10.1080/10810730.2021.1916658.

update your VoC data by collecting new feedback and testimonials. This ensures that your responses remain relevant and credible.

I teach sellers to think about collecting Voice of Customer stories as mini case studies, which are 3-4 sentence case studies that allow them to quickly highlight the positive result. This approach forces them to make the mini case study relevant to the prospect by focusing on the end result benefit for the customer. By doing so, they not only provide a concise and impactful narrative but also ensure that the prospect can quickly see the relevance and potential benefits of your solution.

For example, instead of a lengthy explanation, a mini case study might look like this:

"A CFO at XYZ Corp was initially concerned about our implementation time, but within three months, they reported a 25% increase in efficiency and a seamless integration with their existing systems.

This increase in efficiency meant that projects finished ahead of time and under budget, earning the CFO a significant bonus and enabling their direct report to get a raise based on the seamless integration."

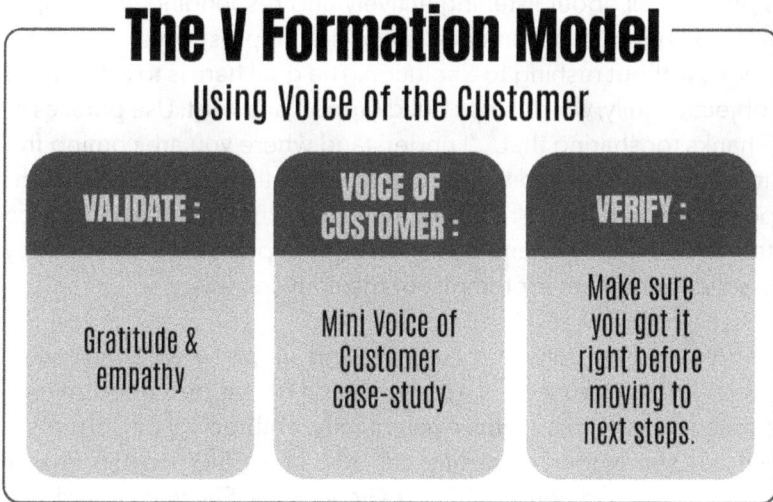

The V Formation Model
Using Voice of the Customer

VALIDATE :	VOICE OF CUSTOMER :	VERIFY :
Gratitude & empathy	Mini Voice of Customer case-study	Make sure you got it right before moving to next steps.

Between the cold calls I've made and the over ten million made by the teams I've led and trained, I think I can confidently claim that I've heard every objection in the book. Having a repository of compelling customer stories ready to share made the positive impact of pivoting from "I," "my," and "our" language undeniable. It led to the development of the V-Formation: Validate, Voice of Customer, Verify Model that I now use and teach.

Deploying the V-Formation Model

Building on the power of using the VoC to effectively address objections, the V-Formation Model offers a structured approach to enhance this technique. By integrating the steps of Validate, Voice of Customer, and Verify, this model ensures that sales conversations are not only empathetic but also strategically directed toward positive outcomes. The V-Formation Model leverages the insights gained from the Voice of Customer to handle objections with a blend of understanding and evidence, helping sales leaders guide their teams through challenging conversations and fostering trust with prospects.

Step 1: Validate

The first step is crucial for making the prospect feel genuinely heard. This phase is all about listening actively and responding with empathy. Sales reps should focus on understanding the prospect's concerns and emotions without rushing to a solution. The goal here is to acknowledge the objection fully, which helps build rapport and trust. Use phrases such as "Thanks for sharing that," "I understand where you are coming from," or "It seems like we need to spend a bit more time on that point." These responses show that you're taking their concerns seriously and are committed to addressing them. By validating the prospect's viewpoint, you set a solid foundation for the rest of the conversation.

Fifteen years ago, traits like curiosity and empathy were not seen as essential for sales success. I surely wouldn't have described myself as empathetic at the time. However, quietly embracing those traits was effective. I remember a specific call with the Chief Human Resource Officer (CHRO) of a Fortune 500 CPG company. She was overwhelmed and listed numerous frustrations. Instead of jumping into problem-solving mode, I paused, took a deep breath, and simply said, "That sucks." I then waited. I could hear her take a deep breath on the other end. She started laughing and said, "Yes, yes, it does."

This simple acknowledgment of her frustrations changed the dynamic of the conversation. I didn't diminish her feelings or jump quickly into problem-solving mode. Instead, I shared my honest reaction, acknowledging that it was a sucky situation. This moment lowered her resistance and allowed me to build a deeper connection. We had a productive conversation after that, and she eventually became a client, provided a valuable testimonial, and referred peers.

According to Marcus Chan, best-selling author and B2B sales influencer, it's essential to empathize and validate concerns by saying things like, "I hear this a lot. I'm sorry you feel that way. It sounds like this has been very frustrating." This approach helps prospects feel heard and can make them more open to discussing solutions.

Step 2: Voice of Customer

The second step involves presenting a mini case study that illustrates how similar objections have been resolved for other customers.

Context: Customer's relatable problem or challenge.

Action: How you solved the customer's problem.

Result: Specific benefits your customer achieved.

We've covered the how to collect and use VoC at length, so let me just share one more framework to support this step of the V-Formation Model. If you're still finding it difficult to come up with a mini case study, you can use the CAR Method - Context, Action, Result - to create a concise and impactful narrative.

Context: Set the stage by describing the situation or problem faced by a previous customer. This helps the prospect relate to the example and see its relevance. For instance, "A company similar to yours was concerned about the long implementation time."

Action: Detail the specific actions taken to address the problem. This shows how your solution works in practice and highlights your capability. For example, "We streamlined their process by deploying a dedicated support team to ensure a smooth transition."

Result: Share the outcomes or benefits achieved. This part demonstrates the effectiveness of your solution and provides tangible proof of its value. For instance, "As a result, they saw a 30% improvement in efficiency within the first three months, which significantly enhanced their overall productivity."

Using the CAR Method helps in creating a mini case study that feels real and relevant, making it easier for the prospect to visualize how similar solutions could work for them.

MINI VoC CASE STUDY EXAMPLES	
Objection: Have a vendor	**Objection: Too expensive**
I'm not sure if you know Bob, the VP of IT at ABC Trucking. Before we started working with ABC, they were using a competitor too. Bob gave us a chance because he felt safer using one enterprise-grade tool for malware, ransomware & phishing protection. VERIFY.	I talked to a FinTech CISO last week that had the same concern. She was surprised to learn that our modules start as low as $4. Once we dug into her needs, it was easy to create a plan that was within budget for her. VERIFY.

Step 3: Verify

The final step ensures that the prospect feels the mini case study was relevant and determines whether they are ready to move forward. It's important to confirm that the provided information addressed their concern and to get permission to proceed with the conversation. Use questions like, "If we did something similar for you, would that allow us to move forward?" or "If we walked through that outcome in more detail, would that answer your question?" These questions help gauge the prospect's reaction and readiness, allowing you to adjust your approach as needed and keep the conversation on track.

Incorporating techniques to lower the psychological reactance or the automatic, often unconscious self-preservation response triggered when individuals sense that someone is trying to influence or persuade them can be valuable here. Brehm J. W., in his work *A Theory of Psychological Reactance*, argues that the magnitude of reactance increases with the intensity and directness of the threat to freedom.[55] When prospects sense a sales pitch or feel pressured, they often experience psychological reactance, which triggers resistance to the outreach.

Acknowledge and listen actively, showing full attention and respect to the prospect's concerns. Validate their objections, demonstrating empathy and understanding. Leverage social proof by sharing success stories or testimonials that relate to their situation. Finally, offer a solution-oriented approach, working collaboratively to find mutually beneficial solutions rather than focusing solely on overcoming objections. By integrating these techniques into the V-Formation Model, you enhance the effectiveness of your objection-handling strategy and foster more open, productive dialogues with your prospects.

Limitations of VoC and Case Studies

When teaching the V-Formation Model, I get pushback from two groups. One is sales leaders working in earlier-stage organizations where they have few customers and may not have any approved case studies. Two is sales reps who swear they don't have visibility into customer success stories or any of their own stories to tell. I acknowledge why these folks might wonder how they can apply social proof when their product or service has little to no social proof, but everybody has stories to tell.

What, I will admit, alarms me is that 90% of the time, at least one bold seller raises their hand and asks, "Can't we just make it up?" The short answer is no. The longer answer is that there is no reason to lie because you and your team have more insights up your sleeves than you realize.

---

[55] Rosenberg, Benjamin and Siegel, Jason T., "A 50-year review of psychological reactance theory: Do not read this article" (2016). Psychology | Faculty Scholarship. 3. https://doi.org/10.1037/mot0000091.

If you find yourself in a role or company without formal, published case studies, here are two techniques any seller can deploy:

- Share anonymized outputs. Specificity is ideal, but you can still provide details without sharing confidential information. That might sound like, "The Director of Accounting at a billion-dollar luxury goods company shared..."
- Use "wisdom of the crowd" insights, as we've discussed in Chapter 10. What sellers underestimate is how much information they collect during their research and calls. If you can't use an anonymized insight, try a wisdom of the crowd comment like, "I talked to over thirty Sales Directors, all of them mentioned..."

A Cautionary Case Study: The Fyre Festival Fiasco

The Fyre Festival, originally billed as an exclusive, luxury music festival in the Bahamas, became a cautionary tale of how social proof and FOMO can drive people to make irrational decisions. Organized by entrepreneur Billy McFarland and rapper Ja Rule, the festival was marketed as the ultimate VIP experience, featuring top-tier musical acts, luxurious accommodations, gourmet food, and an idyllic island setting.

The marketing campaign for Fyre Festival was nothing short of genius, leveraging the power of social media influencers to create a buzz that quickly spiraled out of control. In December 2016, Fyre Festival's promotional video was released, featuring supermodels like Kendall Jenner, Bella Hadid, and Emily Ratajkowski frolicking on a pristine beach, with promises of a once-in-a-lifetime experience. These influencers posted the video on their Instagram accounts, reaching millions of followers and generating massive hype.

People saw their favorite models and celebrities promoting the event and assumed it must be legitimate. The involvement of these high-profile figures acted as a powerful motivator, convincing potential attendees that Fyre Festival was the place to be.

Despite the exorbitant costs, tickets sold out quickly. The festival's target audience, primarily wealthy millennials and social media enthusiasts, was driven by the fear of missing out on what was being touted as the most exclusive event of the year. The anticipation and excitement built up through relentless social media promotion created a sense of urgency that led many to make impulsive purchasing decisions.

Reality Check: A Sad Cheese Sandwich

As the festival date approached, cracks began to show in the glamorous façade. Behind the scenes, the organizers were woefully unprepared to deliver on their promises. The festival site on the island of Great Exuma was far from ready, with inadequate accommodations and facilities. Despite these glaring issues, the marketing machine continued to churn out images of luxury and exclusivity.

When attendees began to arrive in April 2017, the reality was starkly different from the opulent paradise they had been promised. Instead of luxury villas, they found disaster relief tents. Gourmet meals turned out to be a single slice of American cheese on a dry, stale white bread bun. There was no running water, and the overall infrastructure was in shambles. The highly anticipated musical acts were nowhere to be found, and the entire event quickly descended into chaos.

The fallout from Fyre Festival was swift and severe. Attendees took to social media to document the debacle, sharing photos and videos that contradicted the festival's polished promotional materials. The media quickly picked up the story, and Fyre Festival became a global laughingstock. Lawsuits were filed, and Billy McFarland was eventually sentenced to six years in prison for fraud.

Ethics in Action: What We Must Learn

The Fyre Festival debacle serves as a stark reminder of the power of social proof and FOMO. It highlights how easily people can be swayed by the perceived actions and endorsements of others, particularly when those endorsements come from trusted or admired figures. The festival's organizers manipulated these psychological triggers to create a sense of legitimacy and urgency, convincing thousands of people to part with their money for a product that did not exist.

While the story of Fyre Festival is a fascinating case study in the power of social proof, it is also a cautionary tale about the ethical use of these principles. As sales professionals, it is crucial to use social proof responsibly and honestly. Building trust with your customers should be based on genuine value and integrity, not deception or manipulation.

The drama and disaster that was Fyre Festival should remind us all of the importance of ethical conduct. Use social proof for good. Leverage real testimonials, authentic endorsements, and genuine success stories to build trust and credibility with your prospects. This approach will not only lead to better business outcomes but also foster long-term relationships built on trust and respect.

EDICT Framework

Empathy: Acknowledge and validate the prospect's concerns to build trust.

Define: Clarify exactly what the objection is by asking focused questions. This ensures you respond to the right issue.

Isolate: Confirm that this is the prospect's only concern. For example: "If cost wasn't an issue, would you move forward?"

Curiosity: Ask deeper questions to fully understand why the objection exists, and what matters most to the prospect.

Trial Close: Check if you've resolved the objection and see if the prospect is ready to take the next step.

The EDICT Framework

EDICT is a five-step framework I created to help sales leaders train their teams to respond confidently to objections. It stands for Empathy, Define, Isolate, Curiosity, and Trial Close. Each step is essential for managing objections effectively and guiding the sales conversation toward a positive outcome.

When my sales manager introduced me to the Isolate technique circa 2008, I initially thought it was a misguided approach. My ego flared up. I worried that asking the same question twice would make me appear inept. As a new sales rep, I hadn't yet grasped the value of getting the buyer to agree with me twice. Yet, this technique is why the EDICT framework is so effective. It encourages you to secure agreement twice before moving into problem-solving mode. You can see this strategy reflected in the "Define" and "Isolate" steps.

Step 1 - Empathy:
This is the foundation of EDICT. Demonstrating genuine understanding of the prospect's concerns helps build rapport and trust. Active listening and compassionate responses show that you value the prospect's perspective and are committed to addressing their needs. Empathy involves acknowledging the prospect's feelings and validating their concerns, which sets the stage for a productive dialogue.

Step 2 - Define:
After establishing empathy, the next step is to clarify the specific objection. In the "Define" step of the EDICT framework, it's crucial to understand the exact nature of the objection. Effective handling involves asking targeted questions to uncover the true issue. By asking the right questions, you avoid addressing the wrong issue and get to the core of the objection. This focus helps in pinpointing the issue and preparing a precise response, ensuring that you address the real problem rather than peripheral concerns.

Step 3 - Isolate:
This step involves separating the objection from other potential concerns. The goal is to focus solely on the issue at hand. For instance, if a prospect says, "It's too expensive," you might ask, "If cost were not a factor, would you buy it?" This question helps you determine if cost is the only concern or if there are other underlying issues to address. Isolating the objection prevents distractions from unrelated issues, allowing you to concentrate on resolving the actual concern.

Step 4 - Curiosity:
Probing questions are key in this step. By asking insightful questions, you dig deeper into the objection to uncover its root cause. Curiosity involves exploring the prospect's needs and motivations to gain a deeper understanding of their perspective. This step helps gather more information, allowing you to tailor your response more effectively to meet the prospect's specific needs.

Sujan Patel, Founder of Mailshake, emphasizes that effectively responding to sales objections begins with thoughtful questioning. He explains, "You'll need to ask open-ended questions to help you dig up all the objections before you're in a position to respond effectively."[56]

Step 5 - Trial Close:

This step involves testing the waters to see if the objection has been resolved and if the prospect is ready to move forward. It's about checking whether the proposed solution has addressed the concern and if the prospect is inclined to proceed. Trial closing helps gauge the prospect's readiness and adjust your approach as needed to keep the conversation on track.

With each step building on the last, the EDICT framework equips reps to manage objections with empathy and precision, culminating in a Trial Close where techniques like IF:THEN can reinforce clarity and forward momentum.

IF:THEN in Action

"If we can address your concern about timing, then we can proceed with the implementation plan."

The IF:THEN communication technique can be highly effective during the Trial Close step. It creates clarity and structure by stating terms clearly, such as, "If we can address your concern about timing, then can we proceed with the implementation plan?" This approach reduces ambiguity and helps both parties understand the proposed terms and consequences. It also allows for contingencies, promotes problem-solving, and can defuse tension by framing proposals as conditional rather than absolute demands.

---

[56] Sujan Patel, "How to Overcome the 16 Most Common Sales Objections," *Mailshake*, December 2, 2024, https://mailshake.com/blog/sales-objections-2/.

A related concept is the "contingent agreement," as discussed in Harvard Law School's Program on Negotiation. A contingent agreement involves negotiating "if, then" promises to address uncertainties about future events. For example, if there is doubt about project delivery, a contingent agreement might include penalties for late delivery or reduced rates if the project exceeds the budget.

Lawrence Susskind, in his book *Good for You, Great for Me: Finding the Trading Zone and Winning at Win-Win Negotiation* explains, "A contingent agreement—negotiated 'if, then' promises aimed at reducing risk about future uncertainty—offers a way for parties to agree to disagree while still moving forward."[57] Using trial close techniques like IF:THEN allows sellers to retain their role as a trusted advisor versus a high-pressure seller. The goal is to create space to find win-win outcomes.

By integrating the EDICT framework into your sales process, you ensure a structured and empathetic approach to handling objections. This method not only addresses the real issues effectively but also builds trust and rapport with the prospect.

Application: EDICT Framework:

Objection: Can you call me back in January?

- **Empathy:** "I sure can. That's no problem at all."
- **Define:** "Just to make sure that call is of value to you, it sounds like you're interested and the only thing holding you back from learning more today is just a feeling of being too busy with other priorities?"
- **Isolate:** "Got it. So it sounds like if you weren't so busy, this is a product you'd seriously consider investing in this quarter?"
- **Curiosity:** "Do you mind me asking, what do you think will change between now and next quarter?"
- **Trial Close:** "If we could find a way to address your current priorities, then would you be ready to discuss this further?"

---

[57] Lawrence Susskind, *Good for You, Great for Me: Finding the Trading Zone and Winning at Win-Win Negotiation* (New York: PublicAffairs, 2014).

It empowers sales teams to manage objections with greater confidence and drive more successful outcomes.

Mastering Objections with Curiosity and Confidence

Responding effectively to objections is a crucial part of sales success. In this chapter, we explored methods like the 3C Mindset Approach, 4R Active Listening Framework, V-Formation Model, and the EDICT Framework. These approaches show how using curiosity and confidence can turn objections into chances for deeper, more valuable conversations.

The frameworks I've shared in this book are far from the only successful techniques to respond to objections. They're just a few examples that align with the goal of earning the right to the prospect's attention, time, and consideration. Like my journey from outdated tactics to the 3C Mindset Approach, finding what works best for you might involve some experimentation and adaptation. When I started seeing objections as opportunities to ask more questions and understand the prospect better, my results improved significantly. I want the same for you and your team.

CHAPTER 15

Conducting Discovery Meetings and Building Relationships

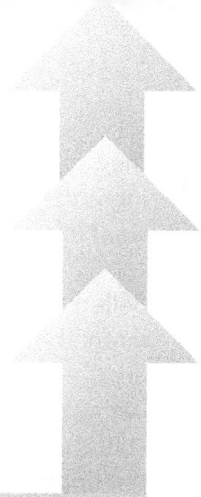

"I've learned that people will forget what you said, people will forget what you did, but people will never forget how you made them feel." –Maya Angelou

I hesitate to use the phrase "unpopular opinion," but you're probably asking yourself, "Why is there an entire chapter dedicated to discovery and hosting an introductory meeting? That has nothing to do with pipeline generation." Well, my hot take: it does.

The fact that most sales processes don't treat it as the final step of earning the right to have your buyers enter a buying process mucks up the rest of the pipeline. The hill I will die on is that the discovery meeting is the final top-of-the-funnel (ToFu) step.

Redefining the Funnel: Where Discovery *Actually* Belongs

This distinction is crucial for effectively managing sales funnels. Qualifying leads through discovery meetings is essential because very few organizations have a process robust enough to ensure only 100% qualified leads attend discovery calls (I've never seen it, but I'm sure it exists somewhere). Even in cases where superficial criteria are met, no discovery has occurred to validate whether the prospect has a problem you can solve, and if they are interested in solving it now. Until you verify this fit, you have a lead, not a qualified opportunity.

By definition, the middle of the funnel (MoFU) is when a buyer is actively in a buying process with you, while the top of the funnel (ToFU) is when they are figuring out if they want to buy from you. The discovery meeting is the critical point where they decide if your solution is the one they want to pursue.

Sellers might view the initial meeting as indicative of serious buying intent, but that's rarely the case, making it a top-of-funnel activity. They are likely meeting with you and a few of your competitors. They are evaluating whether they can handle the problem in-house or stick with the status quo, avoiding external vendors altogether. A discovery meeting is the tipping point where they move from attention and interest to desire and action (an active buying process).

Including discovery meetings in the middle of the funnel can result in dirty data, undermining the effectiveness of your sales process. Consider the value of being able to pull a list of prospects who scheduled a discovery meeting, but:

- Did not attend
- Attended but were not qualified
- Attended but were not interested in entering a buying cycle immediately
- Attended and were qualified but uninterested in learning more
- Attended and resulted in an opportunity because there was a mutually agreed-upon next step

Your re-engagement campaigns would be much stronger if you stopped auto-creating opportunities the moment a discovery meeting is marked as complete, because you could more accurately apply the segmentation principles from Chapter 8. You'll never convince me that an opportunity should be created just because a discovery is attended by a prospect who may or may not be qualified.

In the first half of 2024, only 18% of deals in the pipeline met ICP criteria, according to a report from Ebsta and Pavilion.[58] This statistic underscores the importance of including discovery meetings as a crucial, final step in the top of the funnel to ensure leads are properly qualified before moving further down the sales cycle.

---

[58] Pavilion and Ebsta, *2024 B2B Sales Benchmarks* (New York: Pavilion, 2024), https://www.joinpavilion.com/resource/2024-b2b-sales-benchmarks.

Discovery Is Not a One-and-Done

An easy way to tell if the introductory or discovery meeting is a top-of-funnel activity is to ask if the prospect is also meeting with your competitors. If the answer is yes, and it almost always is, it means they are thinking about buying but haven't decided to buy from you yet. They are evaluating options, comparing solutions, and deciding which provider might best solve their problem. This stage is critical for positioning your solution effectively and differentiating yourself from competitors.

This chapter guides sales leaders on how to prepare their team for these critical interactions. It emphasizes the importance of genuine curiosity, active listening, and asking insightful questions. By focusing on understanding the prospect's needs and challenges, reps can build trust and establish a solid foundation for a long-term relationship.

Including discovery meetings as a top-of-funnel activity ensures a clearer, more accurate sales funnel and enhances your ability to manage and re-engage leads effectively. By treating discovery meetings as part of the top of the funnel, you ensure your sales process is cleaner, more organized, and more effective. This shift in perspective can lead to better data, improved lead qualification, and a more strategic approach to moving prospects through the sales cycle.

If I ruled the World, I'd end the process of opportunity auto-creation the moment a discovery meeting is marked complete and focus on verifying and qualifying leads before moving them further down the funnel.

A rep's job should not be simply to book revenue but to collaboratively architect deals that deploy successfully and positively impact the customer's business, setting up renewals and expansions. This approach will provide more clarity and efficiency in your sales process, leading to stronger and more successful sales outcomes.

Selling Like Sarah: The Power of Uncovering Hidden Needs

Sarah Blakely, the founder of Spanx, exemplifies the power of uncovering hidden needs and providing solutions that people didn't even realize were possible.

Sarah's journey began with a moment of sheer frustration. As she was getting ready for a party, she wanted a smooth look under her white pants, but traditional undergarments weren't cutting it. In a flash of ingenuity, she cut the feet off her control-top pantyhose and discovered a simple but powerful solution to a problem many women faced.

Traditional undergarments were either uncomfortable, ineffective, or unflattering. Women had just accepted these shortcomings because no one had thought to innovate in this space. Sarah's solution wasn't just a new product; it was a revelation. She realized that women didn't need to suffer with uncomfortable undergarments—there was a better way.

When Sarah pitched her idea to potential investors, she encountered skepticism and doubt. Many couldn't see the value in her idea because they didn't understand the problem. But Sarah was talking to women, discovering they had the same need. She asked women what wasn't working and paid close attention to what they said. Those conversations helped her validate the problem, understand the emotional impact, and refine the way she positioned her solution. Sarah's confidence didn't come from her product alone; it came from listening to her customers. She knew that if she could get her product into the hands of women, they would immediately see the benefits. She didn't just sell a product; she sold a solution to a problem that women faced daily.

Sarah's success with Spanx illustrates the importance of understanding your customer and uncovering hidden needs. In sales, it's not just about pushing a product; it's about listening to your prospects and identifying problems they might not even realize have solutions. That starts with asking better questions. Discovery isn't about proving you're smart or qualifying a lead as fast as possible. It's about being curious. It's about getting your prospects to talk openly enough so that you can spot what they've missed or stopped questioning.

Imagine you're in a discovery meeting with a prospect. As you ask questions and dig deeper into their needs, you might uncover pain points they have accepted as just part of their business. Like Sarah, you can offer a solution that changes everything. For example, you might learn that your prospect struggles with managing their sales pipeline effectively. They've accepted the inefficiencies as unavoidable. But with your product, you can show them a better way, one they didn't realize was possible.

During your discovery meetings, focus on mobilizing the buyer, which sales methodology expert, Becc Holland, describes as uncovering hidden problems or blind spots. This aligns with Sarah Blakely's approach, where she educated women about the discomfort they didn't need to endure and provided a revolutionary solution. Next, widen the buyer's perspective by showing them the broader impact of their problems, much like how Sarah demonstrated the transformative benefits of Spanx – not just comfort, but confidence.

It is crucial to instill these principles in your team. Encourage your reps to approach discovery meetings with the intent to educate and uncover hidden needs. Emphasize the importance of listening actively and asking insightful questions. Train them not only to identify but also to articulate the broader impact of the problems they uncover. This method transforms the sales process from a transactional exchange to a consultative partnership.

Sarah Blakely's story of Spanx provides a powerful example of how identifying and addressing hidden needs can lead to groundbreaking success. By applying this mindset in your discovery meetings, you can uncover opportunities to provide immense value to your prospects, transforming their challenges into opportunities for growth and success.

Taking a Trusted Advisor Approach

Being a trusted advisor means you're not trying to push your product. You're working alongside the buyer to accurately define the problem, understand what's at stake, and decide whether it's worth solving together.

A salesperson's job is to educate their prospects. The best discovery calls are those where the seller adds significant value by helping the prospect see their challenges and opportunities in a new light. Holland emphasizes the importance of helping buyers understand aspects of their situation they were previously unaware of, correcting any misdiagnoses, and uncovering missed diagnoses.

According to Holland, "Customers often misdiagnose their problems before and during the sales process. Without a thorough diagnostic conversation, the seller will often prescribe an ineffective solution." She explains that during discovery, it's crucial to identify both misdiagnoses—issues the prospect has identified incorrectly—and missed diagnoses—issues they have completely overlooked. This approach transforms a simple sales call into a valuable consulting session, where you help the prospect understand their situation more comprehensively.

Jill Konrath, in her book *SNAP Selling*, highlights the importance of making your discovery meetings so valuable that your prospects would be willing to pay for the insights you share. She writes, "Think about it. Would your prospects willingly pay $500 for an hour of your time? If not, we've got some work to do." When you've earned that kind of buy-in, you're no longer selling *to* them. You're solving *with* them.

By integrating these techniques, you transform your discovery meetings into powerful sessions that not only gather information but also add value to your prospects. You become a problem solver who brings significant value to their business. You know you're seen as a trusted advisor when your questions slow the buyer down. When they pause and say, "We hadn't thought about that," or "That's interesting, what would you recommend?" the discovery meeting shifts from presentation to collaborative dialogue.

> *"The best sellers I've worked with know how to use discovery to pivot from just another vendor to a trusted advisor."*

The best sellers I've worked with know how to use discovery to pivot from just another vendor to a trusted advisor. Holland's concept of mobilizing the buyer and Konrath's emphasis on delivering invaluable insights work hand-in-hand to ensure that your discovery meetings are not only productive but also profoundly impactful, setting the stage for long-term relationships and successful sales outcomes.

The Google Glass Fumble

In 2013, Google launched Google Glass, an innovative product that promised to revolutionize wearable technology. However, the project failed spectacularly and was withdrawn from the consumer market in 2015. The failure was primarily due to Google's inadequate needs analysis. They assumed that consumers would embrace Google Glass for its technological novelty, but they neglected to conduct thorough focus groups and usability studies. Privacy concerns and practical issues went unnoticed, leading to poor market reception.

Google didn't fail because they lacked innovation. They failed because they assumed they already knew what buyers wanted. That confidence blinded them to what real users actually cared about. Google thought the buyer's job was to adopt the next big tech trend. The real job was to feel confident and safe using wearable tech in public. No one took the time to ask those questions.

They didn't skip discovery by accident. They skipped it because they thought they already had the answers. That same overconfidence shows up in sales when reps try to skip needs analysis and jump straight into telling the prospect how great their product or service is. It keeps sellers stuck selling fancy features and generic advantages because they don't have the knowledge required to match their solution to the prospect's true needs. Holland warns that when we don't pause to challenge assumptions, we risk suggesting an ineffective solution.

It's a stark reminder of what can happen on a discovery call if you don't listen to understand (not respond) so that you can ask great follow-up questions. When you skip an in-depth needs analysis, you miss an opportunity to uncover the root cause of a prospect's pain. Like Google overlooking or not seeking out critical feedback, failing to conduct a robust needs analysis in your sales process can result in misalignment with your prospect's true needs and lost sales opportunities.

The lesson from Google Glass highlights the importance of thoroughly understanding your prospects. It's easy to assume that you have the answers, but without asking the right questions and exploring potential concerns, you will miss critical insights. You may have answers, but they will be to the wrong questions. Google Glass was a multi-million-dollar failure because they built a brilliant solution for a problem they didn't confirm existed. If you're selling without thorough discovery, you're making the same mistake.

This is where needs analysis becomes invaluable. It involves identifying and understanding your prospect's specific challenges, goals, and pain points. This process allows you to tailor your sales pitch to address their most pressing concerns effectively. It means moving beyond surface-level information or questions like, "What keeps you up at night?" and delving into the intricacies of the Jobs to Be Done.[59]

Conducting a thorough needs analysis helps build trust and rapport with your prospects. Effective needs analysis is not just about gathering data; it's about understanding the context in which your prospects operate. It demonstrates that you are genuinely interested in their success and are willing to invest the time to understand their unique situation. This is the foundation of building strong, long-term relationships.

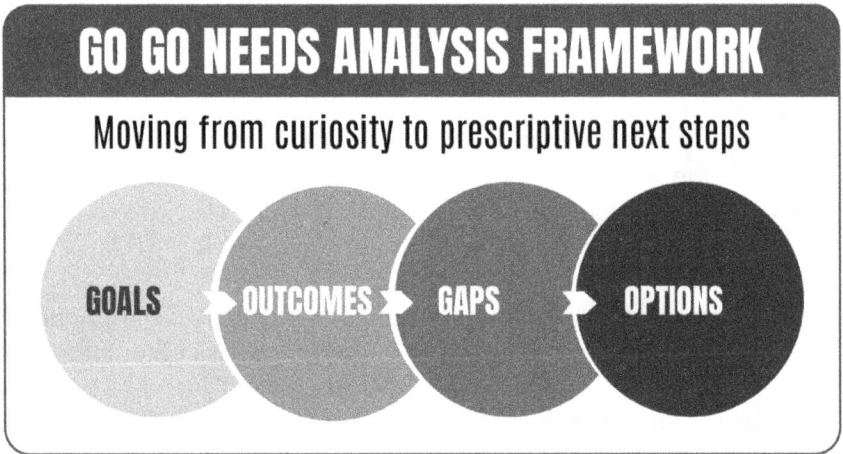

GO GO NEEDS ANALYSIS FRAMEWORK
Moving from curiosity to prescriptive next steps
GOALS → OUTCOMES → GAPS → OPTIONS

Needs Analysis: The Listening Muscle in Action

Needs analysis forms the backbone of effective discovery meetings and helps build strong relationships. By conducting a thorough needs analysis, you can uncover the specific challenges, goals, and pain points of your prospects, allowing you to tailor your sales approach and provide relevant solutions. This approach is critical because it ensures that you are not only addressing the immediate concerns of your prospects but also aligning your solutions with their long-term strategic objectives.

The GO GO Needs Analysis Framework is a structured approach to conducting effective discovery meetings. It stands for Goals, Outcomes, Gaps, and

---

[59] Christensen, Clayton M., Taddy Hall, Karen Dillon, and David S. Duncan. "Know Your Customers' 'Jobs to Be Done.'" Harvard Business Review, September 1, 2016. https://hbr.org/2016/09/know-your-customers-jobs-to-be-done.

Options. This framework helps ensure that you cover all principal drivers of your prospect's situation and provides a road map for understanding their needs comprehensively.

Goals: Identify your prospect's goals and needs. This involves understanding what they aim to achieve and why these goals matter.

Example Questions:

- "What are the main objectives your team is focusing on this quarter?"
- "Can you share more about the strategic goals you're aiming to achieve this year?"
- "What prompted you to look for a new solution at this time?"
- "It sounds like six to seven things are competing for your attention. Of those priorities, which is the most important to get right in the next six months?"
- "What has created an appetite to explore other solutions?"
- "What are you hearing from the executive leadership team about strategic goals for [year]?"
- "You said that X was your top priority. Help me understand what makes that so important to get right?"
- **Outcomes:** Understand and confirm the outcomes that would signify an ideal future state for the prospect. This involves asking questions that clarify what success looks like for them. These questions tend to be ROI-focused.

Example Questions:

- "What would a successful implementation of this solution look like for your team?"
- "If we could help you achieve [specific outcome], how would that impact your overall business goals?"
- "What specific results are you hoping to see from this project?"
- "It sounds like IF [ideal future state], THEN would that be worth [fast-tracking, budgeting for etc.]?"
- "If we are chatting a year from now and this project went perfectly, what would that mean for the work you do on a daily basis?

Gaps: Highlight the gaps between the prospect's current state and their goals or outcomes. This involves helping them see where their current strategies or solutions are falling short. These questions tend to be COI-focused.

Example Questions:

- "What challenges are you currently facing that prevent you from achieving your goals?"
- "How effective are your current solutions in addressing these challenges?"
- "Where do you see the biggest gaps in your current strategy?"
- "How confident are you in your existing team's ability to solve for [xxx]?"
- "What happens if you don't go forward with this project right now?"
- "Based on your scenario modeling, what would the fallout of [COI] be?"

- "Can we estimate how much is being lost by not acting on [insert problem]? Generally, when I do the math, folks find the cost of X is Y. Are you open to taking a few minutes to map out what the cost of not acting on [problem] would be at [Company]?"

Options: Present the options available to capture the positive outcomes, close the gaps, and agree on the next steps. This is where you ask final questions to better understand how to best move the sales process forward and then prescribe your solution as the means to achieve their goals.

Example Questions:

- "If we could show you a way to overcome [specific challenge], would you be open to discussing next steps?"
- "What criteria are you using to evaluate potential solutions?"
- "If we can put together a risk and compliance proposal that maps out how to win back 10% + of lost customers, THEN would that be enough to justify budget ask?"
- "Sounds like you're open to putting together a business plan in front [colleague]. IF I can help you create that to make sure you're 100% confident in the plan, THEN is this something you'll advocate this month?"
- "What are your top decision-making criteria? Which of those is most important?"

Applying the 3C Mindset Approach to Needs Analysis

The Pain Point Exercise is a practical application of the GO GO framework. It's designed to uncover the broad goals that prospects want to achieve, delve into specifics, highlight gaps, and explore options. This exercise can be instrumental in identifying the most pressing pain points and turning them into selling opportunities. The exercise begins by identifying the broad goal that the prospect wants to accomplish, such as increasing revenue or improving operational efficiency. Once this goal is identified, the next step is to delve into specifics by asking about their goals and desired outcomes. This helps uncover the pain points, such as a lack of leads or high customer acquisition costs.

After identifying the pain points, it's crucial to highlight the gaps and options. This involves discussing where the prospect's current solutions fall short and what potential improvements can be made. Finally, understanding why the prospect will act now instead of later is essential. This could be due to external factors like a deadline or internal factors like a shift in priorities. Integrating the Pain Point Exercise with the GO GO framework ensures a thorough and structured approach to needs analysis. It allows sales reps to uncover deep insights and tailor their solutions effectively.

Active listening is a crucial component of needs analysis. It involves fully engaging with your prospect, understanding their concerns, and responding thoughtfully. The 4R Active Listening Framework, which we covered earlier, guides this process: Reinforce, Restate, Resist, Relevance. By actively listening, you ensure that your prospect feels heard and valued. This not only helps in gathering accurate information but also in building trust. Remember, effective needs analysis is as much about listening as it is about asking questions.

Active listening involves more than just hearing words; it's about understanding the underlying emotions and motivations. When a prospect expresses concern about budget constraints, for example, it's essential to acknowledge their worry and explore it further. "I understand that budget is a concern. Can you share more about your current spending and what financial constraints you are facing?" This approach not only addresses the objection but also provides deeper insights into the prospect's needs.

Ask Deeper: The 3Cs Framework and Objection-Rooted Discovery

Earlier in the book, I introduced the 3C Mindset Approach - Curiosity, Conversation, Conclusion - for responding to objections. This framework is also vital during needs analysis. When prospects raise questions or concerns, lead with curiosity to understand the root cause. Engage in a conversation to explore their perspective further, and finally, reach a conclusion that addresses their concerns. For instance, if a prospect is hesitant about the cost of your solution, you could say, "I understand that budget is a concern. When you say financial constraints, what does that look like?" This approach shows that you are not just trying to overcome the objection but want to understand their concern and are genuinely interested in finding a solution that works for them.

False Assumptions: Don't Blame It on the Sauce

The story of Dr. Barry Marshall and Dr. Robin Warren is a powerful example of the importance of using curiosity to lead discovery. For many years, the medical community believed that peptic ulcers were caused by stress and diet, particularly spicy foods. If there were superlatives given out for "most likely to have a mini bottle of Tabasco loose in the bottom of their purse," you should always vote for me in that category, which means I won't stand for spicy food slander.

The conclusion that spicy foods cause ulcers was a foregone conclusion. In sales, we make these same kinds of assumptions every day. We assume when a prospect says, "we need to get better at cold calling," that the answer is to pitch them on your cold calling solution. We assume that because the last nine buyers we talked to were interested in AI, the tenth will be. Those assumptions create blind spots.

In the case of spicy food slander, Marshall and Warren weren't satisfied with the commonly held explanation. They observed that many patients with peptic ulcers also had a bacterial infection in their stomach lining, caused by *Helicobacter pylori*. This was a curious observation, as the prevailing belief was that no bacteria could survive in the acidic environment of the stomach. Driven by curiosity and a commitment to uncover the true cause of peptic ulcers, Marshall and Warren conducted a series of experiments. They cultured *Helicobacter pylori* from patients with ulcers and even went as far as to ingest the bacteria themselves. Marshall developed gastritis, proving their hypothesis that the bacterium was responsible for the inflammation that led to ulcers.

They resisted the urge to accept a commonly held belief just because it had been repeated for decades. That kind of discipline—pausing to ask if the obvious answer is actually correct—is what the Resist step of the 4R Active Listening Framework is all about. Sellers must do the same when a prospect shares a common concern or voices a need that the seller has heard dozens of other prospects share. You cannot assume the same superficial need has the same meaning for every prospect if you want to move from being just another seller to a trusted.

Sellers who don't resist the urge to assume end up treating symptoms instead of solving the root problem. They pitch features that don't map to business needs. They offer pricing before diagnosing value. And just like the medical community before Marshall and Warren, they end up managing surface-level issues instead of fixing what actually matters.

By asking tough questions, Marshall and Warren's research revolutionized the treatment of ulcers, shifting the focus from managing symptoms to eradicating the bacterial infection with antibiotics. This story exemplifies the power of not settling for superficial conclusions, and in 2005, their work was recognized with the Nobel Prize in Physiology or Medicine.

Just as Marshall and Warren's commitment to thorough investigation led to a groundbreaking discovery, conducting a deep needs analysis in sales can uncover hidden opportunities and insights that might otherwise be missed. This approach can be the difference between a missed opportunity and a successful sale. It underscores the importance of curiosity, asking deeper questions, listening actively, and never settling for the obvious or superficial answer.

It's crucial to instill the importance of asking great questions and conducting deep needs analysis within your team. The ability to ask the right questions and understand a prospect's needs is what sets successful salespeople apart from the rest. This practice not only builds trust and rapport with prospects but also leads to more effective and tailored solutions.

Needs analysis must be rooted in genuine interest. Sellers have to care about helping their buyers achieve a positive outcome. Without that, needs analysis feels like a self-serving barrage of questions instead of an advisory conversation. When your sales team approaches each discovery call with the intent to understand and help, they are more likely to uncover valuable insights that can drive meaningful conversations. This deep understanding forms the foundation of strong, long-lasting relationships with clients.

And, if you're wondering, my favorite off-the-shelf hot sauce is Crystal's. My favorite specialty is Bajan Hot Pepper Sauce, and yes, I've tried TRUFF, and yes, it's delicious, but it'll never be my number one. [*]

Great Questions Build Great Salespeople

The importance of asking great questions cannot be overstated. Questions that delve into the prospect's business challenges, strategic

---

*Author's note

goals, and current solutions help paint a comprehensive picture of their needs. According to Gong Labs, "You're most likely to nail your discovery call when you ask between 11-14 targeted questions." [60] Targeted questions, by definition, cannot be generic (meaning don't show up to every call with the same exact list of 14 questions), and they are not a list of qualifying questions. Targeted questions show you understand the prospect's operating environment and have been listening to the pain points they've already shared on the call. This thorough understanding allows your team to position your product or service as the ideal solution to bridge the gaps identified during the needs analysis.

To help your team optimize those 11 – 14 questions, print this GO GO cheat sheet:

GO: GOALS & OUTCOMES

GOALS
Identify your prospects goals and needs.

QUESTION EXAMPLE:
It sounds like 6-7 things are competing for your attention of those priorities, which is the most important to get right in the next 6 months?

OUTCOMES
Understand & confirm which outcomes would result in an ideal future state.

QUESTION EXAMPLE:
It sounds like IF [ideal future state], THEN that would worth [fast-tracking, budgeting for etc]?

GO: GAPS & OPTIONS

GAPS
Help your prospect understand the gaps between their current state & ideal future state

QUESTION EXAMPLE:
How confident are you in your existing team's ability to solve for [xxx]?

OPTIONS
Prescribe options and agree to next steps.

QUESTION EXAMPLE:
IF we could walk you through how to accomplish [x], THEN would you agree that it makes sense to schedul a follow-up call?

---

[60] "11 Top Sales Discovery Call Tips for 2023: Gong Labs Sales Insights." Gong, July 3, 2024. https://www.gong.io/resources/labs/here-are-the-11-best-discovery-call-tips-youll-read-this-year/#:~:text=This%20is%20grossly%20oversimplified.,an%20issue%20the%20buyer%20raised.

Hosting Great Discovery Calls: Where Curiosity Meets Structure

Hosting great discovery calls is essential. By mastering the art of asking great questions and leveraging the GO GO Needs Analysis Framework, you can uncover your prospects' true needs, build stronger relationships, and position your solutions effectively. Top B2B sales professionals don't push their product; they understand their prospects' needs and show how their solution can meet those needs effectively. By implementing these practices within your sales team, you can drive successful outcomes and achieve long-term success.

Call Preparation: Conversation, Not Interrogation

Preparation is crucial for a successful discovery call. It's not a check-the-box information-gathering activity. Sellers need to demonstrate that they value the prospect's time and have done their homework by coming to calls with a point of view (POV) about how they can help. Strong call preparation gives you the context to connect the dots between your solution and what matters most to the prospect. It allows you to come in with a point of view, not just a list of questions.

Discovery Call Preparation Worksheet

My pre-call preparation has helped me close deals with much of the Fortune 500. Here's a breakdown of how you can earn the right to your prospect's time by showing up prepared:

Account Preparation

1. **Financials**

   - Review the company's financial statements, recent earnings reports, and any financial news. Understand their financial health and key performance indicators.
   - Example: "I noticed in your latest earnings report that your revenue increased by 15%, but there was a notable drop in your operating margin. Can you tell me more about the factors contributing to this?"

2. News

- Stay updated with the latest news about the company. Look for recent announcements, press releases, and news articles.
- Example: "I read about your recent acquisition of XYZ Company. How is the integration process going, and what challenges have you faced so far?"

3. Competitors

- Identify the company's main competitors and understand their market positioning. This will help you contextualize your solutions.
- Example: "How do you differentiate yourself from your main competitor, ABC Corp, especially regarding customer service?"

This principle underlines the need to not only uncover hidden pain points but also educate prospects about the broader impacts and potential solutions. The goal of preparation is to show up to the call educated and with a POV. Instead of asking "What are your priorities?" a well-prepared seller can ask, "Based on my research, I'm guessing [X] or [Y] are top-of-mind for you right now. Is that where we should focus this call, or what is more pressing?"

Preparation is how you earn the right to lead the conversation. It shows the buyer that you've taken the time to understand their world before asking them to share it with you.

On the next page, you will find the Discovery Call Preparation Worksheet I used as an enterprise seller and sales leader. By following this comprehensive preparation approach and adding additional categories needed for your product or service, you not only demonstrate respect for your prospect's time but also position yourself as a knowledgeable and trustworthy advisor. Showing up prepared is how you earn the right to your prospect's time and attention, making it more likely they will see the value in what you offer. Achieving this level of impact signifies a truly meaningful discovery meeting.

This approach builds strong relationships and significantly increases your chances of closing deals. When you prepare well, the conversation shifts from an interrogation to a two-way strategy session.

Case Study: Transforming Discovery Calls from Transactional to Trusted Conversations

In 2024, the CEO of a fast-growing SaaS company came to me with an ambitious goal. He wanted his sales team to increase their discovery call win rate from 28% to 45%. The organization had already been working hard, making acquisitions, launching new solutions, and building a strong reputation in their market. But the transactional style of their outbound selling was holding them back. Discovery calls felt like rehearsed pitches, not genuine conversations, and showed in their numbers.

This CEO believed in something different. He wanted his sales team to create value at every touchpoint. He saw discovery calls as an opportunity to give prospects real insights and helpful advice, even if they didn't buy. His commitment was clear: no more canned scripts, no more rushed conversations, and absolutely no hard-selling tactics. Instead, he empowered his team to

4. **Industry Trends**

- Research current trends and challenges in the company's industry. This will allow you to discuss broader market influences affecting their business.
- Example: "With the rapid advancements in AI technology, how do you see your industry evolving in the next few years?"

5. **Customer Industry Trends**

- Understand the trends and challenges faced by the company's customers. This insight can help tailor your solutions to better meet their end-user needs.
- Example: "Given the increasing demand for sustainable products among your customers, how are you adapting your supply chain practices?"

6. Previous Interactions

- Review any past interactions your company has had with the prospect. This includes previous meetings, emails, and touchpoints.
- Example: "In our last conversation, you mentioned challenges with your CRM system. Have there been any updates or improvements since then?"

7. Company Information

- Familiarize yourself with the company's history, mission, values, and key executives. This background knowledge can help build rapport.
- Example: "I see that your company was founded in 1995 and has grown significantly since. What core values do you believe have driven this success?"

become trusted advisors. The goal wasn't just to sell. It was to create relationships built on expertise and genuine curiosity.

This resonated deeply with the sales team. Far from resisting change, these sellers were eager for it. They wanted to learn. They wanted to share valuable knowledge with their prospects. They knew that old-school, pressure-driven tactics weren't working. They were hungry for tools and strategies to have smarter conversations.

My job was to help them make this shift. It was time to build a discovery call process that earned the right to the buyer's attention and consideration, every single time.

A New Mindset: Preparation as a Foundation

Before the sellers could have better conversations, they needed a better process behind the scenes. Preparation became central to the conversation strategy. Discovery calls are often treated casually. But when your aim is a 45% close rate, casual doesn't cut it. The new process began the moment the prospect booked their call online.

As soon as a discovery call hit an AE's calendar, a series of carefully choreographed actions kicked off. We updated the confirmation sequence to highlight the priority the prospect stated when booking the meeting to show they were paying attention.

We rolled out a structured pre-call checklist so the AEs could spend time on research that lent them authority with the prospect. They reviewed the prospect's LinkedIn profile, checked recent company news, and tapped into past interactions. This was about going deeper to genuinely understand who they were about to speak with.

They weren't prepping to pitch. They were building a detailed road map to guide a meaningful conversation. By the time they logged into Zoom, the AE had developed a point of view about what mattered most to the prospect and had a thoughtful plan in place to deliver value.

Turning the Discovery Call Into a Conversation

The new discovery calls began differently than before. Sellers started with a clear, concise agenda, but instead of immediately pitching features, they confirmed their understanding of the prospect's key challenges. They would say, "From what I understand, your main priority right now is [known priority]. Does that sound right?" This subtle shift immediately changed the

8. Social Media Activity

- Check the company's social media channels for recent posts, announcements, and engagements. This can provide real-time insights into their current focus and initiatives.
- Example: "I noticed your recent LinkedIn post about launching a new product line. Can you share more about the inspiration behind this launch?"

Prospect Research

1. Pertinent Conversations

- Identify what the prospect has been discussing that relates to the problem your solution addresses. This shows you're attuned to their current concerns.
- Example: "I saw your recent post about data security concerns. How

are you currently addressing these issues within your organization?"

2. **Connections**

- Look into mutual connections who can provide insights or vouch for your credibility. This can help establish trust.
- Example: "I noticed we both know John Doe, who spoke highly of your leadership. How do you know John?"

3. **Work History**

- Review the prospect's professional background and career progression. This can help you understand their expertise and approach.
- Example: "I see you've been with XYZ Company for five years, and you previously worked in a similar role at ABC Corp. How has your

energy of the call. The prospect felt heard right from the start.

From there, the AE could better prioritize the conversation highlights. The real dialogue started with dedicated time for discovery, where the seller was not sharing their screen. This was a conversation, not a presentation or interrogation. The AE's role was to actively listen, not to respond, but to truly understand. Smart, insightful questions guided the discussion, exploring the prospect's current processes, pain points, and goals.

The AE's job wasn't to sell solutions at this stage. It was to uncover deeper context and clarify the real business impacts at stake. The answers helped them frame the rest of the call. By carefully listening and then using that understanding to ask even smarter follow-up questions, they proved their expertise without ever pushing a sale.

Only after thoroughly exploring the prospect's needs did the AE move into a focused, tailored demo. They kept the demo limited to the two or three most relevant features. Rather than simply demonstrating product functionality, sellers tied each feature directly back to the prospect's stated problems. Instead of pushing capabilities, they shared real customer stories and outcomes, which helped build immediate credibility.

Throughout the demo, the AE continued to ask thoughtful questions and sought feedback. By listening intently to each response, the seller adjusted their approach. This reinforced the fact that the call was about the prospect's needs, not just their own product.

A Value-Based Close, Not a Hard Sell

The call's conclusion was simple, clear, and respectful. The AE reconfirmed the prospect's understanding of the value they'd receive, outlined a recommended next step, and openly asked about hesitations. Rather than shying away from objections, they leaned into them through careful listening and strategic questioning. For example, they asked, "Is there anything we haven't covered that would help you feel confident moving forward?"

If the prospect was ready, the next step was straightforward. If not, the AE ensured a specific follow-up call was scheduled with clearly defined objectives. No ambiguity and no loose ends. This disciplined approach kept the sales process moving forward with respect for the prospect's timeline.

Underneath this new discovery call framework was something even more important: the company's cultural commitment. The CEO

experience there influenced your current strategies?"

4. **Knowledge About Your Company**

- Determine what the prospect already knows about your company from past interactions. This helps avoid redundancy and focus on new information.
- Example: "You mentioned attending our webinar last month. What aspects of the presentation resonated most with you?"

5. **Interest Triggers**

- Identify what initially sparked the prospect's interest in your company, such as a webinar, cold email, or referral.
- Example: "I understand you were referred to us by Jane Smith. Can you share what specifically piqued

your interest in our solutions?"

6. **Preparation to Earn Their Time**

- Think about how you can demonstrate value and relevance from the very beginning. Prepare to show that you have a deep understanding of their needs and challenges.
- Example: "Based on my research, I've identified three key areas where our solution could significantly improve your operational efficiency. I'm excited to discuss these with you."

emphasized from the beginning that these calls were about creating real value, regardless of whether the prospect bought.

Sellers felt empowered. Prospects felt genuinely supported. They weren't being sold to; they were being listened to, understood, and advised.

The results spoke for themselves. By aligning process, preparation, and listening skills, the team quickly moved closer to their ambitious goal of a 45% win rate. More importantly, discovery calls transformed from a transactional chore into meaningful conversations that elevated the entire sales team's approach.

Discovery is where most deals are won or lost. If your salespeople treat it like a quick qualification call, you end up with dirty data, a weak pipeline, and rushed demos that don't convert. When they show up prepared, ask better questions, and use discovery to educate and uncover hidden needs, everything changes. Strong discovery isn't just how you close more deals; it's how you build real trust and long-term relationships.

Part 3

Operationalizing Success

CHAPTER 16

Creating Repeatable Processes to Ensure Durable Growth

> *"We are what we repeatedly do. Excellence, then, is not an act, but a habit." –Aristotle*

Creating repeatable processes is key to scaling success and achieving long-term growth. In a rapidly changing sales environment, a repeatable process isn't a rigid formula but rather a dynamic framework that enables your team to adapt quickly while maintaining consistency. When your team establishes repeatable habits, they're more equipped to deliver consistent results.

This chapter provides a blueprint for developing processes that can be consistently applied and refined, with a focus on continuous learning and adaptation. Sales leaders will learn how to establish a culture where processes are regularly reviewed, tested, and optimized, keeping pace with changing market conditions and customer needs.

3 Steps to Creating Repeatable Processes

- Define Key Activities for Success.
- Build Repeatable Processes and Document Them.
- Build a Culture of Continuous Improvement.

Step 1: Define Key Activities for Success

In 2008, I was a new sales manager with a team of six. I'd been promoted into sales management after a mere six months in my job, after my manager had been unceremoniously shown the door.

At the time, I was working in a transactional sales environment, and despite managing a team of six, I also had a quota. Additionally, I was responsible for hiring, onboarding, training, sales operations, account management, etc. When folks talk about a full-cycle role, I don't think they've ever imagined something as full-cycle as this. We were not supported by human resources, sales enablement, or revenue operations. We were expected to figure it all out by ourselves.

As you might guess, I was overwhelmed. I was working long days. I felt like I was always busy. I also felt like I wasn't getting much done.

I started watching YouTube videos, hoping to learn the secret to adding more hours to my day, and I did, sort of. I stumbled across a video of Peter Turla,[61] a nerdy former NASA scientist, talking about time management and setting priorities. He shared a story from his early days at NASA, where he looked at his colleagues who were sitting at organized desks, leaving work at five PM, and delivering more results than Peter was. Peter interviewed his colleagues and discovered that the difference between how they were working and how he was working was that they had clearly stated priorities and organized their days accordingly.

At the time, I felt like I had a dozen priorities. What was most important – hitting my quota, making sure my team was to quota, making sure I backfilled my head count, division-wide sales enablement responsibilities, or something else entirely? I felt like I was juggling a dozen responsibilities, and some of them seemed to be at odds with one another.

The Power of Knowing Your Key Result Area

When I heard Peter talk about feeling constantly busy at work but not being quite sure what he even accomplished at the end of the day, I was

---

[61] Channel Makers, "11 Essential YouTube Video Title Tips," YouTube video, 11:58, published April 7, 2020, https://www.youtube.com/watch?v=1rFMWRYnT18.

captivated. He went on to talk about the idea of a Key Result Area (KRA). Your KRA is a North Star priority. It is the single most important result you are working toward. I used this new concept to uncover that the most important priority for me was enabling my team to hit quota.

If my team were hitting quota, a lot of the other tasks clamoring for my attention would be less urgent. If my team was hitting quota, it meant that we were locked into profit generating habits, which means I was likely to also hit quota and have high rep retention. If my reps were happy and stayed in seat, I could spend less time hiring and onboarding.

I shared the KRA concept with my team, who were also feeling overwhelmed by the demands to set meetings, close deals, and manage the clients. They used it to dial in their focus as well. We had a newfound clarity on where to spend our time and energy. As a result, we outperformed our peers.

Shortly after unlocking the power of knowing my KRA, I was exposed to the Eisenhower Matrix, which Stephen Covey popularized in his *New York Times* bestselling book, *The 7 Habits of Highly Effective People*. It's a powerful time management tool invented, or at least attributed to, President Dwight D. Eisenhower. The Matrix plots urgent, not urgent, important, and not important across four quadrants. We don't have the space to deep-dive time management best practices (although maybe that will be my next book). However, I encourage you to spend the time doing a prioritization audit for yourself and your team to help create the space to adopt the proven formula for pipeline generation you've just learned.

Primer Exercise: Time Management

The three most important questions to answer for yourself to get started are:

First, what is my Key Result Area (KRA)?

A KRA is not a moonshot goal - it helps you identify the most important work that you need to get done to support *your* goal. It is a singular North Star professional goal.

Next, ask yourself: What are the activities that directly support my Key Result Area?

Be specific and use the Eisenhower Matrix to understand what tasks are truly important in the context of your KRA.

Just as important as identifying the activities that support your KRA is asking: What can I automate, delegate, or delete?

Building a profit generating pipeline requires you to be laser-focused. Focus comes from understanding what you need to do less of, as much as it comes from knowing what you want to do more of.

Understanding that it can be extremely tempting to focus more on metrics (e.g., number of dials or number of emails) over behaviors and results, I encourage you to take the time to identify which activities truly drive revenue and results.

Peter Drucker, a man often credited with "inventing management," shares this insight: "Efficiency is doing things right; effectiveness is doing the right things." By zeroing in on essential activities (KRA activities), you create efficient, effective processes.

Step 2: Build Repeatable Processes and Document Them

Documentation is critical to making any process repeatable. Clear guidelines and an accessible, shared source of truth ensure best practices aren't just concepts. They become habits your team can follow. When each team member operates from the same framework, the result is a consistent, effective process that scales without sacrificing quality.

Most sales teams are eager to scale. But scaling a process that isn't repeatable creates chaos. If your system can't be followed consistently with reliable outcomes, it isn't ready for growth. Before you add more sellers or increase your outbound volume, you need a foundation that can withstand that kind of pressure.

I always err on the side of overcommunication and simplicity when building standard operating procedures. Not because sellers lack skill, but because if a process is easier to follow, it's easier to stick with. And if it's easier to stick with, it gets used.

Earlier in the book, we saw how Emily earned Kevin's trust by coaching him through his discomfort and skepticism. Kevin wasn't a seller who naturally embraced structure. He resisted scripting. He preferred to lean on charm instead of process. However, when Emily took the time to listen to him, coach him with data, and model the behavior she wanted to see, Kevin began to trust her. When she introduced a new outbound messaging framework and asked him to follow a specific sequence of steps, he didn't roll his eyes. He followed it. Not because the process was perfect, but because he trusted the person who gave it to him to have made data-backed decisions that supported his success. Structured processes are not enough: your team also needs to believe in the system. That's the moment sales leaders should be aiming for. Trust doesn't make change effortless, but it does make it possible.

> *"Trust doesn't make change effortless, but it does make it possible."*

When that trust is in place, documentation becomes a multiplier. It gives your team a consistent way to execute, while creating room for judgment and flexibility. Process documents aren't meant to be rigid scripts. They're living tools. They anchor your team to what's working now, while giving you space to evolve with the market and the needs of your customers.

Document what works. Make it visible. Make it accessible. Make it clear enough to follow without guesswork. Then focus on adoption with the understanding that change doesn't happen overnight.

Step 3: Build a Culture of Continuous Improvement

If repeatability is the foundation of scalable sales, then continuous improvement is what keeps that foundation stable as trends and the market shift. The processes you've worked so hard to build aren't meant to be locked away in a dusty folder. They're meant to be lived, coached, trained, tested, and iterated.

That starts with building a culture where your team doesn't just follow the process but understands it, contributes to it, and sees the value of improving it over time.

Six Sigma research shows that companies with strong continuous improvement cultures "outperform peers by 20% or more on key financial metrics."[62] McKinsey notes that the increased capacity and efficiency from continuous improvement can be worth two to three times the value of the cost improvements alone, as it enables organizations to enhance customer experience, increase employee engagement, and improve cross-functional collaboration.[63]

Creating a culture of continuous improvement starts with psychological safety, as we discussed throughout chapters 1 to 3. Reps need to know they can try new things, share honest feedback, and ask for help without fear of judgment. If your team doesn't feel safe to fail, they won't feel empowered to improve. This is especially important when you ask them to test and iterate sales processes. They need to know that bringing data to the table - even if it shows a technique didn't work - is not a sign of failure but a sign of growth.

When sellers feel supported and respected for their contributions, they're more likely to engage deeply, experiment thoughtfully, and commit to the process of getting better. Psychological safety isn't a nice-to-have. It's the foundation that allows your team to refine, improve, and scale what works.

To move from chaos to clarity: define key activities for success, build repeatable processes and document them, and build a culture of continuous improvement.

---

[62] Team, Editorial. "Continuous Improvement Strategies: A Guide to Sustainable Business Excellence." SixSigma.us, May 19, 2025. https://www.6sigma.us/kaizen/continuous-improvement-strategies/.

[63] "How Continuous Improvement Can Build a Competitive Edge." McKinsey & Company. Accessed June 20, 2025. https://www.mckinsey.com/capabilities/people-and-organizational-performance/our-insights/the-organization-blog/how-continuous-improvement-can-build-a-competitive-edge.

Train, Coach, Test, Repeat

Train your team to execute the process consistently, but also coach them one-on-one to refine how they execute based on their individual strengths. Maybe one rep delivers high-converting emails but struggles with live calls. Another thrives on the phone but skips too many LinkedIn touches. Use coaching to help them optimize within the process rather than abandon it entirely. Process and performance aren't separate. When you train and coach through the lens of the process, you drive improvement that scales.

But coaching alone isn't enough. You can't just trust your gut when it comes to refining processes. You must follow the data.

Every sequence, every segment-specific value prop, every touchpoint generates insight. Start by tracking conversion rates at each stage of your pipeline so you can identify where deals are falling off. Analyze engagement by channel and use that insight to double down on what's working. Look at time-based behaviors. Does your team convert more meetings when they follow up within 24 hours? Does the response rate tank when sellers stack too many touches too quickly? Let the data show you.

The data doesn't replace your judgment. It enhances it. You're not building custom rules for every situation. You're building a repeatable system that gets smarter every time you use it.

Let Data Be Your Co-Pilot

Earlier in this book, we talked about creating a baseline. Having a data-backed baseline is what makes experimentation meaningful. Once you have a defined process and trackable benchmarks, your team is empowered to test creative ideas. A rep can try a bold new subject line or swap in a video message instead of a second call, not because they're guessing but because you've trained them to run controlled tests and measure impact against the standard.

That's how you create a culture of continuous improvement. You build a repeatable formula. You train and coach the team to ensure they trust and can follow the formula. You collect and follow the data to iterate on your processes.

Repeatable processes become scalable when they are actively coached, consistently measured, and continuously improved. When repeatable processes are embraced and improved over time, they create the foundation for something bigger – long-term, durable growth.

Durable growth only happens when your processes are clear, repeatable, and consistently followed by your team. Avoid the shiny objects and silver bullets that promise short-term wins. Almost always, those short-term wins come at the expense of your long-term growth.

Following the proven formula you've learned in this book will empower you to create long-term, durable growth. The early steps of the formula teach your team how to build a focused outbound strategy. They learn to segment their territory, create buyer-centric value propositions, and build the strategic foundation of a micro-campaign. From there, they learn how to write sales copy that earns attention, build sequences that earn the right to follow up, and reach prospects across multiple channels in their channel of choice. And once those messages land, the formula helps you guide your team to earn trust in a discovery call, respond to objections with an attitude of gratitude, and deliver personalized insights that drive revenue.

Putting It All Together: From Chaos to Clarity

Every chapter in this book is connected. While all of it works in isolation, the power is in stacking all of the concepts together. You can't scale outbound if your reps don't know who to reach out to, where to find them, and what to say. You now hold the key to help them unlock those insights.

When you create documentation, deliver training, and coach consistently, you turn good ideas into standard operating procedures. Getting extremely clear about your Key Result Area gives you and your team a North Star priority, the single most important result you're working toward.

Follow the data, and invite your team into the process of refinement. This is how you build a single source of truth that evolves with your market and your team - a resource far more powerful than a dozen slide decks sitting untouched in a folder. This approach turns tactics into systems, systems into habits, and helps you build a sales organization that earns trust, drives revenue, and delivers results you can count on.

You got this.

CHAPTER 17

Bias Toward Action

"The most effective way to do it is to do it." –Amelia Earhart

The Power of Action

Throughout this book, we've explored companies and individuals who faced pivotal moments where swift, decisive action was the difference between thriving and becoming obsolete.

Netflix didn't succeed by having the best idea. They succeeded because Reed Hastings saw changing customer behaviors and took immediate action, testing and iterating relentlessly until streaming became the future of entertainment. Meanwhile, Blockbuster hesitated, clinging to an outdated model until it was too late to recover.

Tiger Woods wasn't content with his record-breaking victory at the 1997 Masters. He didn't wait until his competitors caught up. Instead, he proactively dismantled and rebuilt his swing, enduring temporary setbacks because he knew a bias toward action was essential. His willingness to evolve before being forced to change was the hallmark of true greatness.

AND1 burst onto the basketball scene, not because they had the deepest pockets or biggest stars, but because they acted boldly. They bypassed traditional advertising and met their audience on streetball courts and with homemade mixtapes. They met their customers where they were, earning loyalty that money alone couldn't buy.

Calculated Progress over Perfection

What each of these stories underscores is a fundamental truth in leadership and growth: a bias toward action isn't just a competitive advantage, it's a necessity.

As we explored in Chapter 2, growth is scary. Change won't always feel comfortable, and that's okay. Fear of making mistakes or choosing the wrong direction can be paralyzing, but hesitation is often riskier than decisive action. The market rewards those who act, learn, and iterate quickly. Success doesn't come from perfect predictions; it comes from taking informed risks and rapidly learning from the outcomes.

I've benefited from a bias toward action throughout my career. A few times it led me to fail fast, like when I ran a $10,000 direct mail campaign that got a 1.7% reply rate and a single qualified lead. However, it's mostly allowed me to leapfrog my career and the goals of my team. An idea I find myself coming back to is that you can only learn so much by knowing; the rest you have to learn by doing. Now is the time for doing.

Bain's research highlights that organizational drag (bureaucratic processes and slow decision-making) costs the U.S. economy more than $3 trillion a year. Companies that reduce organizational drag by fostering a bias for action recover significant productive power and growth potential.[64] Leaders who cultivate a bias for action by delegating, moving resources quickly, and committing to decisions outperform slower competitors.

You stand at your own crossroads. You've absorbed the proven formula outlined in this book, you understand the buyer-centric methodology, and, by following Kevin and Emily's journeys, you've seen that embracing new ways of working leads to durable growth. Championing a pivot to strategic, buyer-first selling requires courage, consistency, and effort, but it's worth it.

Leading Through Change: A Sales Leader's Role

We've talked candidly about the challenges of leading through change. You've considered the courage it takes to try something new and confronted the fear of failing. The reality is that growth demands decisive action and always involves risk. Your team might resist at first, just as Kevin initially resisted Emily's process changes. Your calling as a sales

---

[64] Boogaard, Kat. "What Is a Bias for Action (and How Do You Build It)?" Marlee. Accessed June 20, 2025. https://getmarlee.com/blog/bias-for-action.

leader is not to avoid risk; your calling is to lead your team through it, with empathy, transparency, and courage.

Evolving your outbound strategy won't always feel easy, but you know by now that ease rarely leads to lasting success. Growth comes from being willing to challenge assumptions, test new approaches, and pivot when the market demands it. That is your edge. Whether it's rethinking your messaging, trying a fresh format, or showing up in unexpected places, lasting success belongs to those who are willing to act before they're forced to.

Creating a buyer-centric, strategically aligned, highly effective outbound approach takes time, courage, and commitment. You will face setbacks along the way, but the cost of inaction is far greater. The examples you've seen prove it's worth the effort. When you invest in building repeatable processes, earn your team's trust, and follow the data, you create something durable - a pipeline that generates profits and sustains success.

It's more than a process; it's a proven formula. You've earned the right to lead this change. Now, the only step left is to act.

Kevin and Emily: Where Are They Now

Throughout the book, the story of Kevin and Emily illustrates how these principles play out in real life. Kevin's initial struggle and eventual success under Emily's thoughtful leadership showed what happens when leaders invest in coaching, trust-building, and carefully designed processes. Kevin embraced the structured sales practices Emily introduced and thrived. His growth revealed deeper insights into his own strengths and aspirations.

Although he experienced tangible success in his outbound sales role, Kevin recognized that high-volume SaaS sales wasn't aligned with his career goals. Reflecting honestly on the type of work he was most passionate about, Kevin wanted a role that emphasized meaningful, long-term client relationships. He decided to apply for an account management job at a company that sold to small businesses. This new role allowed his personable nature and the selling skills that he had cultivated under Emily's mentorship to blossom. This shift to account management provided Kevin greater professional fulfillment because he was able to focus on a small number of important client relationships.

Kevin's growth wasn't just a testament to Emily's leadership. It was a mirror reflecting back her own evolution. Emily still vividly remembers the moment Kevin landed his first major deal using the structured approach they had practiced relentlessly together. It was more than a sales win. It was tangible proof of the trust they had built and a turning point for both of them.

Through Kevin, Emily saw clearly how adaptability and empathy were not merely leadership ideals, but essential practices that shaped real careers and lives. She learned that successful leadership means uncovering and prioritizing the unique needs of each team member, creating a supportive, inclusive environment. Witnessing Kevin's evolution helped Emily see the broader impact of her leadership style and the effectiveness of the *Earn the Right* mindset - meaningful success in sales and leadership comes from earning trust and recognizing that the best outcomes happen when human values guide professional actions.

For Emily, stepping into a VP of Sales role was a significant career milestone. She envisioned building an environment where hundreds of "Kevins" could find their true calling, grow confidently, and feel deeply valued. While it took her a while to find her footing as a sales leader, Emily was now in a position to help reps achieve their personal career goals, which (she hoped) meant inspiring some of them to become the next generation of sales leaders.

Kevin and Emily's story, at its heart, offers a timeless reminder: that investing deeply in genuine human relationships is not only a cornerstone of sales excellence but the very foundation of meaningful leadership and professional growth.

Why It Matters to Me

Throughout my career, I've been both Kevin and Emily. I've felt firsthand the frustration of being handed outdated sales tactics and a list of leads, asked to perform without real guidance or meaningful support.

Unlike Kevin, I never had a leader who invested deeply in my growth or provided me with a clear, proven process to follow. Instead, I pieced together what worked through trial and error, often brute-forcing my way to success. Later, stepping into leadership myself, I became Emily. I had to figure out how to effectively coach, guide, and support my own teams, despite never experiencing that type of mentorship myself.

Arriving at the clarity and confidence behind the *Earn the Right* approach wasn't a straightforward path. It required me to revisit and challenge long-held beliefs I'd internalized about what makes someone success-ful in sales. I had to intentionally reject the outdated methods I'd been taught and lean into the uncertainty that comes with embracing new, untested ways of working, even when it felt uncomfortable or risky.

At the start of my career, I was proud of being a sales chameleon. I was certain it was a strength that I could easily pivot from selling to a Fortune 250 CFO based in New York in the morning to a power plant manager down in the deep south in the afternoon. It felt like a superpower to find a fit-for-purpose way to connect with buyers, whether it was a 4-figure transactional sale or a 6-figure consultative sale. That confidence was eventually beaten out of me by recruiters and hiring managers who told me that it was a weakness. They insisted that what really made sellers and sales leaders worth hiring was having 10+ years of experience sell-ing the exact same type of product to the exact same type of ICP.

Unfortunately, after years of hearing that a strength I coveted was viewed as a weakness, I started believing it.

Everything changed in 2017 when I began my entrepreneurial journey. This journey forced me to create my own frameworks and name my methodologies, and it allowed me to see my professional experiences in a new light. I realized something important. My career has taken me from working within a massive global corporation to being employee number one at a bootstrapped startup. I've applied my knowledge to transactional one-call closes as successfully as I've applied it to consulta-tive subscription models. I've come to understand that the sales funda-mentals that I teach work in every situation because I'm not teaching tricks and tactics to steal attention; I'm centering the buyer to learn how to earn attention.

I was uncovering fundamental truths that consistently delivered results. Far from being a weakness, this range of experiences actually made me uniquely qualified to identify what truly works in sales.

That is what you are seeing here, a blueprint that has worked, and continues to work, in the pursuit of building a profit generating pipeline. Creating and embracing the *Earn the Right* approach came from rejecting ineffective methods, experimenting boldly (and sometimes failing), and gradually uncovering strategies rooted in integrity, trust, and authentic human connection.

This mindset and the structured formula it inspired have transformed my professional path and personal perspective on sales, leadership, and business relationships. My greatest hope is that by sharing this formula, I can empower you to experience that same transformative clarity and growth, building a career you're proud of while creating results that truly matter.

Act Now for Lasting Growth

Profit Generating Pipeline has guided you through redefining sales leadership with a buyer-first approach. Together, we explored a buyer-centric pipeline creation method, transforming the typical sales process into a deeply relational and highly effective system built on trust, value, and relevance.

With a refined approach, your team will learn to personalize at scale by balancing quantity and quality. The result is a pipeline that consistently delivers meaningful relationships and measurable outcomes.

At the core of this method is a powerful mindset shift: you must earn the right to ask for your prospect's attention, time, and business by showing up with relevance and integrity.

Your ability to build and scale a profit generating pipeline is tied directly to your leadership and commitment to these core values. Empower your sales team to embrace a culture of curiosity, consistency, and continuous improvement. Create repeatable processes anchored in clear documentation and reliable data. Foster an environment that rewards creativity and accountability, ensuring everyone feels psychologically safe enough to experiment, learn, and grow.

By embedding these practices into your sales culture, you position your organization for sustainable, durable growth. You're not just generating pipeline – you're cultivating trust, earning credibility, and establishing lasting relationships that lead to long-term revenue growth. This proven formula empowers your team to drive consistent results and positions your organization as a trusted partner in the eyes of your customers.

Your core takeaway should be clear: lasting success in sales leadership doesn't come from tricks, tactics, or demanding more activity. It comes from intentionally earning trust, prioritizing data-backed selling practices, and deeply investing in your people. By applying structured, repeatable processes with empathy-driven mentorship, you will foster meaningful relationships, lasting growth, and sustainable outcomes starting today. Your role goes beyond generating pipeline. You're shaping careers, building connections, and creating an environment where your team feels inspired to deliver their best.

Earn trust, lead authentically, and build something remarkable.

IMPLEMENTATION AIDS

Putting What You've Learned Into Practice

"Promise me you'll always remember: You're braver than you believe, and stronger than you seem, and smarter than you think."
– Winnie the Pooh

Hosting a Sales Book Club Discussion

In Chapter 1, I shared that I run a monthly Business Book Club. Leslie's Book Club is now in its fourth year and has become a valued space to candidly share professional milestones and mistakes.

If you're considering replicating that dynamic by hosting a book club for your team. I've put together a dozen questions to get you started. Change management is one of the toughest and most important jobs of a sales leader. Creating space for understanding and transparent conversation is a meaningful step in pursuit of that goal.

Questions for Your Book Club Discussion:

1. After reading *Profit Generating Pipeline*, what is one belief you had about sales or leadership that has changed or been challenged?
2. What specific technique or strategy from the book do you plan to apply immediately in your own work? How do you anticipate it will help?
3. The book emphasizes earning trust in every interaction. Discuss practical ways you can better earn trust with your buyers or team this week.

4. Are there ideas in the book that you feel might be difficult to implement in your own organization? Discuss why and explore potential solutions.
5. How do the concepts of micro-campaigns and Value-Based Segmentation fundamentally shift traditional sales thinking?
6. How might you adjust your messaging strategy to reduce friction and cognitive overload for your prospects?
7. Leslie emphasizes integrity throughout her methodology. What does selling with integrity look like in practical terms for you?
8. How do you envision outbound sales evolving in the next five years based on trends discussed in this book?
9. As a group, discuss the varying ways each of you interpreted Leslie's definition of *Earn the Right* and why perspectives might differ.
10. Identify a moment or idea from the book that pushed you out of your comfort zone. Why did it challenge you, and how might you grow from it?
11. After finishing this book, what skills or mindsets do you feel more motivated to develop?
12. If you could ask Leslie one follow-up question about her strategies or experiences, what would it be?

Investing in Continuous Improvement

Taking the time to read this book shows tremendous commitment, but the hard work begins now that you've finished. To help put what you've learned into action, I've shared a few resources throughout the book. All of them are listed in the next pages. You can download them using the QR codes. Please also consider connecting on social media or setting up a time to discuss working together.

Connect on Social Media

I post regularly on social media as well. Please consider following me on your favorite social media channel for regular updates, sales tips, and strategy.

LinkedIn: https://www.linkedin.com/in/leslievenetz/

TikTok: https://www.tiktok.com/@salestipstok

YouTube: https://www.youtube.com/@b2bsalescoach

Hire Leslie for Sales Strategy Consulting, Training, Sales Keynotes, and More

If you'd like to learn about having Leslie support you while you build a profit generating pipeline or hiring Leslie to lead sales training with your team, please reach out on www.salesledgtm.com or book a meeting using the QR code.

Book a free 15-minute call with Leslie to explore working together here:

Implementation Aids: Downloadable Workbooks and Guides

- **PATH Goal Setting Worksheet**
  www.salesledgtm.com/leadership
  Use this guided exercise to help your sales team plan for short-term to mid-term goals.

- **Source of Motivation Exercise**
  www.salesledgtm.com/leadership
  Use this simple exercise to better understand how to care deeply about your salespeople and invite trust.

- **Micro-Campaign Worksheet**
  www.salesledgtm.com/value
  Step-by-step guide for launching targeted micro-campaigns. Use this to build an ICP segment and craft a segment-specific value proposition.

- **COI and ROI Cold Email Templates**
  www.salesledgtm.com/value
  Use these four email templates and sample copy as inspiration for your team's sales emails.

- **Strategic Guide to Voicemails**
  www.salesledgtm.com/value
  A deep dive into voicemails: when to use them, what to say, and how to spark curiosity.

- **4R Active Listening Framework**
  www.salesledgtm.com/value
  Train sellers to actively listen, respond with empathy, and build rapport in real time.

- **Cold Call Objection Handling Workbook**
  www.salesledgtm.com/value
  Equip your team with over 40 sample responses to 13 of the most common cold call objections.

Author Bio

Leslie Venetz is a globally recognized B2B sales expert, award-winning corporate sales trainer, and founder of The Sales-Led GTM Agency. With nearly two decades of experience, her expertise spans B2B SaaS and service-based organizations selling across every sales motion, from transactional to consultative. Having successfully sold to and trained teams navigating diverse price points, industries, and ICPs, she is one of the few experts uniquely qualified to enable sales teams across multiple go-to-market motions. Leslie helps teams earn trust, drive revenue, and build a profit generating pipeline through effective prospecting and strategic selling.

Leslie has personally made more than 250,000 cold calls and has influenced more than ten million through her training programs. Her methodologies are used by thousands of sellers to refine their prospecting strategies, handle objections with confidence, and lead sales conversations that consistently convert. A sought-after keynote speaker, she has delivered hundreds of high-impact sales workshops and presentations across four continents, earning a reputation as one of the most influential voices in modern sales.

A LinkedIn Editorial Top Voice and top one percent sales thought leader, Leslie's insights have been viewed more than 100 million times, influencing sales leaders and sellers worldwide. Her expertise has been featured in The Wall Street Journal, Success Magazine, and other top business publications. She has received more than twenty prestigious industry honors, including the 2024 Sales Innovator of the Year, Top Four 2024 Finalist for GTM Advisor of the Year, and recognition as a Five-Time Global Top Fifty B2B Sales Thought Leader.

A pioneer in modern sales education, Leslie's resources have been downloaded thousands of times, helping sellers and leaders execute high-impact strategies. She is redefining what it means to be an ethical, effective, and high-performing sales professional.

www.ingramcontent.com/pod-product-compliance
Lightning Source LLC
Chambersburg PA
CBHW050455190326
41458CB00005B/1297